Global Problems in Sexual Offenses

Global Problems in Sexual Offenses

Edited by

Rahime Erbaş

LEXINGTON BOOKS
Lanham • Boulder • New York • London

Published by Lexington Books
An imprint of The Rowman & Littlefield Publishing Group, Inc.
4501 Forbes Boulevard, Suite 200, Lanham, Maryland 20706
www.rowman.com

86-90 Paul Street, London EC2A 4NE, United Kingdom

British Library Cataloguing in Publication Information Available

Library of Congress Cataloging-in-Publication Data

Names: Erbaş, Rahime, editor.
Title: Global problems in sexual offences / edited by Rahime Erbaş.
Other titles: Global problems in sexual offenses
Description: Lanham : Lexington Books, 2022. | Includes index. | Summary: "Sexual offences pose severe violations of human rights that necessitate criminal law intervention in every democratic society. This edited collection analyzes sexual offences throughout multiple jurisdictions in terms of attrition rate"—Provided by publisher.
Identifiers: LCCN 2022011956 (print) | LCCN 2022011957 (ebook) | ISBN 9781793652034 (cloth) | ISBN 9781793652041 (epub)
Subjects: LCSH: Sex crimes (International law) | Child sexual abuse—Law and legislation. | Rape—Law and legislation.
Classification: LCC KZ7162 .G56 2022 (print) | LCC KZ7162 (ebook) | DDC 345/.0253—dc23/eng/20220531
LC record available at https://lccn.loc.gov/2022011956
LC ebook record available at https://lccn.loc.gov/2022011957

Contents

List of Cases

II Kž 271/2020–4 [2020] Supreme Court of the Republic of Croatia

II Kž 276/2020–4 [2020] Supreme Court of the Republic of Croatia

II Kž 416/2019–4 [2019] Supreme Court of the Republic of Croatia

II Kž 63/2019–5 [2019] Supreme Court of the Republic of Croatia

Bevacqua and S. v. Bulgaria, App no. 71127/01 (ECtHR, June 12, 2008)

Case C-79/11, *Criminal proceedings against Maurizio Giovanardi and others* [2012], ECR, ECLI:EU:C:2012:448

Case 490/20 *V.M.A. v Stolichna obshtina, rayon 'Pancharevo'* [2021] ECJ

Cass. civ. (2), January 21, 2020, K.S.

Circular of the Prosecutor of the Supreme Court 7/2021

Corte di cassazione, judgment of January 25, 2007, no. 1841

Corte di cassazione, judgment of September 28, 2011, no. 42393

Corte di cassazione, judgment of March 23, 2013, no. 14085

Corte di cassazione, judgment of March 18, 2016, no. 11591

Corte di cassazione, judgment of March 23, 2016, no. 31340

Corte di cassazione, judgment of May 10, 2017, no. 33049

Corte di cassazione, judgment of May 20, 2017, no. 45947

Corte di cassazione, judgment of July 11, 2018, no. 43565

Corte di cassazione, judgment of October 16, 2018, no. 6355

Corte di cassazione, judgment of July 10, 2020, no. 27590

Corte di cassazione, judgment of September 8, 2020, no. 28838

Corte di cassazione, judgment of December 4, 2020, no. 3250

Corte di cassazione, judgment of December 11, 2020, no. 5623

Corte di cassazione, judgment of December 17, 2020, no. 7136

Corte di cassazione, judgment of February 10, 2021, no. 21047

Corte di cassazione, judgment of February 18, 2021, no. 24124

Corte di cassazione, judgment of March 24, 2021, no. 12158

Corte di cassazione, judgment of April 30, 2021, no. 19314

Corte di cassazione, judgment of May 28, 2021, no. 34390

Corte di cassazione, judgment of September 22, 2021, no. 37460

Corte di appello di Firenze, judgment of March 4, 2015, no. 858

Decision no. 327/2020 of the Brăila Court

Decision of the Supreme Court of Macedonia, KZh br. 166/83

First instance court of Kalamata (2010) 7 Poiniki Dikaiosini 813

First instance Court of Edessa 60/1984

First instance court of Thessaloniki 103/1981

High Court of Cassation and Justice, *Casefile no. 3/2005*, decision no. III/2005

I.C. v. Romania App no 36934/08 (ECHR May 24, 2016

J. L v. Italy, App no 5671/16 (ECHR, May 27, 2021)

Judicial Council Thessaloniki 1170/2005

Judgment of the Supreme court of Macedonia, KZ, No. 109/84.

Judgment of the Supreme court of Macedonia, KVP, No. 80/98.

M.C. v. Bulgaria App no 39272/98 (ECHR, December 4, 2003)

M.G.C. v. Romania App no 61495/11 (ECHR, March 15, 2016)

Mraović v. Croatia App no 30373/13 (ECHR May 14, 2020)

Mixed Jury Court second instance Thessaloniki 246/2015

Mixed Jury Court Aigion 17/2018

Mixed Jury Court Athens 512/2016

Mixed Jury Court Athens 212/2018

Mixed Jury Court Athens 120/2020

Mixed Jury Court Athens 258/2020

Opuz v. Turkey, App no 33401/02 (ECHR, June 9. 2009)

P.I. v Oberbürgermeisterin der Stadt Remscheid [2012] C 348/09, ECLI:EU:C:2012:300

Second instance Judicial Council Thessaloniki 182/2014

Supreme Court of Macedonia, *Collection of Judicial Decisions 1980–1984, Book III* (Skopje 1985)

Supreme Court of Macedonia, *Collection of Judicial Decisions, Book II* (Skopje 1980)

Supreme Court of Macedonia, *Collection of Judicial Decisions, Book VII* (Skopje 1999)

T.M. and C.M. v. the Republic of Moldova, App no. 26608/11, (ECtHR, January 28, 2014).

The Macedonian Supreme Court Judgment KVP No.80 from 1998

The Superior Council of Magistracy, Plenum, Decision no. 127, July 27, 2021 on the approval of the Joint Thematic Report no. 20–2770 / 20–2771 of the Judicial Inspection

Tribunale di Lecce (2), January 29, 2021 (February 15, 2021)

Tribunale di Milano, November 25, 1999, El Namr [2000] 2, Diritto Immigrazione Cittadinanza, 148

Tribunale di Milano, March 9, 2004 [2004] 2, Foro italiano, c. 435

Tribunale di Milano, January 24, 2008, B S.p.A.

Tribunale di Milano, Judgment of December 16, 2009, no. 15359

Tribunale di Verona, April 14, 2010, Obaseki Gertrude, Omoruyi Ogowen, Ekogiawe John Osagie, n. 979 [2011], 2, Rivista italiana di diritto e procedura penale 838

U-III/5295/2019 [2020] Constitutional Court of the Republic of Croatia

United States v Chambers, 642 F.3d 588 (7th Cir. 2011)

Volodina v. Russia, App no. 41261/17 (ECtHR, July 9, 2019).

Yargıtay Ceza Genel Kurulu, Date: 11.22.2018, E. 2017/394, K 2018/555

Yargıtay Ceza Genel Kurulu, Date: 01.23.2020, E. 2017/206, KÇ 2020/21

Yargıtay, 14. CD., Date: 04.24.2012, E.2011/4954, K.2012/4688

Yargıtay, 5. CD, Date: 06.28.2007, E. 2007/7056, K. 2007/5422

Yargıtay, 5. CD, Date: 05.04.2006, 4003/3857

Yargıtay, 5. CD, Date: 2.16.2006, E. 2006/306, K. 2006/901

Yargıtay, 5. CD, Date: 09.21.2006, 7131

Yargıtay 5. CD, Date: 04.29.1982, 800/1354

Z. v. Bulgaria App No 39257/17 (ECHR May 28, 2020)

List of Legislations

Council of Europe, Council of Europe Convention on preventing and combating violence against women and domestic violence (2011)

Council of Europe Treaty Series - No. 210, "Explanatory report to the Council of Europe Convention on preventing and combating violence against women and domestic violence" (2011)

Council of Europe Convention on Protection of Children against Sexual Exploitation and Sexual Abuse (2007)

Council of Europe, "CETS 201 - Explanatory Report to the Council of Europe Convention on the Protection of Children against Sexual Exploitation and Sexual Abuse" (2007)

Council of Europe, Convention on Cybercrime (2001)

Council Framework Decision 2004/68/JHA of December 22, 2003, on combating the sexual exploitation of children and child pornography. OJ, L 13/44 of January 20, 2004

Criminal Code of the Socialist Republic of Romania (adopted on June 21, 1968)

Directive 2011/93/EU of the European Parliament and of the Council of December 13, 2011, on combating the sexual abuse and sexual exploitation of children and child pornography, and replacing the Council Framework Decision 2004/68/JHA.

Directive 2012/29/EU of the European Parliament and of the Council [2012] establishing minimum standards on the rights, support and protection of victims of crime, replacing Council Framework Decision 2001/220/JHA

European Parliament Resolution, 2001/2035, Female genital mutilation (2001)

Explanatory Report to the Council of Europe Convention on the Protection of Children against Sexual Exploitation and Sexual Abuse (2007)

German Code of Criminal Procedure (StPO)

Greek Criminal Procedure Code

Greek Penal Code

Italian Code of Criminal Procedure

Italian Penal Code

Italian Law No. 69 of July 19, 2019, named "Red Code" (*Codice Rosso*)

Italian Legislative decree June 8, 2001, n. 231

Italian Law October 1, 2012, n. 172: ratification and execution of the Convention of the Council of Europe for the protection of minors against sexual exploitation and abuse, signed in Lanzarote on October 25, 2007

Macedonian Criminal Code

Macedonian Criminal Procedure Code

Macedonian Law on justice for children

Lanzarotte Committee, "Opinion on Article 23 of the Lanzarote Convention and Its Explanatory Note" (2016)

Law no.135/2010 on the Code of Romanian Criminal Procedure

Parliament of Republic of North Macedonia, Draft Law on Amendments of the Criminal Code

Resolution 2011/33 adopted in 2011 by the Economic and Social Council on Prevention, Protection and International Cooperation against the Use of New Information Technologies to Abuse and/or Exploit Children

Romanian Criminal Code of 1936 (Named Criminal Code "Carol II")

The Serbian Criminal Code (Official Gazette RS No 85/2005, 88/2005 – corr., 107/2005 - corr., 72/2009, 111/2009, 121/2012, 104/2013, 108/2014, 94/2016 and 35/2019)

Serbian Criminal Procedure Code (Official Gazette of RS, No 72/2011, 101/2011, 121/2012, 32/2013, 45/2013, 55/2014 and 70/17)

Serbian Family Law (Official Gazette of RS, No 18/2005, 72/2011, 6/2015)

Serbian Gender Equality Law (Official Gazette of Serbia No 52/2021 of May 2021)

Serbian Law on Free legal aid (Official Gazette of RS, No 87/2018)

Serbian Law on prevention domestic violence (Official Gazette of RS, No 94/2016)

Sexual Offences Act (2003)

Treaty on the Functioning of the EU (as amended by the Treaty of Lisbon)

Turkish Penal Code of 2005

United Nations Convention against Transnational Organized Crime (2000).

United Nations, Convention on the Rights of the Child (1989)

United Nations, Declaration on the Elimination of Violence against Women, proclaimed by General Assembly resolution 48/104 of December 20, 1993

Acknowledgments

I would like to express my profound thanks and gratitude to all contributors of the book. Further, I sincerely thank to Dr. Ed Johnston for his valuable support and guidance in this edited project. I am also grateful to my dear colleagues, Professor Valentina Bonini, Anu Sivaganesan, Dr. Chara Chioni-Chotouman, and Dr. Ebru İbiş. I count myself among the privileged ones for having such wonderful colleagues.

I do thank my family for their patience and belief.

I would also like to thank Becca Beurer, Sara Noakes, Kellie Hagan, and Catherine Herman for their guidance and precious help.

Introduction

Sexual offenses pose severe violations of human rights that necessitate criminal law intervention in every democratic society. In other words, regarding these violations, criminal law holds its *prima ratio* character and the role of criminal law cannot be replaced by any civil or administrative law remedy or a simple compensation. Impunity or lenient punishment enjoyed by perpetrators appears as a fundamental concern with respect to sexual offenses. Low(er) reporting rates and high attrition rates of the reported cases through the criminal justice system lie at the point of origin of this edited book collection. Attrition in sexual offenses remains a major problem in many jurisdictions. Attrition, from the perspective of criminal law, is not only caused by issues in criminal procedure, like a lack of victim support or insufficient evidence, but is primarily linked to the respective definition of sexual offenses.

This book considers the attrition problem from both a substantive criminal law and criminal procedure law perspective, as well as benefitting criminological and victimological perspectives. As such, it aims to provide comparative analyses as regards sexual offenses within some jurisdictions in terms of attrition rate. The central question of the edited book is how the cases attrite through their passage in the criminal justice system in different jurisdictions.

Before starting the analysis, two contrasting features of sexual offenses in terms of the sphere influencing these crime types should be noted: First, on the one hand, sexual offenses are the ones which are hugely influenced by society, culture, and political power. Second, these crimes, on the other hand, have been under the influence of global contemporary trends regarding sexual freedoms, especially owing to the contributions by the Council of Europe (CoE), the European Union (EU), and the United Nations (UN).

The societal and cultural influence/pressures do indeed still play a greater role in the approach to sexual offences, regarding both in regulation and prosecution of them. For example, stereotypes that are deeply rooted in society in the form of common myths such as: victim of sexual offences are always female(s), or sexual offences take place outside of marriage, or that the victim has an obligation to manifest a resistance, or a woman accepting a gift by a man shows she consented to sexual acts and many others that are impediment to combatting sexual violence. These myths are not just maintained by society, but they also affect the victim's decision to seek justice, as well as the judiciary's approach to victims and the police's attitudes towards victims. Therefore, sexual offenses are still among less-reported crimes, which leads to high attrition rates in many jurisdictions. In fact, from the view of a comparativist in criminal law, because of societal influence/pressures and the great importance of local culture in sexual crime, sexual offences appear as suitable types of crime for a comparative criminal law analysis and as such to gain deeper insights into diverse jurisdictions and to gain insights into the differences within a given jurisdiction. This edited book thus gives the opportunity to a set of different jurisdictions, Croatia, Greece, Italy, North Macedonia, Romania, Serbia, and Turkey, to present their peculiarities stemming from their society, culture, politics, historical facts and even religion, while presenting their solutions to the global problems of sexual offences. These chapters also cover a comparative look into the other jurisdictions such as the United Kingdom, Germany, the Netherlands, and the United States. Part I of this book entails five chapters dedicated to the analysis of regulation and prosecution of sexual offences in some national examples.

With this objective in my mind, chapter 1 is based on the proposition that the high attrition rate in sexual offenses is primarily linked to our definition of sexual offenses. It highlights several major reforms, which the legislation of sexual offenses experienced in Turkey over the past two decades. Through this passage, the legal language has changed very much. One of the core problems regarding sexual offenses is the legal language itself. As a matter of fact, outdated concepts derived from public morality such as "pudicity," "chastity," "honor," and "virginity," and so on, were removed, and Turkish lawmakers opted for objective (neutralized) criteria. However, this new way of regulating leads to the other problems. Chapter 1 focuses on these problems stemming from the regulation of sexual offenses, after the two iterations of amendments of the Turkish Penal Code in 2005 and in 2014.

Similarly, chapter 2 discusses the grounds for the occurrence of high attrition rates in sexual offences in Greece, that is, limited complaints and even fewer convictions, by jointly considering substantive and procedural criminal law. Indeed, in this chapter, the author firmly advocates the importance of adopting a victim-centered holistic approach to these types of crime. Further, this chapter is significant also in terms of showing the latest approaches to regulation in these types of crime, because Greece amended its Penal Code and Code and Criminal Procedure in 2019. It displays unambiguously, the transformation of the regulation of sexual crime in Greece, in the long time span from 1834 to 2019.

Chapter 3 goes further by widening the scope of research, and as such it addresses sexual offences in the Republic of North Macedonia by the criminological and victimological aspects as well as the substantive criminal law and procedural law aspects. The comprehensive official statistical data from North Macedonia, which explicitly demonstrate the high attrition rate in this country. In addition, this chapter displays that the North Macedonian criminal law still maintains the traditional approaches to sexual offences, as do many other jurisdictions. Indeed, the existence of coercion by the perpetrator and manifestation of resistance by the victim, are the decisive, core element in regulating sexual offenses; this in turn implies the traditional coercive model. Indeed, because coercion is a necessary element of sexual assault, there is a criminal type of sexual intercourse with a helpless person, just as in Romanian and Serbian law as will be displayed in chapters 4 and 5.

The traditional approaches to regulation of sexual offenses are even more visible in Romanian criminal law, as demonstrated in chapter 4. This chapter underlines the evolution of the legislative changes in the area of sexual offenses in Romania: from socialist law to the influence of EU law. In an attempt the comprehend the roots of this traditional approach, the chapter also considers the psychosocial traits of the Romanian people, the social evolution of the family, and the trends for the future. It shows the transformation of regulations on these offences during the last three decades. Nevertheless, it reaches the conclusion that the current legal framework does not generate efficient results in dealing with sexual offences in Romania. This explains the reason why the law is constantly changing in Romania, especially over the last three decades.

As for the influence of global contemporary trends, sexual offences have undergone many reforms in many jurisdictions at different times and with different approaches around the world. The first wave occurred, regarding the legal good that sexual crime violates. Simply put, these crimes were, until recent decades, considered "offences against morals." It is only in the early 2000s that we observe that sexual offences were subject to a paradigm shift in Europe, with the focus of regulation being placed not on crimes against public morals, but on crimes against individual freedom. The second remarkable wave regards consent in sexual offenses. Especially with the advent of the *MeToo movement*, issues surrounding consent are at the center of the debate. The traditional coercive model, which implies that sexual offenses can be committed only by force, and as such, it necessitates the resistance of the victim, has begun to disappear in some jurisdictions, such as Germany, Spain, and Sweden.

Globalization has, in fact, played a greater role in changing and modernizing extant national legislation to a certain degree. Particularly, sexual offences' link with gender-based discrimination and the vulnerability of sexual offense victims, especially children, the Council of Europe's conventions and the EU directives touch sexual offense regulation issues. To illustrate, the Council of Europe Convention on preventing and combating violence against women and domestic violence, the Istanbul Convention (The Istanbul Convention), the Council of Europe Convention on Protection of Children against Sexual Exploitation and Sexual Abuse (the Lanzarote Convention), and the Directive 2011/93/EU of the European Parliament and of the Council of 13 December 2011 on combating the sexual abuse and sexual exploitation of children and child pornography, and replacing Council Framework Decision 2004/68/JHA. In addition, this edited book collection dives into sexual offences with a particular focus on gender-based discrimination as a part II.

The Lanzarote Convention and the EU Directive 2011/93 are comprehensively analyzed in terms of (cyber) grooming, a contemporary form of sexual abuse of children regarding the case study on Croatia case in chapter 5. This chapter deals with EU and CoE standards relating to the criminalization of solicitation of children for sexual purposes or child grooming. The chapter calls for a holistic approach to grooming and comprehensive protection for children by meeting the necessity, in the sense that international standards are adequately and effectively fitted into the national legal regulation framework. What is the most interesting thing in the chapter on Croatia is, the author dives into the case study by re-examining grooming through the lens of international/regional documents, as well as considering selected jurisdictions such as the United Kingdom, Germany, the Netherlands, and the United States.

The Istanbul Convention has had a remarkable influence on the reshaping of sexual offences legislations, as well as on the prosecution of these crimes. For example, abolishing marital immunity, introducing both female genital mutilation and forced marriage as separate offences. Consequently, part II includes three chapters covering case studies, one from Serbia and two from Italy. Among the countries that have ratified the Istanbul Convention, there are quite different levels of implementation: some have profoundly revised their legislations and created efficient systems, while others still cope with political and cultural resistance.

In that regard, chapter 6 considers gender-based and domestic violence as one (umbrella) concept to discuss sexual crime regulations as an area to fight against. It analyzes sexual offences in Serbia with a particular focus on the Istanbul Convention. After Serbia ratified this Convention in 2013 and after its inception on August 1, 2014, sexual crime regulations experienced the transformative power of the norms of the convention; as such, it brought significant improvements to the national Criminal Code in Serbia in 2016 and underpinned recent attempts at legislation. However, it shows the high attrition rates in these crimes due to the traditional definition of rape and its evidentiary requirements. Most importantly, it argues that legal frameworks incorporate stereotypes in gender differences and double standards in morality in Serbia, as is the case in many other jurisdictions.

Chapter 7 delves into psychological aspects of sexual offenses within close relationships. It discusses the possible impacts of the victims' vulnerability on criminal proceedings by providing the statistical evidence, showing for Italy that sexual offences within such relationships entail a high number of unreported cases. It is based on the proposition that the victims' attitudes may create an obstacle to the judicial assessment of sexual offences. Further, it analyzes the psychological aspects by considering the Italian rules, especially the so-called "Red Code" of 2019 that aims to punish violent crimes with severe penalties, as well as the Istanbul Convention's relevant provisions, because sexual offenses within close relationships may amplify gender-based discrimination.

On this exact point, chapter 8 brings one of the most severe forms of gender-based violence to light, that is, female genital mutilation. It addresses this phenomenon through a philosophical and religious analysis on a world scale. It analyzes a series of Muslim Hadiths, with an emphasis on the theory of sacrifice. Thereafter, the focus of the chapter shifts to a comparative legal analysis between various jurisdictions, especially in light of the Istanbul and Lanzarote Conventions. Finally, it displays the Italian legal landscape with a special focus on the provisions of its Criminal Code.

This edited book collection adopts a holistic and integrated approach within the criminal justice system targeting global problems regarding sexual offenses and covers gender-based discrimination dimensions of sexual offenses. It acknowledges that narrow definitions of sexual violence in the regulation of sexual offenses are to be avoided, and international documents governing sexual offenses are to be adopted to fulfill the contemporary requirements as a tool to challenge local stenotypes. It calls for comprehensive protection for victims of sexual offenses in criminal procedure law by taking psychological dimensions of such violence into consideration. In so doing, the book aims to come up with concrete solutions in every chapter to the global problems of sexual offenses, with a particular focus on the attrition phenomena.

I hope the readers enjoy the book.

PART I

Regulating and Prosecuting Sexual Crimes Some National Examples

Chapter 1

Challenges in Regulating Sexual Offences in Turkey

Rahime Erbaş

Sexual offenses have always been in the public interest in Turkey, particularly after the daily news reports on gruesomely committed sexual offenses, like sexual homicide or sexual abuse of children. As such, generally speaking, these offenses have been viewed as major areas for penal populism, and respectively, a repressive approach in legislation toward these offences has prevailed.[1] Quite the opposite, in the application of the new Penal Code of 2005, the Turkish judges displayed a less punitive approach toward sexual offenses by imposing a minimum punishment from penalty scales in the crime definitions.[2] Thus, year after year, the sanctions for sexual offenses turned out to be substantial jail terms. Indeed, after the 2014 amendments, sanctions for these offences became more severe.[3] At the same time, attrition rates in sexual offenses remain a major problem.[4] The judicial statistics of the last five years shows that nearly half of the cases at the trial phase involving sexual offenses resulted in convictions.[5]

Attrition, from the perspective of criminal law, is not only caused by criminal procedural system-related issues such as a lack of victim support or insufficient evidence. In fact, it is primarily linked with how to define sexual offences. Although there has been little interdisciplinary cross-over between criminal law, criminology, and other related fields in terms of regulation of these offences in Turkey, the legislation of sexual offences has undergone several major reforms in the past two decades. Most particularly, sexual offences have been considered a novelty in criminal law reform from the beginning of the 2000s. Indeed, the reform bought paradigm shifts as leading to a transition regarding legal interest for sexual offences from public morality to sexual integrity, as such, as crimes against individual liberty in a more extensive category.[6] In so doing, the legal language considerably changed, and as such the outdated concepts derived from public morality such as "pudicity," "chastity," "honor," "virginity," and so on, were removed.[7] This shift has been highlighted by Turkish scholars as an achievement. Indeed, this shift in legal interest represents one substantial development for a jurisdiction. However, because of the removal of these outdated and settled concepts, the main question as how to efficiently regulate sexual offences arose. Respectively, when defining sexual offences, lawmakers opted for the objective (neutralized) criteria,[8] which refer to individual's sexual integrity and freedom and mainly consist of "the age of victim (i.e., age of consent)," "whether there is a bodily sexual contact between victim and offender," and "the grade of bodily sexual contact." Although this systematic regulation of sexual offenses is praised,[9] these new criteria brought out other problems, debates, and even legal loopholes for some cases. Here comes in the question of how to conceptualize and evaluate consent in formulating sexual offenses as another substantial development for a jurisdiction to reduce attrition, which does not attract sufficient notice of Turkish scholars. In fact, the definition of crime is the primary place where legal interest can be reflected to the fullest extent.[10]

In the Turkish Penal Code, the core sexual offenses in the protection of sexual freedom and integrity for both adults and children as "crimes against individual's sexual integrity," which are also considered sexual offenses *sensu stricto*, detailed below:

Art.102: Sexual assault
Art.103: Sexual abuse of children
Art.104: Sexual intercourse with a minor aged between 15 and 18
Art.105: Sexual harassment

There are other crime types that can be considered sexual offenses *sensu lato*, such as crimes against public morality, as they are likely to offend the standards of decency in a given society. However, they include not only sexual acts like pornography, but forcing children and adults or encouraging them for exploitation in prostitution and also begging. The first one is the crime of shameful sexual acts (Art. 225), having sexual intercourse in public spaces or exposure of one's intimate parts (exhibitionism; public nudity). The other is the crime of obscenity (Art. 226), which corresponds to pornography-related crimes. For example, giving a child the products that contain sexually explicit images, texts, or words, or showing a child that content, to read or make a child listen to them. Or publishing or mediating the publication of the obscene images, texts, or words through the press and broadcasting constitute the crime of obscenity. As for prostitution, engaging in prostitution is not a crime, but forcing and encouraging someone to act as a prostitute or facilitating the way of acting as a prostitute is a crime from two years up to four years' imprisonment and fine (Art. 227). To illustrate, Art. 227/2 states that "in order to make own living partially or completely by benefiting from the earnings of the person dragged into prostitution is also considered an incentive act to prostitution." If the victim is a child, the punishment is higher, from four years up to ten years imprisonment (Art. 227/1).[11]

This chapter, however, confines itself with the crime of sexual assault (Art. 102), which punishes the violation of the bodily integrity of adults through sex acts, and as such it stands as a fundamental (general) sexual crime type in the Turkish law. In an effort to analyze consent in sexual offenses, this chapter displays the transition on legal interest for sexual offenses from public morality to sexual integrity as the owner of sexual autonomy for the consent (II). After considering the legal interest as a foundation, it provides an overview on regulation of sexual offenses in the penal code for those who are non-familiar to the Turkish system (III). Then it moves to the core issue: the role and legal qualification of the consent in the application of sexual assault (Art.102). Because the Penal Code contains no words such as "the consent" or a similar one and instead it states, "violating someone's bodily integrity through sex acts" in Art. 102, which has also aggravating and mitigating forms, this study discusses the consent issue in the context of the verb "violate." The evaluation of the consent in the case-law will be analyzed (IV). It considers nonconsensual sexual acts against a spouse as a sexual assault in Turkey (V). Finally, it provides conclusive remarks (VI).

TRANSITION FROM PUBLIC MORALITY TO INDIVIDUAL'S SEXUAL FREEDOM

The acceptance that sexual offenses are not a matter of public morals, but primarily a matter of the individual's sexual freedom[12] and integrity has a relatively short history in Turkey, just as it does in many other jurisdictions. Modern sexual offense legislation in Turkish law have been influenced by the French and Italian approaches. The 1858 Ottoman Penal Code was an adaptation of French Code pénal of 1810, well known as Napoleonic Code. The French and the Ottoman Penal Code are described as "liberal revolution" and "authoritarian reform" as well as "medieval and early modern interpretation of sexual offences."[13] In so doing, it is argued that the French and Ottoman codes transferred "women's bodies into public,"[14] and sexual offenses were regulated as "attacks on morality" (Arts.197–201).[15] In the same vein, in Turkey's first penal code, which was in force between 1926–2005, these crimes were classified under the section titled "crimes against public morality and family order," which was harshly criticized by scholars.[16] Sexual offenses were based on a range of outdated concepts derived from public morality, such as "pudicity," "chastity," "honor," and "virginity,"[17] which Turkey, in 1926, modeled on the Italian Penal Code of 1889.[18] To illustrate, because of the concept of "virginity," it was assumed that rape could be committed only by men.[19] Besides, rape was regulated with the traditional coercion approach, and as such the courts sought for proof of the resistance of the victim.[20] Marital rape was not considered a sexual crime, rather as a crime of maltreatment of family members. Further, after the 1936 amendments influenced by the Italian Penal Code of 1930 (Rocco Code), which was regarded as a product of a fascist regime,[21] the rape-marriage law did exist in that period because marriage could be used as a tool to recover public morality. Later, this influence was viewed as a fascist legal transplant from Italy to Turkey.[22]

Considering sexual offenses as crimes against public morality did not only represent a certain approach, but also it led to legal loopholes for the violation of someone's sexual freedoms. For example, as the code articulated sexual assault as rape (as intercourse), an oral sexual act could only be punished under the crime of injury, not a sexual crime.[23]

In 2005, the new Penal Code, which was an outcome of a great consensus[24] in parliament, represented major changes in these crimes because it involved the paradigm shifts. Above all, it classified these crimes as "crimes against individual's sexual integrity," and it did remove these outdated concepts from the law. As *Miller* stated:

> By the first years of the twenty-first century, both international law and European law had changed. Indeed, by 2005, various international legislative commissions had started defining rape in precisely the terms . . . Meanwhile, French, Italian, Turkish and other nation-state based jurists were coming to understand rape explicitly as an issue of bodily integrity, identity, and dignity, highlighting the victim's subjectivity, and marginalizing or in some cases eliminating completely the role of violence, penetration, or the penis.[25]

Some argue that the title of the section where sexual offenses are defined should be as crimes against sexual freedom instead of sexual integrity, because integrity as a term implies a physical inviolability in Turkish law just as crimes against physical integrity like injury.[26] However, as Dressler points out that "rape is viewed today not only as a crime of violence, but also as a privacy/autonomy offense."[27]

As a novelty of the new code, for example, the rape-marriage law was repealed, virginity examination was stipulated as a crime, and marital rape was criminalized.[28] As such, it aspired to modernize Turkish law regarding sexual offenses; albeit these crimes have remained as crimes which are the most often amended crime types in the Penal Code. However, a lobby for re-introduction of the rape-marriage law for the underage in Turkey is highly active through the remarkable amount of petitions to Parliament and social media activities, although the studies show that Turkish society, regardless of their political opinion, is overwhelmingly against such marriage.[29]

These novelties in both legal interest and legal language firstly encounter a resistance to change among some academics. To illustrate, some argue that the former Penal Code's regulations for sexual offenses were almost mistakenly freely shaped, and a remarkable amount of case-law on these regulations were produced by the Turkish Court of Cassation (*Yargıtay*) from 1926 to 2005, which represents a long period of experience.[30] To this view, the deficiencies and problems that occurred due to today's application of these regulations of the former code could have been modified, but through the introduction of the new Penal Code, all these experiences were thrown away without providing any grounds.[31] Further, they argue that there is no legal ground or reasoning in the explanatory memorandum of the new penal code as to why sexual offenses are regulated in the new code as a crime of individual sexual integrity instead of public morality.[32] Still, some senior criminal law scholars use the term "the undamaging of pudicity" (in Turkish "*ırza geçme*").[33] They even propose a draft for changing sexual offenses by which sexual assault is named as "the undamaging of pudicity," just as it existed in the former code.[34] This kind of resistance explains the reasons why young Turkish scholars still over-highlight the shift in legal interest as an achievement.

A PROGRESSIVE APPROACH TO SEXUAL VIOLENT ACT TYPES IN THE CODE

After the outdated concepts from rape law in Turkey, like "pudicity," "chastity," "honor," and "virginity," and so on, and the traditional coercion model regarding consent, were removed, the main question as to how the sexual offences could be formulated in the code arose. The objective criteria in formulating sexual offences were applied, which are welcomed by Turkish scholars.[35] These have mainly two standpoints as "the age of victim (i.e., age of consent for children)" and "the severity of sexual integrity violating acts." The age and sex of the offender has no role in classifying the sexual offenses.[36] Further, it makes no difference whether the sex of the victim and offender is the same or not. The marital or private link between the victim and offender has no role either.[37]

A primary standpoint in formulating sexual offences appears as the age of the victim. That is to say, whether the victim is an adult or child and if the victim is a child, at which age the child is a decisive element. The child refers to a person who has not yet reached the age of eighteen under Turkish Penal

Code. In terms of sexual offenses, the children are divided in four categories as follows: (1) any child under fifteen years old, (2) any child above fifteen years old, but is not legally competent, (3) any child above fifteen and legally competent, but being subject to any coercion, threat, deception, or any other means affecting the will to being part of sexual act, and (4) any child above fifteen and legally competent, and part of sexual intercourse without any coercion, threat, deception, or any other means affecting the will.

For the first, second, and third group of children, their ability to consent to any sexual act is not accepted at all. In other words, it is presumed that these three groups of children cannot recognize the legal meaning and consequences of the consent to sexual act. Any sexual act, regardless of whether there is a penetration or any instantaneous bodily sexual contact such as a sudden tweak on someone's cheek with sexual purpose, is considered sexual abuse of children (Art. 103). As for the fourth group, having a sexual intercourse without exercising any coercing is punished (Art. 104). Now it stands as the most debated and problematic sexual crime types in Turkish law, even if it is ex parte prosecuted crime since 2005.[38] Why a consensual sexual intercourse with children between the ages of fifteen and eighteen requires punishment has been controversial topic in Turkey since 1953, when this act was introduced as criminal act. It questions even whether *the legal value* protected through this crime regulated in Art. 104 is merely the sexual immunity of the child or public morality. The prevailing opinion among Turkish scholars is that this crime serves the public morality,[39] and this undermines the achievement of the criminal reforms in 2000s as a shift in legal interest from public morality to individual sexual freedom. The unspoken idea behind criminalizing consensual sexual intercourse with children between the ages of fifteen and eighteen lies on the incest debate.[40] Consensual incest among the competent adults has never been stipulated as a crime in Turkey, although there were heated debates in parliament both in the Ottoman and in Republic times, and the European oriented penal codes which were adopted by Turkey covered incest as a crime. In the last debate in parliament in 1953, the incest as a crime was rejected, but this act was introduced as a crime, although it did not exist on the agenda of Parliament.

The only legal room for children's sexual freedom is recognized only for the fourth group, limited to sexual acts which do not reach the level of sexual intercourse like kissing. Indeed, because the sexual intercourse level without coercion is ex parte prosecuted crime, the children may choose to not file a complaint. For a long time, there was a dispute as to who is eligible for filing a complaint as child or parent,[41] the Court of Cassation settled the dispute by accepting only child as the sole owner of the complaint right, which is a right heavily dependent on personality in Turkish law. However, the dispute over determining who the victim is and who the offender is in such instances, consensual sexual intercourse still remains an unsolved problem. Even if the case cannot be prosecuted due to the lack of complaint, theoretically the act stands as a crime. Besides, although the legal age is the completion of the age of eighteen under the Turkish Civil Code, the legal age for marriage is seventeen as a general rule (Art. 124/1). As for extraordinary circumstances, the children who are sixteen may be allowed by a decision from the court (Art. 124/2). Further, "marriage renders a person being of full legal age" (Art. 11/2). De facto marriage of children who are not yet of a marriageable age is a major problem in Turkey, which is known as "child brides."[42]

As a secondary standpoint in formulating sexual offenses, the code applies a two-level approach to sexual violent acts: bodily sexual contact and non-bodily sexual acts between a victim and suspect."[43] In the case of bodily sexual contact, the core act for sexual assault is "violating someone's bodily integrity through sex acts" in Art. 102/1, whereas it is "sexual abuse of child." The core acts are segmented by severity into four general categories, which are parallel-listed for sexual assault (Art. 102) and sexual abuse of children (Art. 103).

In protecting the child's sexual inviolability and freedom, the code mainly stipulates two main types of crimes: sexual abuse of children (Art. 103) and having sexual intercourse with children between the ages fifteen and eighteen (Art. 104). Therefore, sexual assault, which is regulated in Art. 102, is applied for the case involved the adult victims, but deliberately it does not explicitly state the victim as adult in the crime definition. As such, it stands as a fundamental (general) crime type and it is applied to some rare cases involving child victims, where specific child protective sexual offenses cannot be applied because of the legality principle. Particularly in the case of a mistake on the age of the victim, which is called *mistake of fact*, the offender may be punished under this general crime type as sexual assault (Art. 102).[44]

This four-layered segmentation covers acts as two main act forms and one mitigating and one aggravating form. The first main act is any bodily sexual contact without inserting an organ or other object into the body; the second is any bodily sexual contact while inserting an organ or other object into the body.[45] The mitigating form is the instantaneous and intermittent bodily sexual contact without inserting an organ or other object into the body *(Sarkıntılık)*. The aggravating form is any bodily sexual contact with inserting an organ or other object into the body and causing the death of the victim—sexual homicide—the heaviest form of the sexual offences which requires the heaviest punishment (*aggravated lifelong sentence*[46]). These acts are stipulated parallel to the acts in sexual abuse of children (Art. 103), but in sexual abuse of children by referring to the act as sexual abuse as opposed to violating of sexual integrity in adult cases.[47]

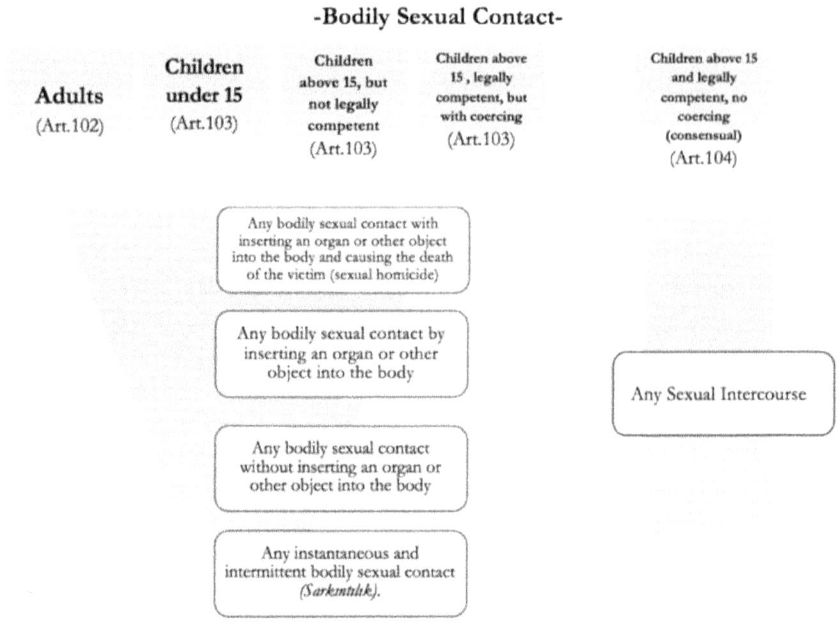

Figure 1.1. Art. 102—Sexual Assault, Art. 103—Sexual Abuse of Children, and Art. 104—(Consensual) Sexual Intercourse with a Minor Aged between 15 and 18.

The code mentions the fifth type of sexual act as "having sexual intercourse" for the children between the ages fifteen and eighteen who have the ability to recognize their behavior's legal consequences, whereas sexual assault and sexual abuse of children is referred to as "inserting an organ or other object into the body." Why this difference is made is criticized by some scholars.[48]

To be more precise, this act is stipulated as "having a sexual intercourse without exercising any force, threat or any other restrictions on consent" in Art. 104. If this act including children between the ages fifteen and eighteen is not consensual, this constitutes another crime: sexual abuse of children (Art. 103), just as the other children below fifteen years old and the other children between the ages fifteen and eighteen who do not have the ability to recognize their behavior's legal consequences.

If the sexual act is non-bodily, like uttering words, this act constitutes sexual harassment (Art. 105), regardless of the type of tools used by the offender. The victim can be children as well as adults. It can be committed face to face or virtual or by any other communication means.

It was assumed that bodily sexual contact is more severe than non-bodily sexual contact. However, when it comes to the sexual violence, in some cases the unjustness of non-bodily sexual contact could be heavier than bodily

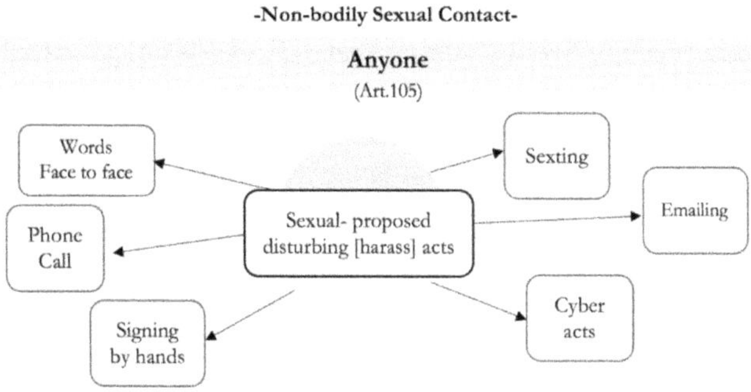

Figure 1.2. Art. 105—Sexual Harassment.

sexual contact. For example, in cyber sexual assaults, there is non-bodily sexual contact at stake. The non-bodily sexual contact refers to sexual harassment, which is the lowest punished form of sexual offenses. In particular, in cyber sexual abuse of children, there is a great concern of lenient punishment for the offender.[49]

CONSENT AND DEFINING THE VIOLATION OF SEXUAL INTEGRITY

In regulating sexual offenses, "the consent" stands as a decisive element, in particular for adult victims. In comparative law, three main approaches in reflecting on consent in sexual offenses have existed as: "the traditional coercion model," "no means no model," and "only yes means yes model." The traditional coercion model, which causes to a seek for resistance of the victim by the courts, is the oldest one and has prevailed in many jurisdictions like in Germany, France, Italy, Spain, and Turkey for a long time. Because it was accepted that sexual offenses are crimes against public morality, it is the obligation of the victim to show a resistance against the sexual offender.[50]

Today, however, a new tendency against it appears, for example, Germany switched to "no means no model" after "Cologne attacks"[51] in 2016[52]; Sweden[53] and Spain[54] shifted to "only yes means yes model" in order "to put more emphasis on consent."[55] However, many countries still preserve the traditional coercion model.[56] Further, there are some critiques of these two new models by saying that the question whether "no" always means "no" cannot be avoided entirely and that "yes" may not always mean "yes" in every case.[57]

As for the Turkish criminal law, first and foremost, all sexual crime types are regulated on the basis/presumption of lack of consent or as acts contrary to the will of the victim.[58] In terms of child victims, the non-existence of the consent is already presumed, but Turkish Penal Code in 2005, is based on the same presumption also for the adult victims. In 2018, The *GREVIO*[59] report welcomed this presumption by stating that " . . . [D]efining sexual violence against adults [sexual assault, Art. 102] as an offense based on the absence of freely given consent without requiring the use of force" is a significant progress in terms of being in compliance with the Istanbul Convention.[60] However, in conceptualizing sexual offenses, the Penal Code contains no word in the crime definition of sexual assault such as "nonconsensual," "without consent," "coercively," "forcibly," "against the will,"[61] which traditional rape regulations contain in many jurisdictions.[62] The consent is given a legal qualification in the application by the judge. There are two main approaches as to the legal qualification in sexual crime. The prevailing approach among judiciary and scholars is that consent serves as a justification reason because the existence of the consent later justifies violent sexual act.[63] This implies a traditional approach to the consent in these crimes in Turkish law.

The minority, but an emerging approach in Turkey, considers it as a part of objective element of the crime (*actus reus*).[64] This new approach considers that conducting sexual acts which are based on someone's consent refers there is no violent act since the beginning. This is the more accurate approach when considering regulation structure of the new Penal Code, which is based on the presumption of a lack of consent. The existence of consent itself prevents any unjustness for sexual freedom and integrity. That is to say, being nonconsensual is an existential part of these crimes which is embedded into the word "violating." In Turkish law, the judge does not seek whether the act is nonconsensual (the will of the victim is defeated or affected) or not, rather they must seek for whether the victim consented or not (the act is consensual or not).[65] Therefore, it can be inferred that the Turkish law is closer to the "only yes means yes model."

To illustrate, in a case from 2018, an eighteen-year-old woman went to a flat with three men. They were all drunk. The victim unexpectedly began to shout and yell at them. The defendants claimed that they had consensual sexual intercourse with the victim. The local court viewed no reason to consider the intercourse nonconsensual, seeing that she was eighteen years old, and she voluntarily went to this flat and her shouts and yells were the result of alcohol. Therefore, the court acquitted the defendants. The Court of Cassation overruled this judgment by holding that the defendant could not prove that the victim had consented, especially seeing that the victim shouted and yelled, even if she was drunk.[66]

When examining the core act which consists of aggravating and mitigating forms, it is conceptualized as "violating someone's bodily integrity through sex acts" in Art. 102/1. However, the code does not define this act or provide any kind of example that could be considered within the scope of this Article.

The only word that the Penal Code explicitly uses is "violating." The word "violating" is not a neutral act, rather it is an act which implies an opposition or even resistance by the person whose bodily integrity is breached by this act.[67] The nonconsensual feature of the sex act is embedded in the "violating" act. As such, whether the victim resisted on it or not is not sought, and "non-forcible form of non-consensual sexual intercourse"[68] is punished within the crime of sexual assault.

Coercion is not an element of this crime. Coercion like threats, deception, or any other means affecting the will is a mean to commit sexual offenses.[69] But, if the offender exercises coercion against the victim to break the resistance of the victim for commission of sexual assault, the offender will not be punished also due to crime of injury as long as coercion does not lead the aggravating form of injury such as injury leading to loss of organ function, permanent scars on face or death of the victim, and so on.[70] Further, fraudulent conduct such as introducing oneself as a physician in order to violate the victim's sexual integrity in the name of medical examination refers to contradiction of the will of person.[71]

In the case-law, the Court of Cassation makes a distinction among the grades of the act (in four-layered segmentations in figure 1). For the primary act, "violating someone's bodily integrity through sex acts without inserting an organ or other object into the body" and also for its mitigating form, "the instantaneous and intermittent bodily sexual contact without inserting an organ or other object into the body" *(Sarkıntılık)* (Art.102/1), the court does not seek whether there is any coercion, threat, deception or any other means affecting the will or not. Violating bodily integrity contrary to the will of the victim is sufficient.[72] However, when it comes to aggravated form, any bodily sexual contact with inserting an organ or other object into the body (Art.102/2), the court seeks for the existence of the means (e.g., any coercion, threat, and deception) affecting the will of the victim.[73] This shows that the traditional coercion model is still in practice.

The official explanatory memorandum of the Penal Code for the crime of sexual assault (Art. 102) considers that this act is an infringement of someone's bodily (physical) autonomy through a "carnal act" (sexual or lustful; in Turkish *şehevi*) which was historically coined as *carnaliter cognovit* (carnal knowledge[74]). The carnality feature of the act is objectively determined.[75] As such, an objective link between the act and the act's carnality is sought.[76] For example, the act is in the form of sexual arousal or in the form of its link sexual organs or parts of the body.[77]

Some local courts mistakenly interpret the provision and additionally seek for a subjective desire of the perpetrator. This paves a way toward impunity for the sexual offender. In a recent case, in 2020, the defendant damaged the vehicle which he rented from a car firm and did not pay damages. The owner (the victim) filed a complaint for a compensation in civil court. The defendant arranged a meeting in a secluded place with the owner with other people. When they were alone, the defendant told the victim to prepare 40,000 Turkish Liras by Wednesday by pointing a gun towards him. The victim, in fear, told that he could bring only by Thursday. The defendant agreed, but told he then wanted to secure the money. He yelled at him, "take off your clothes!" When the victim refused, the defendant fired a gun toward the ground near the legs of the victim. Then he took photos of the victim naked, and told him grab his penis. The victim had to do in fear, meanwhile the defendant was taking photos. Then the defendant told the victim to insert his penis into his mouth, but the victim said, "I cannot do this." Then the defendant rubbed himself against the back of the victim in position for anal intercourse, but he did not insert, but took photos as if he was. In this case, the local court held that the defendant did not act with sexual desire, but he aimed at securing money for robbery, which exposes thread against bodily integrity as well as property. Therefore, it decided for the acquittal of sexual assault (Art.102). However, the Court of Cassation's Sixth Criminal Chamber overruled the acquittal, but the local court insisted in its previous judgment. Then, the Court of Cassation's Assembly of Criminal Chambers re-overruled the local court's judgment. It stated that the defendant's acts were directed to the erogenous zones of sexual sensitivity, which objectively violated the bodily (physical) autonomy in terms of sexual inviolability. As such, this is more than the thread for bodily integrity in a crime of robbery. Also, the assembly noted that the defendant took various photos to secure the crime of robbery, he further kept forcing the victim to grab his penis, and then he rubbed himself against his back. To the assembly, this exactly depict the sexual lustfulness of his acts.[78] Further, given that even the instantaneous and intermittent bodily sexual contact without inserting an organ or other object into the body is stipulated as a form of sexual assault, the local court's judgment for acquittal implies miscarriage of justice and leads to attrition.

Further, solely acting in this way constitutes sexual assault already, and whether the offender satisfies his/her sexual desire or not is not an element of this crime.[79] Further, whether the victim's bodily integrity is damaged or not is not an element of crime. For example, caressing someone's hair in a lustful way constitutes already sexual assault.[80] The Court of Cassation (*Yargıtay) considered the following acts as sexual assault (Art. 102/1): "grabbing the buttocks of the victim walking on the road,"*[81] "hugging the victim's waist,"[82] and "touching the breasts of the victim while she was sitting on her seat in public transportation."[83]

MARITAL RAPE: A MODERN PERSPECTIVE?

In Turkish law, there is no "marital immunity rule"[84] in sexual offenses, at least in the view of the legal framework. However, in practice, when it comes to sexual violence within a marriage, sexual myths play a deeper role than they do in cases where there is no marital link. The myths such as "rapists are strangers" or "a spouse cannot be an offender of sexual offences against a spouse" prevail in Turkish society, which leads to impunity of the perpetrators. Marital rape as a crime of sexual assault committed against the spouse is one of the most serious and hidden problems experienced in Turkey, because it is assumed that spouses have a martial obligation to meet each other's sexual desires to some certain level.[85] This is harshly criticized by arguing that if a spouse has a right to ask for sexual relationship, then the other spouse has a right to reject. Feminists in Turkey state that this is because of the patriarchy in society.[86] Many women do not have any awareness that marital rape stands as a crime, even if today the awareness has been increasing.[87] The former Penal Code did not recognize that marital rape is a crime. Instead, it was considered as a crime of maltreatment of a family member, which protected the legal value of family order, not an individual legal interest.[88]

In 2005, a new approach was adopted, and family status makes no difference when it comes to the link between victim and offender. In other words, the marital link between the offender and the victim has no role from the view point of the Penal Code after 2005, because sexual offenses refer to a violation of an individual's sexual freedom and integrity, not public morals.[89] However, the Penal Code makes a distinction regarding prosecuting conditions whether it shall be *ex officio* or *ex parte* prosecuted, which is highly criticized among scholars.[90] The official explanatory memorandum of the Penal Code for the crime of sexual assault (Art. 102) states that;

> These acts which constitute the aggravating form of sexual assault [any bodily sexual contact with inserting an organ or other object into the body, Art. 102/2], can also be committed against spouse. Marriage union imposes mutual obligations to each other to satisfy their spouse desires as well as the duty of loyalty to each other. Nonetheless, even within the marital union, it is doubtless that there are both medical and legal limits in terms of demands for such desires. The acts carried out against a spouse by violating these limits and as such constitute the quality of the sexual assault crime require criminal sanctions. However, in this case, the investigation and prosecution rely upon on the complaint of the victim spouse.[91]

Accordingly, the act which reads as "any bodily sexual contact with inserting an organ or other object into the body" (Art. 102/2) is prosecuted ex parte where the victim is a spouse, whereas it is an ex officio crime for other victims. But, as for the less severe act, which reads as "any bodily sexual contact without inserting an organ or other object into the body," it is ex officio prosecuted crime for every victim regardless of status. Therefore, regarding spouse victims, the more severe act is ex parte prosecuted leading to the controversial arguments among scholars.[92] Whereas some scholars argue that the less severe form of the crime makes no distinction as to status of victim, and as such it can be committed against the spouse,[93] others argue that it cannot be committed against a spouse.[94] The Istanbul Convention, in Art. 36/3, states that sexual assault committed against former or current spouses or partners is to be criminalized.[95]

CONCLUDING REMARKS

The criminal justice system's contribution to high attrition rates in sexual offenses begins with its way of defining sexual offenses and most significantly its approach to the role of consent in both the penal code and the application of sexual offenses. Indeed, crime definitions with particular focus on the consent issue come to the attention especially after cologne attacks in Germany, in 2016, and it became a matter of lively debates in many jurisdictions. This study considered the Turkey's case from several major reforms in 2000s to today's substantive criminal law problems of the sexual offenses surrounding consent issues. In so doing, it mainly confined itself with the crime of sexual assault (Art. 102), the sexual crime involving bodily sex acts against adults.

It is obvious that the paradigm shifts of the 2000s regarding legal interest for sexual offenses from public morality to sexual integrity and as such removing the outdated concepts is still over-highlighted among the Turkish scholars as an achievement of the Penal Code in 2005. On the contrary, the question as to whether the definition of sexual offenses in Turkish law sufficiently could reflect on this legal interest—individual sexual freedom and integrity remains mostly overlooked. The core problems of the former Penal Code such as seeking resistance of the victim in the case law, unawareness of marital rape among women backed up with myths, the ongoing lobby for re-introduction of the rape-marriage law for the underage in Turkey remains persistent. Although the overall systematic regulation of sexual offenses of the new code is to be appraised, the new criteria in formulating sexual offenses as whether the sexual act is in the form of a *bodily sexual contact* or a *contactless act* is problematic, as it cannot reflect on the weight of unjustness of the sexual acts in every case. In some cases, contactless acts may be more severe than acts with bodily sexual contact as with cyber grooming.

Based on the issues conveyed in this chapter, it can be concluded that reformulating crime definitions or amending the existing ones in the short term may not bring solutions to the problem of sexual offenses. Indeed, changing the habits of the judicial authorities to interpret the law and the presumption of society on individual sexual freedom are more difficult parts of combating high attrition rates in sexual offenses. Therefore, a long-term solution should be sought. Consequently, the criminal elements need to be more explicitly written than the principle of legality requires because sexual offenses, which are under the dynamic effect of society and state, necessitate bold and long-term determinations.

REFERENCES

Literature

Artuk, M. E., Gökcen, A., Alşahin, M. E., and Çakır, K., *Ceza Hukuku Özel Hükümler* (18th ed., Adalet, 2019).

Aygörmez, Uğurlubay G. A., "Cinsel Suçlara İlişkin Güncel Maddi Hukuk Sorunları," in Gülsün Ayhan Aygörmez Uğurlubay (ed), *Alman ve Türk Hukukunda Cinsel Suçlar ve Cinsel Suçları Önleme Stratejileri* (Oniki Levha 2019).

Baş, E., "Türk Ceza Hukukunda Cinsel Taciz Suçu," *Ankara Üniversitesi Hukuk Fakültesi Dergisi* 65, no. 4 (2016).

Battaglini, G., "Fascist Reform of the Penal Law in Italy," *Journal of Criminal Law and Criminology* 24, no. 1 (1933), https://scholarlycommons.law.northwestern.edu/cgi/viewcontent.cgi?article=2386&context=jclc, accessed May 22, 2021.

Bayraktar, K., et al., *Özel Ceza Hukuku*, vol. 2 (Oniki Levha 2017).

Çağırkan, B., "Child Brides and Its Importance in Terms of Social Roles in Turkish Society: The Case of Bitlis," *Balkan and Near Eastern Journal of Social Sciences* 4, no. 1 (2018), http://ibaness.org/bnejss/2018_04_01/06_Cagirkan.pdf, accessed August 17, 2021.

Centel, N., "5237 Sayılı Türk Ceza Kanunu'nda Cinsel Saldırı Suçu ve Cinsel Suçlar Değişiklik Tasarısı'nın Değerlendirilmesi," *Türkiye Barolar Birliği Dergisi* 24, no. 99 (2012).

Demirel, M., "Ceza Hukukunda Rızanın İki Boyutu: Tipikliğe Engel Olan Rıza ve Hukuka Uygunluk Nedeni Olan Rıza," *İstanbul Hukuk Mecmuası* 78, no. 3 (2020).

Dönmezer, S., *Kriminoloji* (9th edn, Adalet Bakanlığı 2020).

Dressler, J., "Understanding Criminal Law," (6th ed., LexisNexis, 2012).

Dülger, İ., "Cinsel Özgürlüğe Karşı İşlenen Suçlardan Irza Geçme Suçu" (PhD Thesis, Selçuk University, Konya 1998).

Dursun, S., "Türk Ceza Hukuku'nda Cinsel Suçlara Genel Bir Bakış," *Ceza Hukuku Dergisi* 9, no. 24 (2014).

Erem, F., *Soyunu Sürdürebilmek Özgürlüğü* (Sevinç Matbaası 1980).

Hafızoğulları, Z., and Özen, M., *Türk Ceza Hukuku Özel Hükümler Kişilere Karşı Suçlar* (2nd ed., US-A Yayıncılık 2011).

Hörnle, T., "The New German Law on Sexual Offenses," (October 1, 2016) 1, 10, https://ssrn.com/abstract=2999677, accessed August 17, 2021.

İlkkaracan, P., "Changing Turkey's Laws to Improve Women's Rights," https://opendocs.ids.ac.uk/opendocs/bitstream/handle/20.500.12413/12596/ilkkaracan_2008_changing.pdf?sequence=1, accessed April 4, 2021.

Jabrayilova, S., "The Distinctive Features of Sexual-Related Offences: Statutory Rape V. Marital Rape," *Ankara Law Review* 9, no. 1 (2012), http://dergiler.ankara.edu.tr/dergiler/64/1768/18722.pdf, accessed May 15, 2021.

Kırbaş, Canikoğlu S., "Feminist Bir Perspektifle Türk Ceza Kanunu'nda Cinsel Saldırı Suçu," *Fe Dergi: Feminist Eleştiri* 5, no. 1 (2013).

Koca, M., and Üzülmez, İ., *Türk Ceza Hukuku Özel Hükümler* (6th ed., Adalet 2019).

Miller, R. A., *The Limits of Bodily Integrity* (Ashgate, Hampshire, 2007).

Mollamahmutoğlu, S., and Savaş, V., *Yargısal ve Bilimsel İçtihatlarla Türk Ceza Kanununun Yorumu,* vol. 2 (Sevinç Matbaası 1985).

Tane,r F. G., *Türk Ceza Hukukunda Cinsel Özgürlüğe Karşı Suçlar* (2nd ed., Seçkin 2020).

Özbek, V. Ö., Doğan, K., and Bacaksız, P., *Türk Ceza Hukuku Özel Hükümler* (15th ed., Seçkin 2020).

Selçuk, S., "Cinsel Dokunulmazlığa Karşı Suçların Yapısı ve Bir Öneri," in Mahmut Koca, İzzet Özgenç, İlhan Üzülmez, and M. Emin Alşahin (eds), *Prof. Dr. Mehmet Emin Artuk'a Armağan* (Seçkin 2020).

Tezcan, D., Mustafa Ruhan Erdem, and R. Murat Önok, *Teorik ve Pratik Ceza Özel Hukuku* (18th ed., Seçkin 2020).

Ünver, Y., "Türk Maddi Ceza Hukukunda Cinsel Suçların Eleştirisel Olarak İncelenmesi," in Yener Ünver (ed) *II. Türkiye Slovenya Uluslararası Hukuk Sempozyumu-Cinsel Suçlar ve Evlilik Hukuku* (Seçkin 2013).

Üzülmez, İ., "Yeni Türk Ceza Kanunu'nda Cinsel Saldırı Suçu," in Bahri Öztürk (ed), *3. Yılında Yeni Ceza Adalet Sistemi* (Seçkin 2009).

Yalçın, Sancar T., "Dilin Kadına Yönelik Şiddetteki Rolü" (vol 3, Hukuk Kurultayı, Ankara Barosu Yayınları 2006).

Yeldan, D., and Taneri, G., *Cinsel Suçlarda Beraat* (2nd ed., Seçkin 2020).

Yıldız, A. K., *5237 Sayılı Türk Ceza Kanunu* (İstanbul Barosu Yayınları 2007).

Yokuş, Sevük H., *Türk Ceza Hukuku Özel Hükümler* (3rd ed., Adalet 2020).

Legislations and Other Resources

Adalet İstatistikleri Yayın Arşivi, https://adlisicil.adalet.gov.tr/Home/SayfaDetay/adalet-istatistikleri-yayin-arsivi, accessed September 2, 2021.

Council of Europe, Council of Europe Convention on preventing and combating violence against women and domestic violence [The Istanbul Convention] (Council of Europe Treaty Series - No. 210, Istanbul, 11.V.2011) https://rm.coe.int/168008482e accessed August 17, 2021.

GREVIO's (Baseline) Evaluation Report (GREVIO/Inf(2018)6, 2018) 8, https://www.google.com/search?client=safari&rls=en&q=GREVIO%E2%80%99s+(Baseline)+Evaluation+Report&ie=UTF-8&oe=UTF-8, accessed May 24, 2021.

Melissa Eddy, "Germany Passes 'No Means No' Law After Cologne Attacks *The New York* Times" (New York, July 7, 2016), https://www.nytimes.com/2016/07/08/world/europe/germany-rape-law.html, accessed April 24, 2021.

TCK 103 Çocuk Cinsel İstismarı Affina Karşı Kadın Platformu, Bilgi Dosyası (July 9, 2020) 3,http://www.tdb.org.tr/ekler/TCK103_09.07.2020.pdf, accessed April 19, 2021.

The explanatory memorandum of Art. 102, The Grand National Assembly of Turkey (Türkiye Büyük Millet Meclisi), "Türk Ceza Kanunu Tasarısı ve Adalet Komisyonu Raporu (1/593)," 508, https://www.tbmm.gov.tr/tutanaklar/TUTANAK/TBMM/d22/c059/tbmm22059119ss0664.pdf, accessed September 2, 2021.

"Sweden Approves New Law Recognising Sex without Consent as Rape," BBC (London, May 24, 2018), https://www.bbc.com/news/world-europe-44230786, accessed April 24, 2021.

Zoe Tidman "'Only Yes Means Yes': Spain Plans New Rape Law to Put More Emphasis on Consent," *Independent* (London, March 3, 2020), https://www.independent.co.uk/news/world/europe/spain-rape-law-only-yes-means-yes-consent-bill-a9373256.html, accessed April 24, 2021.

Cases

Opuz v. Turkey, App no 33401/02 (ECHR, June 9, 2009)
Yargıtay Ceza Genel Kurulu, Date: 11.22.2018, E. 2017/394, K 2018/555
Yargıtay Ceza Genel Kurulu, Date: 1.23.2020, E. 2017/206, KÇ 2020/21
Yargıtay, 14. CD., Date:24.04.2012, E.2011/4954, K.2012/4688
Yargıtay, 5. CD, Date: 28.06.2007, E. 2007/7056, K. 2007/5422
Yargıtay, 5. CD, Date: 04.05.2006, 4003/3857
Yargıtay, 5. CD, Date: 16.02.2006, E. 2006/306, K. 2006/901
Yargıtay, 5. CD, Date: 21.09.2006, 7131
Yargıtay 5.CD, Date: 20. 04 1982, 800/135

NOTES

1. Durmuş Tezcan, Mustafa Ruhan Erdem and R. Murat Önok, *Teorik ve Pratik Ceza Özel Hukuku* (18th edn, Seçkin 2020) 391; Handan Yokuş Sevük, *Türk Ceza Hukuku Özel Hükümler* (3rd ed., Adalet 2020), 321.

2. Mahmut Koca and İlhan Üzülmez, *Türk Ceza Hukuku Özel Hükümler* (6th ed., Adalet 2019), 320.

3. For example, in terms of sexual assault of adults (Art. 102/1), whereas in the first version of the Code in 2005, a sex act that does not reach the level of intercourse like touching requires imprisonment from two years up to seven years, after the 2014 amendments it becomes imprisonment from five years up to ten years. At the same

time, in 2014, a mitigated form of this act as the instantaneous and intermittent bodily sexual contact such as one time a sudden touch is introduced. This requires imprisonment from two years up to five years. As for nonconsensual sexual intercourse against adults (Art. 102/2), it required imprisonment from seven years up to twelve years; in 2014, it is stipulated that its punishment cannot be less than twelve years' imprisonment.

4. Didem Yeldan and Gökhan Taneri, *Cinsel Suçlarda Beraat* (2nd ed., Seçkin 2020) 16; Türkan Yalçın Sancar "Dilin Kadına Yönelik Şiddetteki Rolü" (vol. 3, Hukuk Kurultayı, Ankara Barosu Yayınları 2006), 181; See also Selman Dursun, "Türk Ceza Hukuku'nda Cinsel Suçlara Genel Bir Bakış," *Ceza Hukuku Dergisi* 9, no. 24 (2014): 57, 71.

5. Adalet İstatistikleri Yayın Arşivi, https://adlisicil.adalet.gov.tr/Home/SayfaDetay/adalet-istatistikleri-yayin-arsivi, accessed September 2, 2021.

6. Dursun (n. 4) 57.

7. Ibid, 59.

8. Fahri Gökçen Taner, *Türk Ceza Hukukunda Cinsel Özgürlüğe Karşı Suçlar* (2nd ed., Seçkin 2020), 103 ff.

9. Dursun (n. 4) 71.

10. Ibid.

11. See also Gülsün Ayhan Aygörmez Uğurlubay, "Cinsel Suçlara İlişkin Güncel Maddi Hukuk Sorunları," in Gülsün Ayhan Aygörmez Uğurlubay (ed), *Alman ve Türk Hukukunda Cinsel Suçlar ve Cinsel Suçları Önleme Stratejileri* (Oniki Levha 2019), 19, 21.

12. Tezcan, Erdem, and Önok (n. 1) 393; Ali Kemal Yıldız, *5237 Sayılı Türk Ceza Kanunu* (İstanbul Barosu Yayınları 2007) 211; Veli Özer Özbek, Koray Doğan and Pınar Bacaksız, *Türk Ceza Hukuku Özel Hükümler* (15th ed., Seçkin 2020) 325; İlhan Üzülmez, "Yeni Türk Ceza Kanunu'nda Cinsel Saldırı Suçu," in Bahri Öztürk (ed), *3. Yılında Yeni Ceza Adalet Sistemi* (Seçkin 2009) 251; Yener Ünver, "Türk Maddi Ceza Hukukunda Cinsel Suçların Eleştirisel Olarak İncelenmesi," in Yener Ünver (ed) *II. Türkiye Slovenya Uluslararası Hukuk Sempozyumu-Cinsel Suçlar ve Evlilik Hukuku* (Seçkin 2014) 26–27; Sami Selçuk, "Cinsel Dokunulmazlığa Karşı Suçların Yapısı ve Bir Öneri," in Mahmut Koca, İzzet Özgenç, İlhan Üzülmez, and M. Emin Alşahin (eds), *Prof. Dr. Mehmet Emin Artuk'a Armağan* (Seçkin 2020) 737, 739; Seher Kırbaş Canikoğlu, "Feminist Bir Perspektifle Türk Ceza Kanunu'nda Cinsel Saldırı Suçu," (2013) 5 (1) *Fe Dergi: Feminist Eleştiri* 61, 62; Köksal Bayraktar and others, *Özel Ceza Hukuku*, vol. 2 (Oniki Levha 2017), 470.

13. Ruth A. Miller, *The Limits of Bodily Integrity* (Ashgate, Hampshire, 2007), 84.

14. Ibid, 85.

15. Ibid.

16. İbrahim Dülger, "Cinsel Özgürlüğe Karşı İşlenen Suçlardan Irza Geçme Suçu" (PhD Thesis, Selçuk University, Konya 1998), 232–233; Dursun (n 4) 58. In the case of *Opuz v. Turkey (2009),* the applicant stated that "A woman was viewed primarily as the property of society and of the male within the family. The most important indicator of this was that sexual offences were included in the section titled 'Crimes Relating to General Morality and Family Order,' whereas in fact sexual offences

against women are direct attacks on a woman's personal rights and freedoms," *Opuz v. Turkey*, App no. 33401/02 (ECHR, June 9, 2009), para.178.

17. See also Kırbaş Canikoğlu (n. 12) 62 and 63.

18. See also Dursun (n. 4) 59.

19. Sulhi Dönmezer, *Kriminoloji* (9th ed., Adalet Bakanlığı 2020) 165. See also Dursun (n. 4) 62.

20. See Joshua Dressler, "Understanding Criminal Law" (6th ed., LexisNexis, 2012), 574.

21. See Giulio Battaglini, "Fascist Reform of the Penal Law in Italy," *Journal of Criminal Law and Criminology* 24, no. 1 (1933): 278, https://scholarlycommons.law.northwestern.edu/cgi/viewcontent.cgi?article=2386&context=jclc, accessed May 22, 2021.

22. Faruk Erem, *Soyunu Sürdürebilmek Özgürlüğü* (Sevinç Matbaası 1980), 8.

23. Yalçın Sancar (n. 4), 183.

24. Also, the NGOs played a significant role in this achievement during the legislation of the new code. See Pınar İlkkaracan, "Changing Turkey's Laws to Improve Women's Rights," https://opendocs.ids.ac.uk/opendocs/bitstream/handle/20.500.12413/12596/ilkkaracan_2008_changing.pdf?sequence=1, accessed April 4, 2021, Yalçın Sancar (n. 4). 182.

25. Miller (n. 13), 72.

26. Nur Centel, "5237 Sayılı Türk Ceza Kanunu'nda Cinsel Saldırı Suçu ve Cinsel Suçlar Değişiklik Tasarısı'nın Değerlendirilmesi," *Türkiye Barolar Birliği Dergisi* 24, no. 99 (2012): 269, 271–272.

27. Dressler (n. 20), 571.

28. Kırbaş Canikoğlu (n. 12), 62–63.

29. Further, according to this study, 91.8 percent of participant answered the question, "Would you marry your daughter before the age of 18?" as "no." See *TCK 103 Çocuk Cinsel İstismarı Affına Karşı Kadın Platformu*, Bilgi Dosyası (July 9, 2020) 3, http://www.tdb.org.tr/ekler/TCK103_09.07.2020.pdf, accessed April 19, 2021.

30. Zeki Hafızoğulları and Muharrem Özen, *Türk Ceza Hukuku Özel Hükümler Kişilere Karşı Suçlar* (2nd ed., US-A Yayıncılık 2011), 152–153.

31. Ibid.

32. Ibid.

33. Selçuk (n. 12), 739.

34. Ibid, 740.

35. Taner (n. 8), 144. See also Yıldız (n. 12), 213; Dursun (n. 4), 71.

36. Üzülmez (n. 12), 252.

37. Özbek, Doğan, and Bacaksız (n. 12), 326; Üzülmez (n. 12), 252.

38. See Ünver (n. 12), 43–47.

39. Yıldız (n. 12), 224.

40. See also Tezcan, Erdem, and Önok (n. 1), 473.

41. Yıldız (n. 12), 224.

42. Dursun (n. 4), 67. See also Barış Çağırkan, "Child Brides and Its Importance in Terms of Social Roles in Turkish Society: The Case of Bitlis," (2018) 4

(1) Balkan and Near Eastern Journal of Social Sciences 52, http://ibaness.org/bnejss/2018_04_01/06_Cagirkan.pdf, accessed August 17, 2021.

43. See also Dursun (n 4), 59–60; Uğurlubay (n 11), 22.

44. A mistake of the age of the victim often comes to argument as a defense in the court in Turkey. For example, ". . . It is the case that a girl under the age of 15 came to the defendant's house by her own free will. The court notes that it shall be determined whether or not that she is under 15 years could be realized and understood by the defendant under the circumstances they live in . . ." (Yargıtay, 5. CD, Date: 21.09.2006,7131). An old case reads as ". . . As the accused had sexual intercourse with the victim by believing in the age of his partner written on her identity card, he cannot be convicted for that he intentionally committed a crime according to the age of victim redefined in the court" (Yargıtay 5.CD, Date: 20. 04 1982, 800/1354), retrieved from: Sadık Mollamahmutoğlu and Vural Savaş, *Yargısal ve Bilimsel İçtihatlarla Türk Ceza Kanununun Yorumu,* vol. 2 (Sevinç Matbaası 1985), 721–722.

45. See also Dursun (n. 4), 59–60.

46. "Aggravated lifelong sentence" is the heaviest punishment after abolishing the death penalty in 2004 with the Code no 5170, and it refers to serving imprisonment under stricter conditions.

47. Dursun (n. 4), 61–62.

48. Tezcan, Erdem, and Önok (n. 1), 481; Dursun (n. 4), 62.

49. Tezcan, Erdem, and Önok (n. 1), 491; Eylem Baş, "Türk Ceza Hukukunda Cinsel Taciz Suçu," *Ankara Üniversitesi Hukuk Fakültesi Dergisi* 65, no. 4 (2016): 1135, 1169.

50. Taner (n. 8), 114.

51. Melissa Eddy, "Germany Passes 'No Means No" Law After Cologne Attacks *The New York Times*" (New York, July 7, 2016), https://www.nytimes.com/2016/07/08/world/europe/germany-rape-law.html, accessed April 24, 2021.

52. Tatjana Hörnle, "The New German Law on Sexual Offenses" (October 1, 2016) 1, 10 https://ssrn.com/abstract=2999677, accessed August 17, 2021.

53."Sweden Approves New Law Recognising Sex without Consent as Rape," BBC (London, May 24, 2018), https://www.bbc.com/news/world-europe-44230786, accessed April 24, 2021.

54. Zoe Tidman "'Only Yes Means Yes': Spain Plans New Rape Law to Put More Emphasis on Consent," Independent (London, March 3, 2020), https://www.independent.co.uk/news/world/europe/spain-rape-law-only-yes-means-yes-consent-bill-a9373256.html, accessed April 24, 2021.

55. Ibid.

56. For example, Art. 151 of the Azerbaijan Penal Code reads as "[c]oercion of the person to sexual relations, buggery or to committing of other actions of a sexual nature by threat of destruction, damage or withdrawal of property or with use of material or other dependency of the victim (male, female)," retrieved from Sevinj Jabrayilova, "The Distinctive Features of Sexual-Related Offences: Statutory Rape V. Marital Rape" *Ankara Law Review* 9, no. 1 (2012): 81, 87, http://dergiler.ankara.edu.tr/dergiler/64/1768/18722.pdf, accessed May 15, 2021.

57. Dressler (n. 20), 576.

58. Taner (n. 8), 121.

59. GREVIO is abbreviation of Group of Experts on Action against Violence against Women and Domestic Violence. It serves as a monitoring mechanism of the Council of Europe Convention on Preventing and Combating Violence against Women and Domestic Violence Council of Europe, briefly known as the Istanbul Convention.

60. GREVIO's (Baseline) Evaluation Report (GREVIO/Inf(2018) 6, 2018) 8, https://www.google.com/search?client=safari&rls=en&q=GREVIO%E2%80%99s+(Baseline)+Evaluation+Report&ie=UTF-8&oe=UTF-8, accessed May 24, 2021.

61. Dressler (n. 20), 568.

62. Ibid.

63. M. Emin Artuk, Ahmet Gökcen, M. Emin Alşahin, and Kerim Çakır, *Ceza Hukuku Özel Hükümler* (18th ed., Adalet 2019), 373; Ünver (n. 12), 33–34.

64. Muhammed Demirel, "Ceza Hukukunda Rızanın İki Boyutu: Tipikliğe Engel Olan Rıza ve Hukuka Uygunluk Nedeni Olan Rıza," *İstanbul Hukuk Mecmuası*78, no. 3 (2020): 1469, 1518.

65. Taner (n. 8), 121.

66. Yargıtay Ceza Genel Kurulu [The Court of Cassation's Assembly of Criminal Chambers], Date: 22.11.2018, E. 2017/394, K 2018/555, https://www.lexpera.com.tr/ictihat/yargitay/ceza-genel-kurulu-e-2017-394-k-2018-555-t-22-11-2018, accessed May 23, 2021

67. Uğurlubay (n. 11), 26.

68. Dressler (n. 20), 568.

69. Üzülmez (n. 12), 254.

70. Artuk, Gökcen, Alşahin and Çakır (n. 63), 360; Üzülmez (n. 12), 261.

71. Artuk, Gökcen, Alşahin, and Çakır (n. 63), 360. See also Özbek, Doğan, and Bacaksız (n. 12), 329.

72. Yargıtay, 14. CD., Date: 24.04.2012, E.2011/4954, K.2012/4688, retrieved from Taner (n. 8), 120.

73. Taner (n. 8), 120.

74. See Dressler (n. 20), 567.

75. The explanatory memorandum of Art. 102, The Grand National Assembly of Turkey (Türkiye Büyük Millet Meclisi), "Türk Ceza Kanunu Tasarısı ve Adalet Komisyonu Raporu (1/593)," 508 https://www.tbmm.gov.tr/tutanaklar/TUTANAK/TBMM/d22/c059/tbmm22059119ss0664.pdf, accessed September 2, 2021. see also Taner (n. 8), 106.

76. Uğurlubay (n. 11), 24.

77. Ibid.

78. Yargıtay Ceza Genel Kurulu [The Court of Cassation's Assembly of Criminal Chambers], Date: 23.01.2020, E. 2017/206, KÇ 2020/21, https://www.lexpera.com.tr/ictihat/yargitay/ceza-genel-kurulu-e-2017-206-k-2020-21-t-23-1-2020, accessed May 23, 2021.

79. The explanatory memorandum of Art. 102. See n. 74. Artuk, Gökcen, Alşahin, and Çakır (n. 63), 360; Üzülmez (n. 12), 253–254.

80. Artuk, Gökcen, Alşahin, and Çakır (n. 63), 360.

81. Yargıtay, 5. CD, Date: 28.06.2007, E. 2007/7056, K. 2007/5422, https://www.lexpera.com.tr/ictihat/yargitay/5-ceza-dairesi-e-2007-7056-k-2007-5422-t-28-6-2007, accessed May 23, 2021. See also Üzülmez (n. 12), 253.

82. Yargıtay, 5. CD, Date: 16.02.2006, E. 2006/306, K. 2006/901, https://www.lexpera.com.tr/ictihat/yargitay/5-ceza-dairesi-e-2006-306-k-2006-901-t-16-2-2006, accessed May 23, 2021. See also Üzülmez (n. 12), 253.

83. Yargıtay, 5. CD, Date: 04.05.2006, 4003/3857, retrieved from Üzülmez (n 12), 253.

84. Dressler (n. 20), 568.

85. The explanatory memorandum of Art. 102. See n. 74.

86. Kırbaş Canikoğlu (n. 12), 66.

87. Taner (n. 8), 88.

88. Dursun (n. 4), 65. See also Koca and Üzülmez (n. 2), 327.

89. Tezcan, Erdem and Önok (n. 1), 397.

90. Ibid.

91. The explanatory memorandum of Art. 102. See n. 74. For critics, see Ünver (n. 12), 31–32.

92. Tezcan, Erdem and Önok (n. 1), 397; Dursun (n. 4), 65.

93. Yıldız (n. 12), 213; Ünver (n. 12), 31; Taner (n. 8), 91; Dursun (n. 4), 65–66.

94. Üzülmez (n. 12), 256; Koca and Üzülmez (n. 2), 327; Yokuş Sevük (n. 1), 325.

95. Council of Europe, Council of Europe Convention on preventing and combating violence against women and domestic violence [The Istanbul Convention] (Council of Europe Treaty Series - No. 210, Istanbul, 11.V.2011), https://rm.coe.int/168008482e, accessed August 17, 2021.

Chapter 2

Substantive and Procedural Challenges Impeding an Effective Response to Rape

The Example of Greece

Chara Chioni-Chotouman

Sexual offenses, and especially rape, are considered heinous crimes in contemporary societies. Feinberg aptly includes rape in his list of wrongs that are crimes "everywhere in the civilized world."[1] However, paying closer attention to the field we observe that few victims are reporting rape incidents, and even fewer participate in the subsequent criminal proceedings till their end, until a res judicata.[2] Several factors are driving victims away from criminal proceedings. It is undeniable that societal level factors, like the victim-blaming culture and the stigma associated with this offense, play an important role. This phenomenon is also linked with a distrust of the victims towards the formal criminal justice system. The MeToo movement can be considered a result of this rupture, in the sense that the inability of the formal system to respond to victim's needs and expectations enhances the development of informal ways to restore the balance.[3] Strongly connected with the above observations, shortcomings of the legal framework should not be overlooked. Substantive and procedural challenges are both affecting the standards at a declarative level and define the legal practice. In this chapter, the substantive and procedural factors that drive out of the criminal justice system rape victims in Greece and contribute to limited complaints and even fewer convictions will be examined. Due to their close connection with social structure and beliefs, all those shortcomings will be analyzed in their social context.

SUBSTANTIVE LAW—THE OFFENCE OF RAPE

The provision of rape itself influences the number of reports and constitutes an important factor in securing convictions. At a declarative level, it indicates the direction of the system toward either a more conservative and patriarchal approach or a more victim-centered/feminist one that encompasses women's experience. No other legal text addresses the citizens like the Penal Code does, shaped by the society and also shaping it.[4] As a result, the provision of rape not only demonstrates the prevalent social perception of what constitutes an acceptable sexual behavior but also affects the boundary between an unpleasant, even traumatic experience and an illegal one. Moreover, possible shortcomings are particularly affecting the course of criminal cases influencing the number of convictions. In this framework, it is particularly important to review the development of the provision of rape examining the starting point of the relevant legislative choices and the response of the system. The following analysis is divided into two sections, before and after the adoption of the new Greek Penal Code in 2019, which changed significantly the provision (Article 336 PC).

Shortcomings Before the Amendment of the Penal Code

The offense of rape was provisioned in the Penal Law promulgated in 1834. Forcing a man or a woman to sexual intercourse using physical force or threats connected to an imminent danger to life or physical integrity or by rendering the victim incapable to react was considered rape according to Article 273.

It was also provisioned in the Penal Code (PC) of 1950. Before 1984, it was included in the chapter titled "offences against morals". In its initial form punishable with rape was whoever by physical violence or threat of great and imminent danger forced a woman into intercourse outside marriage. Therefore, necessary elements of the crime were the use of physical violence or a threat of great and imminent danger and intercourse taking place outside marriage. Regarding the first element, it was necessary for a conviction to elaborate on how the perpetrator exercised the physical violence or threatened the victim.[5] Manifestation of resistance was also required.[6] Furthermore, sexual acts that did not constitute intercourse, in the sense of penetrative sex, could not be considered as rape,[7] being punishable with a more lenient penalty. The fact that only heterosexual penetrative sex could constitute rape was reinforced by court decisions stating that a woman could only participate by exercising the violence or articulating the threat.[8] Moreover, rape could only refer to a female victim. Lastly, it is evident that marital rape was not treated as a form of rape, with intercourse within marriage being considered as an obligation of the wife.[9] Any other form of sexual abuse against a female or male victim was covered by Article 337, titled “coercion into indecent acts” provisioning that imprisonment of up to ten years should be imposed on anyone that forced a woman or man using physical force or threats connected to an imminent danger to perform or tolerate any other indecent act. This offense foresaw a milder punishment, since imprisonment of up to twenty years could be imposed for the offense of rape.

With Law 1419/1984, the provision was amended combining the two aforementioned offenses (Articles 336 and 337 PC).[10] Thus, the intercourse was not differentiated from other sexual acts, even though the requirement that it should take place outside marriage remained. Moreover, the amendment adopted gender-neutral wording, making it possible for men to also be considered victims of the crime.[11] The fact that the perpetrator should use physical violence or a threat of a great and imminent danger remained as a prerequisite,[12] with the courts often requiring evidence of physical resistance by the victim.[13]

In 2006, a special statute aiming at combatting domestic violence was introduced in Greece following the initiative of women members of the Parliament from various political parties in 2004.[14] With Law 3500/2006, Article 336 was amended to include marital rape, thus eliminating a form of “spousal immunity.” Sexual assaults during the marriage under the previous regime could only be dealt with within Article 330 PC on inflicting violence. However, this provision constituted only a misdemeanor punishable by a maximum two-year penalty and addressed only partially the true nature of this form of sexual abuse. The view that intercourse within marriage constitutes a legitimate right of the husband was prevalent in Greek society until recently, driving victims away from the criminal justice system and leading them to tolerate the abuse.[15]

In conclusion, in Greece, the offense of rape was narrowly conceptualized expressing the dominant view of morality. It is indicative that the marital exception was in force until very recently. The offense of rape was structured primarily with the concept of “intercourse” at its core, influencing to this day the prevailing conception of the offense. It also required even after amendments the use of corporal violence or threats of great and imminent danger, thus leaving outside the protective scope incidents of rape that did not meet the aforementioned requirements. As a result, a lot of incidents were not reported and in case they were, no conviction could easily be secured. However, the case-law over time tried to extend the scope of the provision by eliminating the condition that the victim ought to have actively resisted the perpetrator’s violence.[16] Thus, signs of corporal violence were not considered a prerequisite in the case of a victim that due to shock or fear of the consequences of showing resistance or due to her weak physical strength or other circumstances considered resisting futile. This evolution acknowledged the fact that many victims experience immobility or a "freeze response,"[17] and it can be considered a major breakthrough for victims, who even in absence of signs of physical violence could come forward and report.

The Amendment of the Penal Code in 2019

Greece amended its Penal Code and Criminal Procedure Code in 2019 after approximately seventy years. The lengthy consultations that preceded and the two drafts that were not adopted should be indicative of a carefully considered effort to update criminal law. Indeed, the offence of rape was updated, now also incorporating the absence of consent. However, the adoption of a broad provision, in line with the Istanbul Convention and the ECtHR's case-law, was far from the committee's original standpoint.

According to the initial form of the Article available for public consultation, it was necessary that the act was committed by corporal violence or threat of serious and imminent danger to life or physical integrity.[18] Thus, cases where the threat did not concern the life or physical integrity were not punishable by imprisonment of five to fifteen years. Limiting the scope of threats that could lead to a decision that the offence of rape was committed results in leaving sexual assaults occurring by using extortionate threats unpunished. Psychological violence not related to life or physical integrity or financial threats were also ignored, without taking into account that marital rape often takes place in this framework. This choice also contradicted with the case-law, which evolved to address psychological violence.[19]

A public outcry followed, leading to the proposition of an additional paragraph according to which in case the act was committed under threat of an illegal act or omission, imprisonment of three to five years should be imposed. Extortionate threats thus constituted only a misdemeanor entailing legal consequences that rendered the protection scheme ineffective.[20] There was again a fierce opposition that resulted in a last-minute amendment in the face of the risk that Members of the Greek Parliament could vote down the entire bill containing the new Penal Code and the political cost of standing by such an anachronistic conception of rape. According to this final amendment a nonconsensual sexual act shall be considered rape and imprisonment of up to ten years shall be imposed. For the first time in Greece, sex without consent amounts to rape. It came as a victory of the feminist movement and as a result of the social reflexes which have definitely been evolved. It also set a precedent and a limit for future amendments aiming at going below a certain threshold of protection. The reflexes that were developed partly due to the narrow conception of rape for a long period of time, which left incidents of sexual abuse unpunished, demonstrated to the legislator that society has shifted towards not tolerating sexual abuse in all its forms. Therefore, future amendments aiming at reducing the protection will not be an easy decision.

Nevertheless, there are still several shortcomings leading to fewer victims reporting and fewer cases resulting in a conviction. Firstly, the initial narrow conception of rape in the proposed draft was combined with a new definition of the sexual acts that could lead to the commission of rape, since not all sexual acts amount to rape. Before the amendment, the notion of "indecent acts" was used, which was relatively broad and left a margin of appreciation to the judges. It was a well-processed concept defined in the case-law as any act that objectively offends the common perception of decency and morality and is subjectively directed towards satisfying or stimulating sexual desire.[21] It could include vaginal or anal intercourse as well as other acts replacing it, as the contact of the genitals of the perpetrator with the body of the victim or the touching or rubbing of the victim's genitals.[22] It is evident that judges enjoyed wide discretion examining ad hoc if an act other than intercourse could amount to rape.

The new provision, however, introduced a new statutory term, whose definition is included in the Penal Code. According to Article 336 para.2 PC, sexual intercourse includes copulation and acts of equal gravity. The arising issue is whether we can presume that acts that do not presuppose penetration continue to be illegal and amount to rape. According to the explanatory report of the new Penal Code vaginal and anal intercourse, oral sex, and hand-to-genital contact are included in the new definition, as well as the use of substitute means to commit the aforementioned acts.[23] However, several acts that under the previous regime were indecent, like genital rubbing, remain out of the scope of this new notion. Moreover, even the acts mentioned in this explanatory report it is not certain that will be acknowledged as "sexual intercourse" by case-law since explanatory reports are not binding. This new narrower term enhances uncertainty and fails to incorporate the female experience, which does not connect sexual assault with penetrative sex.[24] It also deprives the court of the necessary discretion in the framework of sexual offences, especially when committed against minors.[25] The case-law seems to address the issue by treating the new notion exactly like the notion of indecent acts, reclaiming its judicial discretion, thus providing an example of judicial activism.[26]

Moreover, the correlation between the nonconsensual rape regulated in Article 336 para 4 PC and sexual intercourse by abuse of position provisioned in Article 343 PC can also lead to fewer convictions. Article 343 PC refers to sexual intercourse occurring, as a result, either of abuse of employment relationship or by taking advantage of the victim's position as a person seeking employment[27] or by a perpetrator abusing her position (prison guards, police officers, teachers, etc.). It is a misdemeanor carrying a penalty ranging between two to five years. The legislator, thus, chose to treat as misdemeanor cases of nonconsensual rape committed by perpetrators abusing their status. This choice is obscure, given that nonconsensual rape constitutes, as analyzed, a felony. Yet, when the perpetrator abuses her position, something that logically would be considered as an aggravating circumstance, then the penalty is reduced.[28] Besides the paradox caused, treating those forms of sexual assault as a misdemeanor has remarkable consequences for the victims. It has to be noted that in the field of substantive criminal law, a misdemeanor is prescribed in five years, and in case the prosecution is initiated during that time, in eight years. Practically, it is not uncommon that the victim remains under the influence and the authority of the perpetrator for a significant amount of time, thus rendering the prosecution time-barred. On the contrary, the felonies are prescribed according to Article 113 PC in fifteen years.

Even the recent introduction of nonconsensual rape in the Penal Code is already under scrutiny. There are already voices against this development, arguing that the notion of consent is too broad and causes legal uncertainty.[29] This tendency may also affect the way in which courts will approach this new provision.[30] What is, therefore, imperative is to further develop and examine the concept of "consent" in the framework of sexual offences. Those arguing that the recently adopted amendment should be abolished fail to address the fact that it constitutes a positive obligation deriving from both the Istanbul Convention and the case-law of the ECtHR.[31] The introduction of nonconsensual rape was neither a novelty nor a "construction" of the feminist movement in Greece. It constitutes a contemporary trend affecting the legislation in many EU countries.[32] This theoretical position though combined with a more conservative political ideology focusing the discussion on evidentiary difficulties and possible false allegations impede the acceptance of the provision, thus discouraging victims and making competent authorities more restraint in cases where violence is absent. A lot of women believe that the law against rape is practically difficult to be applied.[33] They also fear that they will not be believed.[34] In this framework, under researching the relevant developments in other States and adhering to an old conception of rape is only leading in reproducing social stereotypes and rape myths, such as the "real" rape committed by a stranger with the use of force, made to suppress women and control female sexuality.[35]

PROCEDURAL ISSUES

Initiating Prosecution

Until 1984 and Law 1419/1984, for the initiation of prosecution a formal complaint by the victim was required, yet only when the latter was female. For some, this choice was interpreted as a form of exhortation to female victims to cover up the incident,[36] when others prioritized the will of the victim and criticized State's paternalism.[37] This precondition was altered and now the prosecution is initiated *ex officio* irrespective of the victim's gender. Although it is very common for the prosecutor to act after receiving a complaint by the victim, the *ex officio* prosecution was a significant amendment, because for non *ex officio* prosecuted crimes the victim must file a complaint within a period of three months. With the *ex officio* initiation this deadline does not apply. It also enables prosecutors to initiate proceedings after being notified of the commission of an offence, even without a complaint by the victim. Disconnecting the investigation and prosecution from a complaint by the victim is specifically mentioned in Article 55 of the Istanbul Convention, which addresses the reluctance of many victims to file a formal complaint due to fear of retaliation and often feelings of shame, emphasizing at the same time the social impact of the offence of rape.

A formal complaint by the victim remained in the new Penal Code a precondition for prosecutions in the framework of Article 343 PC. In case the perpetrator abused an employment relationship or took advantage of the victim's need to work, the onus was placed on the victim to initiate criminal proceedings. It was a questionable choice given that victims had only three months to report the incident which was recently amended by Law 4855/2021.

Influencing Prosecution

As analyzed, for the offence of rape the prosecution is initiated *ex officio*, thus not contingent upon a complaint by the victim and not influenced by a subsequent withdraw of such a complaint. However, according to Article 344 PC, it is possible for the prosecutor to abstain from prosecution at the request of the victim. In case the prosecution is already initiated, the prosecutor refers the case to the Judicial Council, which may terminate the proceedings considering the victim's statement that the publicity from the criminal prosecution will result in serious psychological trauma. This request can also be examined by the competent court.[38] The aim of this provision is to minimize the secondary victimization and the intrusion in the victim's private life. It was enacted in the aftermath of adopting the *ex officio* prosecution of rape to combine on the one hand the need to deal with the insufferable stigma and the psychological pressure a rape victim can experience in the framework of criminal proceedings and on the other hand the need to minimize the out-of-court-settlements.[39]

In this instance, the interest of the particular victim outweighs the public interest in prosecution. It is a provision leading to attrition since it affects the reports/prosecutions and reports/convictions ratio. It also does not eliminate the risk for out-of-the-court settlements with a strong transactional character between the perpetrator and the victim.[40] For those reasons, there has been a lot of skepticism about this provision, and it has also been proposed to abolish it.[41]

This provision certainly creates a rupture in the public nature of prosecution. It also enables perpetrators to approach vulnerable victims and exert pressure often accompanied by financial incentives. However, it cannot be overlooked that a victim of a serious sexual crime may choose not to relive the trauma, endure the cross-examination and have her life under scrutiny. Allowing the victim's will to influence prosecution contributes to avoiding secondary victimization through the criminal procedure.[42] The victim has the right to heal, and criminal proceedings may interfere with this right.[43] It also facilitates reconciliation and prevents a distressing invasion of criminal procedure in the victim's private life.[44] Moreover, not respecting the victim's will is rather patronizing and does not treat victims as responsible agents, competent to make their own decisions.[45] Furthermore, in practical terms, it is also difficult for prosecutions to continue "victimless" and rather controversial to force a rape victim to testify. A victim in this position will also face a very hostile and insensitive environment at a trial where the prosecutor, the judges, and the defendant will all be against her trying to indicate inconsistencies in her testimony and discredit her in order either to secure a conviction or—in the case of the defendant—to walk free from what seems a very odd trial. Thus, not respecting the will of the victim, in this case, is at the expense both of the victim's interests and the capacity of the system. Consequently, the main issue is not whether Article 344 CP should be abolished or not, but to create a system that can address the needs of rape victims enabling them to participate effectively and minimize the secondary victimization. Ignoring the will of the victim on the continuation of the proceedings while maintaining a hostile to rape victims' system will only exacerbate the issue.

The New Article 228 CCP

Procedures causing anxiety and stress to the victims or questioning their credibility are a significant issue leading them to refrain from pressing charges.[46] Greece just adopted a controversial measure of examining victims of rape, practically expanding the procedure on inquiring victims of trafficking to most sexual offenses' victims.[47] The aim of the new provision is to take an early statement by the victim, who subsequently is possible to not participate at the main hearing.[48] Particularly problematic is the provision that during the examination of the victim by competent authorities a psychologist or psychiatrist serving as an expert witness shall be appointed. She, according to the law, shall assess the perceptive capacity and mental state of the victim and formulate her findings in a written report, which shall form an integral part of the case file. In this process, the victim is explicitly deprived of her general right to appoint her own psychologist or psychiatrist as a consultant. While in the case of victims of human trafficking this procedure has a justifiable basis, the same does not apply for all victims of sexual offences. This psychological or psychiatric evaluation constitutes a mandatory medical examination that contradicts the need to recognize and respect victims enshrined in Article 1 of Directive 2012/29. It is also not in line with Article 20 of the Directive according to which all medical examinations should be kept to a minimum and carried out only where strictly necessary for the purposes of the criminal proceeding. Competent authorities are able, if they consider it necessary, to order a psychiatric expert examination. Adopting this measure *a priori* for all victims of sexual offenses without exception may be perceived by them as an expression of mistrust and discourage them from reporting.

Systemic Deficiencies and Sexual Offenses

Apart from specific issues linked to legislative drafting and political choices affecting the number of sexual abuse incidents reported and brought to trial, certain general issues in the administration of justice should be addressed. The length of the proceedings and the response from the police are not the only systemic deficiencies affecting rape victims. They are though the ones that can have a significant effect on victim's behavior and influence their trust and confidence in the criminal justice system.[49]

The length of the criminal proceedings often discourages victims. In Greece, a *res judicata* for a felony requires approximately eight years, and in case pre-trial detention is imposed on the accused around five to six years. Of course, factors such as the complexity of the case play an important role, but it is common ground that criminal proceedings last an extremely long time.[50] Victims that come forward and report are facing a slow-moving and bureaucratic system. The lengthy proceedings and several delays often caused by the conduct of the defence have psychological as well as financial impact on victims. Moreover, in general, delays affect the public trust in the operation of the criminal justice system. Specifically, in sexual offenses such delays can also compromise evidence and affect both victim's and defendants' ability to recollect the incident. They also lead to an impression of impunity for the offenders, thus having serious implications at a declarative level, ultimately for the position of women in society.[51]

Sexual offences are particularly affecting social peace; therefore, it should be considered instituting a faster procedure for those offenses. Dealing expediently with such offenses will secure evidence, help victims remain and have trust in the process, and eventually will increase the confidence of the public in the system. On the other hand, it will also benefit defendants, since being accused of a sexual offense has tremendous implications in their lives, and it is in their best interest too to promptly conclude the proceedings. In Greece, greatly influenced by the MeToo movement, there is an ongoing discussion about expediently dealing with sexual offense cases. The competent ministry has undertaken to propose a bill on prioritizing those cases. It is a very welcomed development, which has to be more than a paper resolution and practically by overcoming systemic deficiencies lead to handling swiftly serious forms of sexual abuse.

Police authorities at the forefront of the formal criminal justice system are also playing a key role in supporting victims filing a complaint, conducting an effective investigation and referring victims to the appropriate available services.[52] Their first task is to secure the proper investigation of the incident. They should order a forensic examination and collect all the evidence at this close to the event time. It is imperative to explain to the victim the necessity of undergoing a forensic examination even if she has visited a hospital, since in Greece medical professionals as first responders are not collecting any evidence even if the victim explicitly mentions rape. Moreover, their way of approaching and inquiring a rape victim must be appropriate and sensitive to minimize the victim's shame and discomfort.[53] Incidents of discouraging the victim to report must also be eliminated by properly educating police officers on how to approach rape victims or, even better, by establishing a special force entrusted with dealing with sexual offenses. They should also respond effectively irrespective of whether it is a recent incident or not. An incident committed in the framework of a relationship or marriage should be addressed accordingly, despite the tendency from the police to not interfere so aggressively in what they conceive as a "private matter."[54]

Police officers are also entrusted with the task to keep the victims involved in the process. Victims in Greece have after the EU Directive 2012/29 on establishing minimum standards on the rights, support, and protection of victims of crime several rights aiming at keeping them informed and included in the process.[55] Police officers should be familiar with those rights and inform the victim accordingly. Moreover, they also function as a referral point for victims in the framework of a multidisciplinary, holistic response.[56] Awareness of this obligation is pivotal as well as proper education to secure that vulnerable victims receive proper help and guidance. By minimizing the shortcomings in the police response more victims will decide to report and more will feel included and seen, overcoming feelings of fear and doubt, thus regaining their trust in the criminal justice system.[57]

Shortcomings in Safeguarding Victim's Rights

The victim in Greece has an important place in criminal proceedings, equal to that of the accused.[58] However, this enhanced role is contingent upon acquiring a formal role.[59] The victim who does not wish or is not able to become a party in the proceedings has more limited rights. Directive 2012/29 offered victims that do not participate as a party in the proceedings broader and concrete rights predominately at the pre-trial stage. Nevertheless, a great difference remains in Greece between a victim that does not participate as a party and the one acquiring this formal role. The aim of this chapter is not to analyze all the rights conferred to victims and possible shortcomings, since something like that exceeds the limits of this analysis, but to focus on the main shortcomings greatly affecting rape victims and their contact with the criminal justice system.

The Right to Understand and be Understood

After Directive 2012/29, Greece introduced several provisions aiming at guaranteeing the effective communication of victims at their first contact with competent authorities. All those provisions are particularly important for sexual abuse victims, who are usually traumatized and experience feelings of fear and confusion. More specifically, Law 4478/2017 that incorporated Directive 2012/29 compliments the provisions of the Code of Criminal Procedure on victims. According to the law, competent authorities should use simple and accessible language. Initially, national law limited this obligation only to the first contact with the victim, contrary to Article 3 para 2 of the Directive 2012/29 establishing a relevant obligation *from* the first contact. After a reasoned opinion by the European Commission, the relevant provision was amended now including every interaction with the victim.

Moreover, the victim has the right to be accompanied by a person of her choice. It is not an absolute right, with even the directive provisioning certain exceptions.[60] The national legislator though chose to further curtail the right. Firstly, in accordance with the directive, the right is not granted in case it is at the expense of the victim's interest or prejudices the course of the proceedings. According to national law though, persons involved in the investigated act are also excluded, yet without specifying who those persons are. The suspects, who are by definition involved in the act, belong to the first category of exceptions since their presence at the examination of the victim undoubtedly affects negatively the interests of the latter. Thus, this third exception can only refer to witnesses. However, witnesses are also persons that provided help to the victim right after the incident or, in case of sexual abuse, relatives or close friends with whom the victim shared details of the incident. The presence of a person close to the victim can empower the latter and reduce the feeling of shame and discomfort. Therefore, this exception must be interpreted in the light of the interests of the victims and of the proceedings as a whole and not function as a strict rule excluding a priori persons close to the victim, especially at the expense of the latter's interests.

The Right to Receive Information About the Case

Victims of all crimes should be offered all the necessary information to effectively participate in the proceedings and receive support. In this respect, Directive 2012/29 sets a detailed victim-centered framework, with the extent of the information varying according to the specific nature of each case and the needs of the particular victim.[61] Concerning this right, Greece has followed the directive. The relevant information linked with the initiation of the proceedings, namely the procedure for filing a complaint and the victim's subsequent role in it, available legal aid, translation, and interpretation services as well as further support shall be provided by the authorities by their own initiative, not being contingent upon a request from the victim.[62] This is a really important parameter especially for victims of sexual abuse, who being particularly vulnerable should not be placed under the burden of filing petitions to receive information. However, albeit this important step toward greater protection, ways to monitor the granting of the right are not provisioned. Competent authorities are not obliged to prove that they offered the necessary information and not offering them is not linked to remedies or sanctions.

Right to Legal Aid

Participating in criminal proceedings especially as a party requires financial resources. In Greece, the access to legal aid is regulated for all offences by Law 3226/2004, recently amended by Law 4689/2020. It is disputed whether or not it can be granted at the stage before filing a complaint. A more victim-oriented interpretation of the provision's wording allows victims to file a petition for legal aid even at this early stage.[63] In any case, victims can be provided a state-appointed attorney free of charge after filing a complaint and expressing the will to participate in the proceedings as a party. This is, as already mentioned, an important prerequisite for granting a significant number of rights and facilitations to the victim that we also come across in the framework of legal aid.

Beneficiaries of legal aid are also citizens of an EU Member State, third-country nationals, and stateless persons if they have a lawful residence or habitual residence in the European Union. However, granting the right is contingent upon strict financial and criteria and the gravity of the offense. Those limitations combined with the fact that legal aid in Greece faces several shortcomings and often in the framework of sexual offenses is lacking the necessary expertise for dealing with such cases hinder the access to the right.[64]

In Camera Proceedings

High attrition rates in rape can be tackled by rendering the criminal trial a safe environment for victims to participate and testify. The criminal trial constitutes an ordeal to rape victims, as also the ECtHR acknowledges.[65] Encountering the perpetrator again and having to endure questions about private matters, such as previous sexual encounters and relationships, can cause a lot of anxiety to victims of sexual offences.[66] Details of the crime can also cause frustration and feelings of shame, especially in the era of social media where victim shaming can take huge dimensions and such details can be linked with the name of the victim for years, leading to the victim constantly reliving the trauma.[67] Therefore, a public procedure can be very intimidating for victims, that especially after several years just want to move on with their lives and do not have their private lives under public scrutiny.[68] It also affects their testimony since they are influenced by the presence of so many strangers. In this context, providing the possibility to victims to ask for the trial to be held in camera is of paramount importance for them to remain in the process and for safeguarding the quality and accuracy of their testimony.[69]

However, the right to ask for the proceedings to be held in camera is conferred according to Greek CCP only to victims that have the role of the party in the proceedings. As stated in Article 330 CCP, the court may of its own motion or at the request of a party decide to order holding the proceedings, whether wholly or partly, in camera. To define if it is imperative to exclude the public from a trial, the court examines whether the publicity of the hearing is detrimental to the accepted principles of morality or whether special reasons for protecting the private or family life of the parties exist. It is evident that there are the interests of the party that are considered and not the ones of every victim irrespective of her choice to acquire the formal role of the party. Consequently, a victim not participating as a party cannot address the court asking for the exclusion of the public nor can be heard in the process of the court examining such an option in its own motion.[70] It is an omission inconsistent with the necessity to create a safe environment for victims of sexual abuse to come forward and testify in an environment that does not afflict their emotional well-being. It is important for every rape victim, irrespective of her role in the proceedings, to be able to address the court and request the exclusion of publicity and it is equally imperative to be heard in the framework of such a decision by the court.

CONCLUDING REMARKS

Substantive and procedural shortcomings are affecting the response of the criminal justice system and the perception of its efficiency by victims. Whereas some attrition in rape cases is expected and it is even reasonable given the influence of social and psychological factors, it is imperative to create a system that does not exacerbate the phenomenon. For rape victims, addressing the criminal justice system should not seem futile or an ordeal. In this respect, it is of paramount importance to adopt a modern and effective normative framework that covers all forms of rape. Moreover, it is crucial to eliminate all those procedural barriers causing anxiety to victims both at the pretrial stage and at the main proceedings, such as the new article 228 CCP. Respecting victim's rights and adopting a victim-centered holistic approach from the first contact of the victim with competent authorities will also help her see the criminal justice system as a safe and trustworthy environment and not as a completely uninterested and impersonal one.

Finally, the state must adopt a firm stance against sexual assaults. By supporting relevant theoretical research, issuing guidelines for competent authorities and monitoring their prompt and adequate response it will be made evident for victims that they have the right to come forward and address a system that can respond to their experience in a sensitive manner.

REFERENCES

Anagnostopoulos, I., "Prosecuting Rape: A Public or Private Matter?," *Poinika Chronika* 2 (1985) (in Greek).

Aziz, S., "#MeToo—Der Umgang mit Opfern sexualisierter Gewalt," *Juridikum* 1 (2018).

Charalambakis, A., *Criminal Law and Case-law* (Nomiki Vivliothiki 2021) (in Greek).

Chioni-Chotouman, C., "Combating Gender-Based Violence: Greek Criminal Law vis-à-vis European Trends," in Stradella E (ed.), *Gender Based Approaches to the law and Juris Dictio in Europe* (Pisa University Press 2020).

Chioni-Chotouman, C., *Victims' Rights in Criminal Proceedings—The Impact of European Law in Greek Criminal Trial* (Nomiki Bibliothiki 2021) (in Greek).

Dionysopoulou, A., "The offence of rape in the new Penal Code," *Nova Criminalia* 8 (2020) (in Greek).

Doak, J., *Victims' Rights, Human Rights and Criminal Justice: Reconceiving the Role of Third Parties* (Hart Pub 2008).

Elbers, N. et al., "The Role of Victims' Lawyers in Criminal Proceedings in the Netherlands," [2020] *European Journal of Criminology*.

Elholm, T., and Colson, R., "The Symbolic Purpose of EU Criminal Law," in Renaud Colson and Stewart Field (eds), *EU Criminal Justice and the Challenges of Diversity: Legal Cultures in the Area of Freedom, Security and Justice* (Cambridge University Press 2016).

Feinberg, J., *The Moral Limits of the Criminal Law Volume 1: Harm to Others* (OUP 1987).

Harless, S., "From the Bedroom to the Courtroom: The Impact of Domestic Violence Law on Marital Rape Victims," *Rutgers Law Journal* 35 (2003).

Hellmann, D., and Pfeiffer, C., "Epidemiologie und Strafverfolgung sexueller Gewalt gegen Frauen in Deutschland," *Monatsschrift für Kriminologie und Strafrechtsreform* 98, no. 6 (2015).

Hohl, K., and Stanko, E., "Complaints of Rape and the Criminal Justice System: Fresh Evidence on the Attrition Problem in England and Wales," *European Journal of Criminology* 12, no. 3 (2015).

Jordan, J., "Here We Go Round the Review-go-round: Rape Investigation and Prosecution—Are Things Getting Worse Not Better?," *The Journal of Sexual Aggression* 17, no. 3 (2011).

Kaifa-Gbanti, M., "The Basic Principles of the Rule of Law, the New Penal Code and Its Amendments," [2020] Poinika Chronika (in Greek).

Kostaras, A., "Utopia and Reality in the Prosecution of Rape" [1987] Poinika Chronika (in Greek); Catharine MacKinnon, "Feminism, Marxism, Method and the State," in Harding S (ed), *Feminism and Methodology* (Indiana University Press 1988).

Majeed-Ariss, R., et al., "'Could Do Better': Report on the Use of Special Measures in Sexual Offences Cases," *Criminology & Criminal Justice* 21, no. 1 (2021).

Moller, A., et al., "Tonic Immobility during Sexual Assault—A Common Reaction Redicting Post-Traumatic Stress Disorder and Severe Depression," *Acta Obstetricia et Gynecologica Scandinavica* 96, no. 8 (2017).

Moor, A., et al., "Rape: A Trauma of Paralyzing Dehumanization," *Journal of Aggression, in Maltreatment & Trauma* 22, no. 10 (2013).

Nakane, T., "Prosecution Ex Officio or Following a Complaint by the Victim? An Analysis on Offences Related to Violence against Women and Sexual Offences," *New Journal of European Criminal Law* 12, no. 2 (2021).

Northern Greece Law Society, *The Draft of the Manoledakis' Committee—A Solution (?) to the Issues of Criminal Justice* (Sakkoulas Pub. 2013) (in Greek).

Papageorgiou-Gonatas, S., *Current Issues in Modern Criminal Proceedings* (Nomiki Bibliothiki 2015) (in Greek).

Papageorgiou, G., "The Female Victim in the Criminal Justice System," [1990] Efimerida Ellinon Nomikon (in Greek)

Paraskevopoulos, N., and Fitrakis, E., *Sexual Offenses* (Sakkoulas Pub. 2021) (in Greek).

Patterson, D., Greeson, M., and Campbell, R., "Understanding Rape Survivors' Decisions Not to Seek Help from Formal Social Systems," *Health & Social Work* 34, no. 2 (2009).

Pitsela, A., "Kriminalpolitik in Griechenland," *Neue Kriminalpolitik* 27, no. 2 (2015).

Reidy, M., "The Impact of Media Coverage on Rape Shield Laws in High-Profile Cases: Is the Victim Receiving a Fair Trial," *Catholic University Law Review* 54 (2004).

Stefanidou, A., *Domestic Violence* (Nomiki Bibliothiki 2010) (in Greek).

Symeonidou-Kastanidou, E., *Offences against Personal Legal Values* (Nomiki Bibliothiki 2020).

Taylor, C., and Gassner, L., "Stemming the Flow: Challenges for Policing Adult Sexual Assault with Regard to Attrition Rates and Under-reporting of Sexual Offences," *Police Practice and Research* 11, no. 3 (2010).

Tuerkheimer, D., "Beyond #MeToo," *New York University Law Review* 14, no. 5 (2019).

Vavra, R., *Die Strafbarkeit nicht-einvernehmlicher sexueller Handlungen zwischen erwachsenen Personen* (Nomos 2020).

Vetten, L., et al., "Worth Their While? Pursuing a Rape Complaint through the Criminal Justice System," *South African Crime Quarterly* 31 (2010).

Wegerstad, L., "Sex Must Be Voluntary: Sexual Communication and the New Definition of Rape in Sweden," *German Law Journal* 22 (2021).

Wolf, A. K., and Werner, M., "Victims' Rights Looking Good on Paper—How Criminal Prosecution in Germany Fails Victims of Sexual Violence," *German Law Journal* 22 (2021).

NOTES

1. Joel Feinberg, *The Moral Limits of the Criminal Law Volume 1: Harm to Others* (Oxford University Press 1987) 10.

2. See indicatively Deborah Hellmann and Christian Pfeiffer, "Epidemiologie und Strafverfolgung sexueller Gewalt gegen Frauen in Deutschland," *Monatsschrift für Kriminologie und Strafrechtsreform* 98, no. 6 (2015): 527, 531.

3. See in this respect also Deborah Tuerkheimer, "Beyond #MeToo," *New York University Law Review* 14, no. 5 (2019): 1146, 1153, and 1159.

4. See also Thomas Elholm and Renaud Colson, "The Symbolic Purpose of EU Criminal Law," in Renaud Colson and Stewart Field (eds), *EU Criminal Justice and the Challenges of Diversity: Legal Cultures in the Area of Freedom, Security and Justice* (Cambridge University Press 2016), 49ff.

5. Areios Pagos 557/1979 Nomos database.

6. Ibid.

7. For this interpretation of the notion "intercourse," see first instance court of Kalamata 105/2009, *Poiniki Dikaiosini* 7 (2010): 813.

8. See first instance court of Thessaloniki 103/1981 Nomos database stating in relation to the intercourse that the participation of a woman in the offense of rape seems "*impossible due to the same biological construction as that of the victim.*"

9. See also in this respect, Giorgos Papageorgiou, "The Female Victim in the Criminal Justice System," *Efimerida Ellinon Nomikon* (1990): 767, 768.

10. In its new form, article 336 PC stated: *"Whoever with physical violence or with threat of great and imminent danger forces another to extra-matrimonial intercourse or to tolerance or action of an indecent act, is punished with incarceration.*"

11. First instance court of Kalamata, *Poiniki Dikaiosini* 7 (2010): 813.

12. First instance court of Edessa 60/1984 Nomos database.

13. Papageorgiou (n. 9), 768.

14. Andromeda Stefanidou, *Domestic Violence* (Nomiki Bibliothiki 2010).

15. On the correlation between the legislative change and the willingness of victims to report incidents of marital rape, see Hellmann and Pfeiffer (n. 2), 529, on German law.

16. Mixed Jury Court second instance Athens 497/2016 Isokratis database, Mixed Jury Court Athens 153/2015 Isokratis database, first instance Judicial Council of Heraklion 33/2010, *Poinika Chronika* (2012): 374.

17. See about freezing as peritraumatic behavior Avigail Moor and others, "Rape: A Trauma of Paralyzing Dehumanization," *Journal of Aggression, in Maltreatment & Trauma* 22, no. 10 (2013): 1055; Anna Moller and others, "Tonic Immobility during Sexual Assault—A Common Reaction Redicting Post-Traumatic Stress Disorder and Severe Depression," *Acta Obstetricia et Gynecologica Scandinavica* 96, no. 8 (2017): 932.

18. Draft of the new Penal Code, http://www.opengov.gr/ministryofjustice/?p=9808, accessed December 9, 2021.

19. Mixed Jury Court second instance Thessaloniki 246/2015 Isokratis database, Mixed Jury Court Athens 512/2016 Isokratis database, Mixed Jury Court Athens 212/2018 Isokratis database, second instance Judicial Council Thessaloniki 182/2014 Isokratis database.

20. See in detail, Chara Chioni-Chotouman, "Combating Gender-Based Violence: Greek Criminal Law vis-à-vis European Trends," in Elettra Stradella (ed), *Gender Based Approaches to the Law and Juris Dictio in Europe* (Pisa University Press 2020), 205.

21. Areios Pagos 316/2018, 491/2019.

22. Areios Pagos 153/2019, 322/2019, 347/2019, 447/2019, 491/2019.

23. Law 4619/2019, Explanatory Report, 66.

24. See Mixed Jury Court Athens 120/2020 Isokratis database, which explicitly characterizes this new notion as narrower.

25. In favor of this discretion seem to be also Nikos Paraskevopoulos and Eftichis Fitrakis, *Sexual Offences* (Sakkoulas Publications 2021), 41.

26. Areios Pagos 1/2020, Areios Pagos 241/2020, Mixed Jury Court Athens 258/2020, Qualex database; See, however, Aristotelis Charalambakis, *Criminal Law and Case-law* (Nomiki Vivliothiki 2021), 656, who criticizes this case-law.

27. With Law 4855/2021 the phrase "taking advantage of victim's need to work" was amended as mentioned.

28. See also Athanasia Dionysopoulou, "The Offence of Rape in the New Penal Code," *Nova Criminalia* 8 (2020): 4, 5.

29. See for example Maria Kaifa-Gbanti, "The Basic Principles of the Rule of Law, the New Penal Code and Its Amendments," *Poinika Chronika* (2020): 161, and Paraskevopoulos and Fitrakis (n. 25) 113, that even argue that it results to less protection for female victims.

30. For the slow reaction of the judicial system to such amendments, see Sarah Harless, "From the Bedroom to the Courtroom: The Impact of Domestic Violence Law on Marital Rape Victims," *Rutgers Law Journal* 35 (2003): 305.

31. Article 36 of the Istanbul Convention, *M.C. v. Bulgaria* ECHR 2003-XII 3, par. 166; *M.G.C. v. Romania* App no 61495/11 (ECHR, March 15, 2016), par. 59; *I.C. v. Romania* App no 36934/08 (ECHR May 24, 2016), par. 52, *Z. v. Bulgaria* App No 39257/17 (ECHR May 28, 2020), par. 67.

32. See Linnea Wegerstad, "Sex Must Be Voluntary: Sexual Communication and the New Definition of Rape in Sweden," *German Law Journal* 22 (2021): 734, 736.

33. Catharine MacKinnon, "Feminism, Marxism, Method and the State," in Sandra Harding (ed), *Feminism and Methodology* (Indiana University Press 1988), 144.

34. Jan Jordan, "Here We Go Round the Review-go-round: Rape Investigation and Prosecution—Are Things Getting Worse Not Better?," *The Journal of Sexual Aggression* 17, no. 3 (2011): 234, 236.

35. See Rita Vavra, *Die Strafbarkeit nicht-einvernehmlicher sexueller Handlungen zwischen erwachsenen Personen* (Nomos 2020), 81; and Anne-Katrin Wolf and Maja Werner, "Victims' Rights Looking Good on Paper—How Criminal Prosecution in Germany Fails Victims of Sexual Violence," *German Law Journal* 22 (2021): 800, 808.

36. Ilias Anagnostopoulos, "Prosecuting Rape: A Public or Private Matter?" *Poinika Chronika* 2 (1985): 621, 622

37. Alexandros Kostaras, "Utopia and Reality in the Prosecution of Rape," *Poinika Chronika* (1987): 3, 4.

38. Areios Pagos (Full Court) 37/1991, Mixed Jury Court Aigion 17/2018 Isokratis Database.

39. See Elisavet Symeonidou-Kastanidou, *Offences against Personal Legal Values* (Nomiki Bibliothiki 2020), 295.

40. Stylianos Papageorgiou–Gonatas, *Current Issues in Modern Criminal Proceedings* (Nomiki Bibliothiki 2015), 166.

41. See Draft of the new Penal Code—Committee of Prof. I. Manoledakis in Northern Greece Law Society, *The Draft of the Manoledakis' Committee—A Solution (?) to the Issues of Criminal Justice* (Sakkoulas Pub. 2013), 263, with, however, a rather insensitive reasoning stating that the public interest is far more important than the possible psychological trauma of the victim (sic), 373.

42. See Judicial Council Thessaloniki 1170/2005 Qualex database, which states that the trial constitutes a "second rape" for the victim.

43. Lisa Vetten et al., "Worth Their While? Pursuing a Rape Complaint through the Criminal Justice System," *South African Crime Quarterly* 32 (2010): 19, 24.

44. See the reasoning in relation to *ex officio* prosecution, which also applies to the victim influencing the continuation of prosecution in Tomohiro Nakane, "Prosecution Ex Officio or Following a Complaint by the Victim? An Analysis on Offences Related to Violence against Women and Sexual Offences," *New Journal of European Criminal Law* 12, no. 2 (2021): 46, 154.

45. Harless (n. 30), 306.

46. Vavra (n. 35), 73.

47. Issues were outlined by Scientific Council of the Parliament in its report even before Law 4855/2021 was passed, https://www.hellenicparliament.gr/UserFiles/7b24652e-78eb-4807-9d68-e9a5d4576eff/11775701.pdf, accessed December 9, 2021 (in Greek).

48. Cf. article 58(a) of the German Code of Criminal Procedure (StPO), according to which the consent of the victim is necessary for the audio-visual recording.

49. See Debra Patterson, Megan Greeson, and Rebecca Campbell, "Understanding Rape Survivors' Decisions Not to Seek Help from Formal Social Systems," *Health & Social Work* 34, no. 2 (2009): 127, 130, about how the disbelief in formal social systems prevents rape victims from addressing them. See also Wolf and Werner (n. 35), 815.

50. Circular of the Prosecutor of the Supreme Court 7/2021 available at https://eisap.gr/%ce%b5%ce%b3%ce%ba%cf%8d%ce%ba%ce%bb%ce%b9%ce%bf%cf%82-7-2021/, accessed December 9, 2021; Angelika Pitsela, "Kriminalpolitik in Griechenland," *Neue Kriminalpolitik* 27, no. 2 (2015): 202, 204.

51. Katrin Hohl and Elisabeth Stanko, "Complaints of rape and the criminal justice system: Fresh evidence on the attrition problem in England and Wales," *European Journal of Criminology* 12, no. 3 (2015): 324, 325.

52. On the police being the public face of the criminal justice system and the lack of confidence of sexual assault victims in reporting to the police, see Caroline Taylor and Leigh Gassner, "Stemming the Flow: Challenges for Policing Adult Sexual Assault with Regard to Attrition Rates and Under-reporting of Sexual Offences," *Police Practice and Research* 11, no. 3 (2010): 240, 242.

53. See Wolf and Werner (n. 35), 811, for a link between an unprofessional approach by police officers and attrition.

54. See also Harless (n. 30), 309.

55. See in detail Chara Chioni-Chotouman, *Victims' Rights in Criminal Proceedings—The Impact of European Law in Greek Criminal Trial* (Nomiki Bibliothiki 2021), 176.

56. Dir 2012/29, Article 8 par. 2.

57. See Hohl and Stanco (n. 46), 333, for data on how police-victim interaction affects attrition. See also Sonja Aziz, "#MeToo—Der Umgang mit Opfern sexualisierter Gewalt," *Juridikum* no. 1 (2018): 34, 36.

58. Article 70 Greek CCP.

59. Article 63 Greek CCP on supporting the accusation.

60. Dir 2012/29 Art.3 para 3.

61. Dir 2012/29 art.4.

62. Explanatory Memorandum Law 4478/2017, p.13.

63. Chioni-Chotouman, "Victims' Rights in Criminal Proceedings" (n. 55), 191.

64. On the importance of legal representation for the exercise of victim's rights in the case of serious crimes and sexual offences, see Nieke Elbers et al., "The Role of Victims' Lawyers in Criminal Proceedings in the Netherlands," *European Journal of Criminology* (2020): 1, 13.

65. *Mraović v. Croatia* App no 30373/13 (ECHR May 14, 2020), para. 47.

66. Jonathan Doak, "Victims' Rights, Human Rights and Criminal Justice: Reconceiving the Role of Third Parties" (Hart Publishing 2008), 55.

67. See in this respect Megan Reidy, "The Impact of Media Coverage on Rape Shield Laws in High-Profile Cases: Is the Victim Receiving a Fair Trial," *Catholic University Law Review* 54 (2004): 297, 320.

68. See for the issue also Rabiya Majeed-Ariss et al., "'Could Do Better': Report on the Use of Special Measures in Sexual Offences Cases," *Criminology & Criminal Justice* 21, no. 1 (2021): 89, 99.

69. *Mraović v. Croatia,* App no. 30373/13 (ECHR May 14, 2020), paras 45–47.

70. Chioni-Chotouman, *Victims' Rights in Criminal Proceedings* (n. 55), 267.

Chapter 3

Sexual Offenses in The Republic of North Macedonia

Nikola Tupancheski, Gordana Lazhetikj, Aleksandra Gruevska Drakulevski, and Aleksandra Deanoska Trendafilova

A seventeen-year-old girl was raped by her fiancé's cousin—Macedonian media reported in December 2021 and recently a formal accusation for rape was submitted for this case by the Public Prosecution Office—Gostivar to the Court.[1] Just a few days before, an announcement was made that a nine-year-old child was sexually abused twice by a person who falsely introduced himself to be an imam.[2] But the public in North Macedonia was particularly surprised when in August 2021, the Public Prosecution Office submitted accusations for actions of sexual abuse of several children perpetrated by their judo coach.[3]

Undoubtedly, sexual offenses are a serious issue in the criminal law as well as in the practice worldwide. They are specific and related to a number of sensitive subjects, including but not limited to individual freedom, gender equality and position of women in society. Sexual offenses are globally subject of studies and research all the time in criminal law science, criminology, victimology, subject of debates and discussions and of the activities of many civil society organizations for the protection of gender-sensitive issues, sexual violence.[4] The sphere we discuss is extremely complex, since these crimes are often a form of domestic violence,[5] with a dominant gender-sensitive issue. A particularly serious form is sexual abuse of children. In addition to the group of violent forms of sexual offenses, there are acts of a sexual nature where violence is not a "*prima facie*" element of the crime, but the crime itself is opposite to the so-called "sexual morality system."[6] as this expression is used even in the title of the Chapter XIX of the Macedonian Criminal Code—Crimes against Sexual Freedom and Sexual Morality.[7] These offenses are socially and legally unacceptable because they represent unethical acts of abuse that further (potentially) generate serious implications and even consequential violence.

Recently, a process of drafting amendments to the Macedonian Criminal Code (hereinafter: MCC) has been initiated by the Ministry of Justice in order to finally harmonize the criminal legislation of North Macedonia with the Istanbul Convention,[8] which came into force in the Macedonian legislation on July 1, 2018. This chapter addresses particularly sexual offences from legislative aspect as several concepts in the Macedonian positive legislation seem to be inappropriate due to the still present traditional concept of rape in the law. The draft—novelties that at the moment (December 2021) are still not adopted, but are in Parliament Procedure, provide significant changes in line with the contemporary standards of protection of women from sexual violence and radically changing the concept of rape. Additionally, apart from this novelty to the existent Criminal Code, a whole new Criminal Code is in phase of preparation and the initial draft envisages changes even in the title of the Chapter and eradicating the obsolete sexual morality concept.

Further the chapter analyzes the substantive criminal law aspects, the procedural aspects and protection of victims of sexual offences in the Republic of North Macedonia, as well as the criminological aspects and sentencing policy for sexual offences in the Republic of Macedonia. The shortcomings will be highlighted and finally the chapter provides general proposals as concluding remarks.

SUBSTANTIVE CRIMINAL LAW ASPECTS: SEXUAL OFFENSES IN STRICT AND BROAD SENSE

The MCC provisions relevant to sexual offenses constitute Chapter XIX: Crimes against the Sexual Freedom and Sexual Morality (Articles 186–194-a). The title of this chapter itself reflects the dual nature of the object of protection and the two subgroups of crimes related to the more specific object of protection.[9] The first aspect is the freedom of the person, and therefore, the acts against that freedom in area of sexual relations are criminalized. On the other hand, the acts against morality (the general moral views of what is allowed and what is not permissible in the sphere of sexual relations according to the cultural and moral norms) are the second focal point.[10] The moral views and understandings of what the society allows and what does not in this sphere are under constant pressure of the cultural and other sources (e.g., religion and tradition).[11] However, precisely these—the culture, tradition, and so on, are the sources of acts that are criminalized in contemporary legislative amendments (female genital mutilations, for example).[12]

Although most of the offences are part of the aforementioned chapter XIX, several incriminations in another chapter of the MCC have sexual pretext. Namely, the crimes perpetrated for the purpose of sexual exploitation of persons (mostly women) and children are crimes of trafficking and are part of chapter XXXIV: Crimes against Humanity and the International Law[13] (human trafficking and child trafficking). These serious crimes are perpetrated for many possible purposes but the most common in practice is the purpose of sexual exploitation. According to the Annual reports of the National Commission for Combating Trafficking in Human Beings and Illegal Migration, in the period 2014–2020, nearly 80 percent are victims of sexual exploitation and forced marriages.[14]

Chapter XIX, as we already mentioned, does not cover all acts where the motive has sexual nature. This also refers to the cases of pathological sexual expression such as the sexual sadistic murders or human trafficking etc.[15] There are two subgroups of crimes in chapter XIX:[16]

a. Crimes against the freedom of the person and the free decision-making in sexual relations, and
b. Crimes against sexual morality.

This internal systematic of the chapter in two subgroups was established from the moment the Criminal Code of Macedonia was adopted in 1996, five years after Macedonia declared independence and modernized the criminal law but still kept some concepts from the past system. The first subgroup of crimes represents actions directed against the person's free will and these crimes are negation of self-determination to engage in a free sexual intercourse. As such they are violations of the human dignity.[17] Some of these acts additionally consist of elements of exploiting of a position or the vulnerability of the victims. These victims are in fact limited in their freedom of will. These represent crimes against the individual.

A general feature of the second subgroup of crimes is that they primarily go against the general moral order of what is acceptable, allowable in the society. It is obvious that this is a remainder of the extremely traditional view that existed in past in respect to sexual relations that is expressed, as mentioned, even in the title of the MCC chapter XIX itself. However, in the literature it is noted that the protective function of the Macedonian Criminal Law is mainly dimensioned towards protection of the individual and the "moralization function" should be (and is) in fact abandoned.[18]

The concept of sexual intercourse and the concept of "other sexual acts" are constitutive elements of several crimes of this type. The crimes against free decision regarding sexual relations that are the first subgroup of the MCC Chapter XIX are the following:

Rape[19] is considered a classical form of a sexual offense in the Macedonian Criminal Law, for which imprisonment of three to ten years is prescribed for the basic form.[20] The object of protection of this incrimination is the freedom to have sexual intercourse, which is absolute and does not depend on certain qualities or the character of the person: the freedom of decision-making in this sphere of every person is protected. According to the law, the act is committed by a person who, by using force or threatening to directly attack the life or bodily integrity of the victim or the life or body of a person close to the victim, will force the victim to a sexual intercourse or another sexual act. In the Macedonian Criminal Law theory, rape is considered a complex criminal act,[21] consisting of two segments: (1) *coercion,* stipulated as a legal element of rape and (2) *intercourse*, or another sexual act consisting of another type of penetration or genital friction, body touch with sexual connotation, and similar acts. The coercion is performed by using force or threat. The threat consists in making certain that a direct physical attack to the victim or a close person (meaning a person that is engaged in emotionally close relations with the victim-member of family, fiancé, partner, etc.) will take place. The force and/or threat should be eligible to break the other person's existing or expected resistance. Rape presupposes lack of consent of the victim and opposing to the act of intercourse or another sexual act. *The resistance of the victim* is expected to be serious and lasting until the end of the sexual intercourse. This is stipulated in a Supreme Court of Macedonia Judgment from 1974 and this standing is supported until present times.[22] The crime does not exist if the victim does not oppose the intentions of the perpetrator or if she/he does not invest all the efforts to prevent the perpetrator from achieving the goal. There should be no sign that the victim additionally agreed during the intercourse with the act of sexual intercourse; consent excludes the existence of the crime. This is a view in the theory, which is affirmed by the case law as well.[23] *Having the coercion as a constitutive element of the crime is a seriously problematic approach that is expected to be overcome soon with the upcoming novelties of the Criminal Code that are in ongoing process of adoption. According to the draft-novelty, nonconsensual sexual actions (performed without coercion) will be also considered sexual offences.*

A passive subject (victim) is any female or male person over the age of fourteen. If the victim is a person under the age of fourteen, it will be considered a criminal offense of "sexual assault of a child under the age of 14," which is formal title of the offence.[24]

This means that according to the positive Macedonian criminal legislation, the age of consent, at the moment, is fourteen. However, we believe that it is very low, so in the forthcoming amendments of the Criminal Code mentioned above, the age of consent will be elevated to fifteen.[25]

In the crime of rape, it does not matter what the moral qualities[26] of the victim are from the point of view of the society and its previous relationship with the perpetrator, therefore, a person with whom the perpetrator lives in a marital or permanent extramarital union can also be a victim of rape. Aggravated forms of rape constitute the cases when there was an occurrence of severe bodily injury, death or other severe consequences; if the rape was committed by several persons (meaning three or more persons); rape committed in a particularly cruel or humiliating manner (it is the wording of the respective provision; it presupposes existence of additional humiliating elements such as rape in front of the children of the victim), or if the crime is committed out of hatred or against a child over fourteen. The Macedonian Supreme Court in its decisions on several occasions illustrated what rape committed in a particularly cruel or humiliating manner means. For example, in a judgment from 1983, it is stipulated that: "The forced sexual intercourse is committed in an especially cruel and humiliating manner when the perpetrator was hitting the victim for a prolonged time (several hours) with different things all over the body, additionally humiliating the victim."[27] In another judgment,[28] the court also concluded that "Rape in an especially cruel and humiliating manner is performed when the victim's clothes were removed by force and naked she was kept in a pond of water before the intercourse was performed."

The perpetrators of these forms of rape can be sentenced with imprisonment of four to twenty years. It is a very wide range as one can note, but it is also case with many other provisions on different types of crimes. It is unclear why the Macedonian legislator keeps on prescribing very wide ranges for the imprisonment in the Criminal Code. A special aggravated form is also the so-called blackmail rape (potentially sentenced with imprisonment of up to five years).[29]

Sexual intercourse with a helpless person[30] is a criminal offense, where the perpetrator uses the victim's inability to resist—meaning absence of free will and free decision-making. The crime consists in the sexual exploitation of a person who for various reasons is not able to decide freely, and therefore—to oppose the perpetrator. A victim is usually a person who is unable to resist due to a certain mental disability, a person who usually does not understand the meaning of the sexual act. This should, of course not be interpreted as depriving those persons of the freedom of sexual intercourse.[31] The existence or non-existence of an emotional connection is always relevant in order the crime to be confirmed or excluded. Serious forms exist when grievous bodily harm, death, or other serious consequence occurred, or the offense has been committed by multiple perpetrators or in a particularly cruel or degrading manner. The prescribed sentence is imprisonment of up to twenty years, where the minimum varies according to the form—a minimum of eight years for the basic form, a minimum of ten years of imprisonment if the victim is a child aged over fourteen, and a minimum of twelve years for the abovementioned aggravated types.[32] The sentence of shorter duration is envisaged in case only other sexual acts took place.

The sexual assault upon a child under the age of fourteen[33] is one of the most serious and difficult sexual offenses. Hence, criminal law contains a general prohibition on any sexual intercourse with children under the age of fourteen, regardless of gender. Voluntary and violent intercourse or other sexual acts are both criminal offences.[34] This means that this crime exists when the child is forced, but also when he/she voluntarily participates in the sexual intercourse. This means the child's consent is not acknowledged or relevant for the existence of the crime. The notion of another sexual act is interpreted in a broader sense so that it includes all actions of touching but different than the acts covering penetrations. Included are actions that do not mean classical physical contact with the victim's body. According to the Macedonian Supreme Court Judgment KVP No.80 from 1998, sexual assault upon a child is performed even when no coercion exists, if the perpetrator was touching the hair and the neck of the child for the purpose of satisfying a sexual urge.[35] So, in such cases especially the clearly and openly manifested intention of the perpetrator to satisfy the sexual passion should be established as existent.[36] The subjective side (*mens rea*) of the crime consists in the intention and the awareness of the perpetrator that the victim is a child under the age of fourteen. If the perpetrator is not aware of the age of the victim, the crime does not exist. Namely, if the perpetrator mistakenly thinks that the child is over fourteen years of age, it will be considered a real mistake and treated as such.[37] Therefore, the mistake is in favor of the perpetrator and the criminal defense of the mistake will apply. Of course, in every single case, the court *in concreto* will have to establish whether mistake really exists, or the perpetrator is just pretending in order to escape justice. The Macedonian Supreme Court addressed this issue in a Decision from 1983, since the same concept existed in the criminal legislation in that period as well. According to the conclusions of the court, there is no crime in that particular case—where the sexual activities with the victim were consensual, the victim on several occasions previously had left her home and lived extramarital life with men in other places (cities)—which was established by the court as a fact and all these aspects led the perpetrator to believe that she was really over the age of fourteen; furthermore, the perpetrator thought that the victim was fifteen, as he was told that by herself. Having into consideration all these facts, the court concluded that the criminal defense of mistake applies, since the age of consent is a constitutive element of the respective crime.[38] The general (basic) form is sentenced by imprisonment of twelve to twenty years. Aggravated forms are those forms when a severe bodily injury or death occurred or if the act was committed out of hatred or in a cruel or humiliating manner or by several persons. Perpetrators of these types of offenses may be imprisoned from fifteen to twenty years or with life imprisonment.

Sexual intercourse by abuse of the position[39] stands as another sexual offense that aims to protect the individual that is vulnerable from the point of view that the perpetrator stands in position of superiority to her/him. The special circumstance appears as an abuse of the position of superiority in these relations that always has elements of extortion or blackmail, so even if the victim gives explicit consent, essentially, she/he does not have complete freedom of decision. Those who have "power," "superiority" over others, are not expected to abuse such a position. It also means that they should not satisfy their sexual urges by exerting direct or indirect pressure on their subordinates. This offense is committed by incitement of the victim to sexual intercourse or other sexual act or, with such intent, by harassing, intimidating or humiliating the victim.[40] According to the MCC, the perpetrator will be sentenced by imprisonment of five to twenty years. In case the victim is a child over the age of fourteen, the sentence ranges from ten to twenty years of imprisonment.

Fulfilling sexual urges in front of another[41] has been consisted in performing sexual acts in front of another in a public place, whereas an aggravated form is the action performed in front of a child. This offense is punishable by imprisonment of up to one year, but in case a child is involved, the perpetrator may be sentenced with a prison up to twenty years. The protection is primarily directed toward the public, especially children.

The second subgroup of sexual offenses of Chapter XIX are *the crimes against sexual morality*: intermediation in prostitution (Article 191); displaying pornographic materials to a child (Article 193); production and distribution of child pornography (Article 193 –a), inciting a child under the age of fourteen to intercourse or other sexual activity (Article 193-b), and incest (Article 194). These crimes are violations of some protected moral goods or values.[42] In practice, these crimes are very rare and only several annual cases of intermediation in prostitution and in only some years are detected.[43]

From Chapter XXXIV: *Crimes against humanity and international law*, two incriminations are very important and are in practice most often committed for the purpose of sexual exploitation of the victim—human trafficking and child trafficking. The act of committing the basic crime of *human trafficking*[44] is the recruitment, transportation, transfer, purchase, sale, shelter, or acceptance of persons for exploitation through prostitution or other forms of sexual exploitation as well as for other purposes (forced labor, slavery, illicit transplantation of human body parts, etc.) and all this is done by using force, serious threat or other forms of coercion, abduction, deception or abuse of one's position or the state of powerlessness of the victim, the state of pregnancy, special needs, and so on. This form of crime is punishable by four to twenty years of imprisonment. Among the special forms of the crime, it is important to mention the use or enabling another person to use sexual services from victims of human trafficking, punishable by imprisonment of six months to five years. Many other forms of the crime are envisaged in the mentioned provision of Article 418-a.

Child trafficking is a criminal offense covered by the provision of Article 418-d of the MCC.[45] In terms of elements and actions, this crime is similar to the previous one, with the main difference that the victim is a child (person under eighteen years). This crime also includes, among other actions, the intermediation in child prostitution, and along with the many goals of the crime: the illegal adoption, forced marriages (child marriages), and so on, are also envisaged. Imprisonment from eight to twenty years is prescribed for the basic type of this crime, and for some aggravated forms the minimum sentence is twelve years of imprisonment.

The analysis of the Macedonian substantial criminal law frame unequivocally shows that the current system and legislative model regarding sexual offenses in North Macedonia needs serious improvement, as it follows old traditional approaches and concepts that have been abandoned in modern legislations as proved to be inadequate protection of the victims.

In the process of reforms, in this respect the Istanbul Convention is very significant. As mentioned in the introduction, Republic of North Macedonia signed the Istanbul Convention on 8.7.2011. It was ratified by the Macedonian Assembly on 23.3.2018 and entered into force on 1.7.2018.[46] Reservations were put in accordance with Article 78, para. 2 on Article 30, para. 2, Article 44, para. 3, Article 55, para 1., and Article 59.

As a result of the open state policy for promoting gender equality and enhanced protection of women and children in particular, as well as to achieve a higher level of compliance with the international standards in the field, many strategic and legislative initiatives and processes take place in the country in the last couple of years. One of the actions is the process of preparation for implementation of the provisions of the Istanbul Convention in the national legislation.[47] This is in line with the plan that the GREVIO Baseline Report for North Macedonia is scheduled to be published in November 2023, according to the Provisional Timetable.[48]

In respect of the Criminal Code novelties, two processes take place. The first is the drafting of a new Criminal Code by a Working Group appointed by the Macedonian Minister of Justice.[49] The provisional estimations are that it could be enacted by the end of 2022. All the relevant CoE Conventions, EU Directives, Framework Decisions and Regulations will be transposed in order to comply with the European and global standards and values in all relevant areas. The implementation of the Istanbul Convention is taken as highest priority by the Working Group. But, as the adoption of the new Criminal Code might take time and fulfilling some of the obligations from signing and ratifying international treaties should be done in due course, the Ministry of Justice prepared proposals for amendments to the current Criminal Code envisaging, among other provisions, changes in order to introduce new crimes and concepts regarding sexual offenses and other crimes deriving from the Istanbul Convention provisions.

This draft proposal for MCC amendments that is in parliamentary procedure, as mentioned above, includes the following changes:

- Criminalization of all nonconsensual sexual intercourse or other sexual activities without consent;
- Introduction of the crime of sexual harassment;
- Criminalization of the act of instigation to child prostitution as a separate crime;
- Envisaging of the act of stalking as a criminal offense;
- Introduction of the female genital mutilation as a separate crime, and so on.

In addition, the age limit for consented intercourse with a child will be elevated from fourteen to fifteen. If adopted, these new provisions would provide higher protection of children and every sexual activity with a child under the age of fifteen (consensual or without consent) would be considered a crime.

PROCEDURAL ASPECTS AND PROTECTION OF VICTIMS

The Criminal Procedure Code (hereinafter: CPC),[50] provides procedural possibilities for discovering and gathering relevant evidence as a ground for initiating preliminary procedure and submitting the indictment,[51] respectively, as well as measures for motivating the victims to report the criminal offences, such as protection of witness, enlisted rights, help, support, and protection of victims, especially endangered victims and particularly vulnerable victims.[52]

Special Investigative Measures

Regarding most severe criminal offenses that encompass sexual offenses elaborated in this paper, there are some particular investigative techniques and measures. Namely, there are twelve available special investigative measures (SIMs) that can be used when there is a probability that data and evidence necessary for the successful conduct of the criminal procedure will be provided, as well as data regarding a person under international arrest warrant, which otherwise cannot be collected (Article 251 para.1, CPC). The SIMs can be ordered for the most severe offenses, punishable with imprisonment of at least four years (for most of criminal offenses against sexual freedom and sexual morality, as well as other criminal offenses linked with the sexual exploitation, such as human trafficking or child trafficking), but also for some enlisted criminal offenses punishable with lenient sanction, among which are several offenses against sexual freedom and sexual morality—intermediation in prostitution; showing pornographic materials to a minor; production and distribution of child pornography, as well as seduction or other sexual activity of a minor under the age of fourteen. Those SIMs are very helpful especially when the criminal offences are committed by an organized criminal group, or any form of criminal association.

With the purpose to enhancing the discovery and prosecution of these crimes, CPC provides a kind of "motivation" for the perpetrators to cooperate with the investigative authorities.[53] Although the principle of legality stipulates the obligation for the public prosecutor to conduct the investigation,[54] there are several exceptions, among which is the possibility for extended discretion power of the public prosecutor not to initiate criminal procedure when the suspect, as a member of an organized group, gang, or other criminal association, voluntarily cooperates before or after the offense has been discovered or during the criminal procedure, in the case when such cooperation and statement of that person, upon assessment of the public prosecutor, could be essential for the criminal procedure.[55]

Witness protection

When analyzing the possibilities for victims of sexual offenses, the protection of victims as witnesses provided by the CPC, regarding procedural protection measures and by special Law on witness protection,[56] for non-procedural protection measures, shall not be excluded. Depending on the nature of sexual offense, the possibility for witness protection is seen as prerequisite for active collaboration of victim without fear of further consequences, revenge, or re-victimization.[57]

Witness protection, in accordance with the CPC shall be provided upon request of the victim as witness during preliminary procedure or main hearing. The grounds for requesting and accepting witness protection measures are stipulated by the CPC:[58] if the victim or the injured party with giving statement with known identity for the defence would expose himself, or a person close to him, to a serious danger to life, health, or physical integrity. The procedural measures mean a special manner of examination and participation in the procedure, such as using the pseudonym,[59] or by using technical devices for transmitting image and tone which enable transmission of the statement while concealing the appearance of the endangered witness so that his/her face and voice are modified and cannot be recognized. The non-procedural measures are stipulated by the law on witness protection, and they can be applied as an urgent measure during the criminal procedure upon assessment and decision of the public prosecutor.

Aside witness protection, the victims of sexual offenses are provided with appropriate rights and protection after being identified as victims.[60] There is an obligation for the police, the public prosecutor, and the court to take actions with special care, to inform the victim of all available rights and possibilities and to take care of the victims' interests during the procedure.[61]

Special Rights of Vulnerable Categories of Victims

Having in mind the severity of committed crime, the CPC prescribes special rights for the victims of criminal offenses punishable with the imprisonment of at least four years,[62] such as advisor at the expense of state budget funds before giving a statement or submission of a property claim, if there is severe psycho-physical damage or severe consequences of the crime and compensation for material and non-material damage from a state fund under conditions and in a manner prescribed by a special law, if the compensation for damage cannot be provided by the convicted person.

CPC provides special rights of vulnerable categories of victims,[63] among which are: children (persons under the age of eighteen at the time of giving the statement); endangered victims (who by giving a statement or answer to a certain question would expose themselves or a close person to a serious danger to life, health, or physical integrity); and particularly vulnerable victims (due to the age, nature and consequences of the crime, physical or mental disability or other significant health condition, social and cultural past, family circumstances, religious beliefs and ethnicity of the victim, and the behavior of the accused. Family members or friends of the accused to the victim would have detrimental consequences for their mental or physical health or adversely affect the quality of the given statement).

When there is a child victim, the guarantees in CPC and LJC are very similar, so that the court is obliged to determine special procedural protection measure when the child victim needs special care and protection or when the child is a victim of human trafficking, violence or sexual abuse, as well as crimes against humanity and international law or other serious acts against children sentenced with imprisonment of more than four years.[64] As far as witness protection is concerned, LJC is referring to CPC and Law on witness protection.

Relevant factors for providing additional special rights of victims are the nature of the offense and the prescribed sentence. These are: before the examination to talk to a free counselor or a proxy, if he/she participates in the procedure as an injured party; to be examined by a person of the same sex in the police and the public prosecutor's office; not to answer questions that refer to the personal life of the victim and are not related to the crime; to request examination with the help of visual audio means in a manner determined by the CPC and to request exclusion of the public at the main hearing. This provision refers to victims of criminal offenses against sexual freedom and sexual morality, humanity, and international law.[65]

Mediation Procedure

Regarding the mediation procedure, according to the LJC, there is an explicit limitation that referral to mediation is excluded for offences against sexual freedom and sexual morality as well as gender-based forms of violence against women, in accordance with the ratified international agreements.[66] In other words, mediation procedure and other forms of speedy proceeding and shortened procedure are not applicable to sexual offences.

Protection of Child Victims

The juvenile criminal justice system is a separate component of the Macedonian criminal justice system.[67] It is implemented upon the provisions of the law on justice for children (hereinafter: LJC),[68] for all cases when the criminal offense has been committed by the child in conflict with the law.[69] The LJC stipulates the protection of child victims' similar manner as CPC. However, in LJC there is a list of procedural guarantees that the court may determine toward the child victims: use of screens to protect the victim and the witness from the view of the accused; concealment of identity or appearance; giving a statement via video conference; removal of toga and hats; exclusion of the public; video and audio recording of the statement to be used as evidence; video and audio recording of the interrogation which will be used as evidence; taking a statement through an expert person; use of special technical means of communication; and protection of the privacy of the child and his family.

CRIMINOLOGICAL ASPECTS AND SENTENCING POLICY

Relevant data for sexual offenses in the Republic of North Macedonia can be obtained from the Ministry of Interior, as well as from the State Statistical Office (hereinafter: SSO).[70] There are discrepancies in these figures.[71]

According to the data of the Ministry of Interior, in the period 2010–2016, on average, per year there were total of 35.8 perpetrators of rape and 39.4 committed criminal acts. For the same period, there were on average per year 40.7 perpetrators of sexual assault upon a child under the age of 14 and on average per year 37.5 committed criminal acts. Also, the Ministry of Interior presents data on these two *delicta carnis* according to the sector for internal affairs. The data are presented in tables 3.1 and 3.2 in the text below.

The rate of rapes in the country is fluctuating with most rapes in 2017 (55) and the least number in 2010 (28). In some cases, the rape was conducted by several perpetrators.

We can conclude that the Republic of North Macedonia has a low rape rate (on average 1.9) on 100,000 population compared to the other countries in the world. Most of the rapes were committed on the territory of SVR Shtip, Strumica, Skopje, Bitola and Ohrid, which are the biggest cities in the country (see table 3.2).

In 2010, there were 61 cases of sexual assault upon a child under the age of fourteen, followed by a decrease in the following years with slight fluctuations. Most of the crimes were committed on the territory of SVR Bitola, Skopje, Shtip, Strumica, and Veles.

Another relevant source is the SSO. According to its data in the period 2008–2019, crimes against sexual freedom and sexual morality account in the

Table 3.1. Delicta Carnis, 2010–2019. Source: Ministry of Interior (https://mvr.gov.mk/analiza/kriminal/55, accessed December 3, 2021).

	2010	*2011*	*2012*	*2013*	*2014*	*2015*	*2016*	*2017*	*2018*	*2019*	*Average*
Rape	28	41	43	38	45	42	36	55	31	35	39.4
Perpetrators	31	39	36	36	48	33	33	37	35	30	35.8
Rate on 100,000 population	1.28	1.87	1.96	1.73	2.17	2.02	1.73	2.65	1.49	1.69	1.9
Sexual assault upon a child under the age of 14	61	35	34	47	43	38	30	26	32	29	37.5
Perpetrators	71	37	35	51	54	38	28	24	32	37	40.7

Table 3.2. Rape and Sexual Assault on a Child under the Age of Fourteen (2010–2019). Source: Ministry of Interior (https://mvr.gov.mk/analiza/kriminal/55, accessed December 3, 2021).

	R	*SA*	*R*	*SA*	*R*	*SA*	*R*	*SA*	*R*	*SA*	*R*	*SA*	*R*	*SA*	*R*	*SA*	*R*	*SA*	*R*	*SA*	*R*	*SA*
	2010	2010	2011	2011	2012	2012	2013	2013	2014	2014	2015	2015	2016	2016	2017	2017	2018	2018	2019	2019	Average	Average
SVR Skopje	1	7	2	7	8	10	5	8	5	10	10	6	6	5	3	6	5	5	6	6	5.1	7.0
SVR Bitola	3	8	8	8	3	3	4	9	5	3	8	16	4	8	4	2	3	12	4	4	4.6	7.3
SVR Veles	2	7	4	2	3	1	6	3	11	6	3	/	4	2	2	2	1	3	4	1	4.0	3.0
SVR	7	1	5	2	5	4	3	7	5	3	6	1	3	2	2	4	/	2	2	3	4.2	2.9
SVR Ohrid	/	6	/	3	1	3	3	1	10	1	4	3	4	1	8	3	3	2	4	3	4.6	2.6
SVR	4	11	9	6	6	8	7	7	2	3	3	5	6	5	20	4	10	3	4	5	7.1	5.7
SVR Tetovo	4	2	2	/	2	1	2	3	/	8	3	4	3	2	3	1	4	2	3	1	2.9	2.7
SVR Shtip	7	19	11	7	15	4	8	9	7	9	5	3	6	5	13	4	5	3	8	6	8.5	6.9

Table 3.3. Reported (1), Accused (2), and Convicted (3) Adult Perpetrators of Crimes against Sexual Freedom and Sexual Morality, by Year (2008–2019). Source: State Statistical Office (https://www.stat.gov.mk/PublikaciiPoOblast.aspx?id=43&rbrObl=6, accessed December 3, 2021).

	Total			*Crimes against sexual freedom and sexual morality*					
	(1)	(2)	(3)	(1)	%	(2)	%	(3)	%
2008	26409	11310	9503	186	0.70	99	0.88	92	0.97
2009	30404	11905	9801	123	0.40	78	0.66	65	0.66
2010	30004	11239	9169	109	0.36	63	0.56	54	0.59
2011	31284	12219	9810	83	0.27	66	0.54	54	0.55
2012	31860	11311	9042	109	0.34	54	0.48	47	0.52
2013	34436	12297	9539	108	0.31	78	0.63	64	0.67
2014	37164	13699	11683	88	0.24	65	0.47	49	0.42
2015	26069	11951	10312	74	0.28	60	0.50	56	0.54
2016	20502	9320	8172	88	0.43	45	0.48	39	0.48
2017	20582	7423	6273	64	0.31	45	0.61	38	0.61
2018	19779	6829	5857	70	0.35	53	0.78	44	0.75
2019	20106	5370	4712	44	0.22	23	0.43	20	0.42
Average	27383.3	10406.1	8656.1	95.5	0.4	60.8	0.6	51.8	0.6

total number of crimes with, on average per year, 0.4 percent reported, and 0.6 percent accused and convicted adult perpetrators.

There were reported on average per year 95.5 adult perpetrators of sexual offenses; on average per year 60.8 were accused, and on average per year 51.8 were convicted. A decrease in the number of reported, accused, and convicted over the years; slight fluctuations can be noted. In 2019, there was a sharp decrease of the numbers (See table 3.3).

In the last three years of the available data (2017–2019), on average, nearly 85 percent of the accused adult perpetrators of crimes against sexual freedom and sexual morality were convicted (See table 3.4).

We can conclude that for most of the reported cases, there was strong evidence, hence, they resulted in conviction.

In 2019, of the total number of reported crimes against sexual freedom and sexual morality (44), twenty were rapes, thirteen were sexual assaults upon a child under the age of fourteen, two were mediation in prostitution, and nine

Table 3.4. Accused (2) Adult Perpetrators of Crimes against Sexual Freedom and Sexual Morality and Decision, Convicted (3) or Not Convicted (4), by Year. Source: State Statistical Office (https://www.stat.gov.mk/PublikaciiPoOblast.aspx?id=43&rbrObl=6, accessed December 3, 2021).

2017			*2018*			*2019*		
(2)	(3)	(4)	(2)	(3)	(4)	(2)	(3)	(4)
45	38	7	53	44	9	23	20	3

were other crimes against sexual freedom and sexual morality. In 2018, the total number of reported crimes against sexual freedom and sexual morality was seventy. Thirty-three of them were rapes, nineteen were sexual assaults upon a child under the age of fourteen, and eighteen were other crimes against sexual freedom and sexual morality.

There was only one reported female perpetrator of crimes against sexual freedom and sexual morality in 2018 and one in 2019. In 2019, one female perpetrator was reported for mediation in prostitution, and one in 2018 was reported for other crimes against sexual freedom and sexual morality.

In 2018, there were eight unknown perpetrators (11.4 percent), and in 2019 there were four unknown perpetrators (10 percent). So, in most of the cases, the victim knew the perpetrator. Namely, it is a myth that most sexual assaults are committed by strangers. Also, we can conclude that in approximately 10 percent of the cases, the police failed to find the perpetrators of sexual assaults. The data are presented in table 3.5.

Regarding ethnicity, most of the reported adult perpetrators of crimes against sexual freedom and sexual morality in 2018 and 2019 were Macedonians (on average 44 percent), followed by Roma (on average 19 percent), Albanians (15 percent), and Turks and Bosniaks (see table 3.1). The high percentage of reported Roma for committed crimes against sexual freedom and sexual morality can be explained by their cultural characteristics. Namely, Roma men often marry girls under the age of fourteen, and most of them are reported and hence accused and convicted of the crime sexual assault upon a child under the age of fourteen (See figure 3.1).

In the analyzed period (2017–2019), in most of the cases, the decision by the court was conviction. Only in 6 percent (on average) of the cases did the court reach a verdict of acquittal. In less than 5 percent of cases, there was a judgment based on a guilty plea or the investigation was terminated, or the court-imposed security measures (see table 3.6).

In the last three years for which there is available data (2017–2019), on average per year, 5.7 accused adult perpetrators of sexual offences were in detention. Regarding the duration of detention, on average 3.3 accused perpetrators were in detention over three months, on average one was in detention for periods of either 1–2 months or 2–3 months, and on average, 0.3 was in detention up to 3 days (see table 3.7). We can conclude that for *delicta carnis* the court-imposed detention only in 15 percent (on average) of the cases and in nearly 58 percent (on average) the duration of the detention was over three months.

Regarding the judicial penal policy against sexual offenses, on average thirty-four of the accused adult perpetrators were convicted in the period 2017–2019. Another feature of the judicial penal policy is that on average,

Table 3.5. Reported Adult Perpetrators of Crimes against Sexual Freedom and Sexual Morality, Decision and Sex. Source: State Statistical Office (https://www.stat.gov.mk/PublikaciiPoOblast.aspx?id=43&rbrObl=6, accessed December 3, 2021).

	Total		*Crimes against sexual freedom and sexual morality-Total*		*.... Rape*		*.... Sexual assault upon a child under the age of 14*		*.... Mediation in prostitution*		*.... Crimes against sexual freedom and sexual morality-Other*	
	2018	2019	2018	2019	2018	2019	2018	2019	2018	2019	2018	2019
Total	19779	20106	70	44	33	20	19	13	-	2	18	9
Total known perpetrators	11609	12255	62	40	29	19	18	12	-	2	15	7
Female	1204	1384	1	1	-	-	-	-	-	1	1	-
Complaints dismissed	4721	4827	12	12	3	6	2	5	-	1	7	-
Investigation suspended	5	3	-	-	-	-	-	-	-	-	-	-
Investigation halted	154	138	7	3	3	2	4	1	-	-	-	-
Indictment	6729	7287	43	25	23	11	12	6	-	1	8	7
Total unknown perpetrators	8170	7851	8	4	4	1	1	1	-	-	3	2

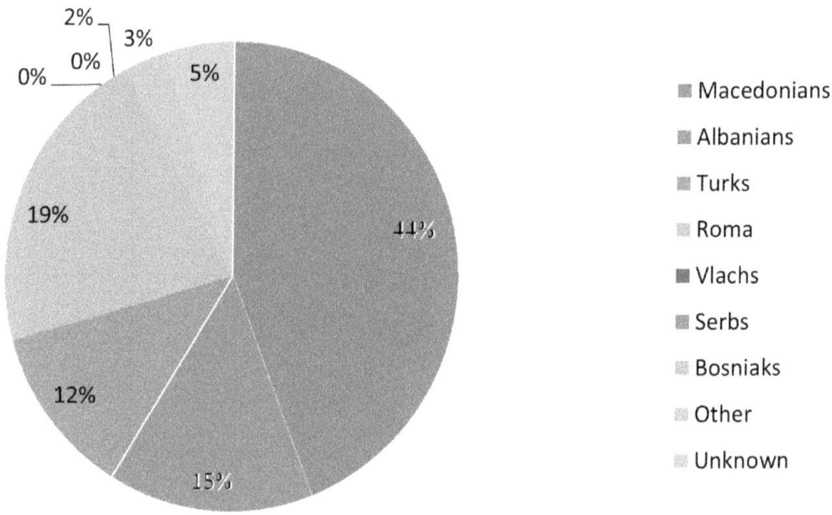

Figure 3.1. Reported Adult Perpetrators' Ethnicity.

76.5 percent of them were imposed punishments, and on average 23.5 percent were sentenced with alternative measures (See table 3.8).

In the period 2017–2019, on average per year, 24.3 convicted adult perpetrators of sexual offences were sentenced to prison. Most of them were sentenced for rape (on average 10.3 convicts); on average per year, 8.3 convicts were sentenced to prison for sexual assault upon a child under the age of fourteen. On average per year, 0.3 convicts were sentenced to mediation in conducting prostitution, and on average 5.3 for other sexual offenses. None of the perpetrators were sentenced to life imprisonment. On average per year, most of the perpetrators of these crimes were sentenced to imprisonment for three to five years (5.3), then, to imprisonment for five to ten years (4.7) and imprisonment for six to twelve months (4.3).

In the analyzed period on average per year, eight perpetrators were sentenced to alternative measures, namely, to probation. On average per year, three convicts were sentenced to probation for rape, one for sexual assault upon a child under the age of fourteen; 0.7 for intermediation in conducting prostitution, and 3.3 for other crimes against sexual freedom and sexual morality. Next, on average, 4.3 were sentenced with security measures (see table 3.9, 3.10).

What's more, no confiscation of property was imposed, and on average in the analyzed period, 1.7 confiscations of objects were imposed.[72] We can conclude that more than 70 percent of the convicted perpetrators were sentenced to imprisonment.

Table 3.6. Accused Adult Perpetrators of Crimes against Sexual Freedom and Sexual Morality and Decision, by Year. Source: State Statistical Office (https://www.stat.gov.mk/PublikaciiPoOblast.aspx?id=43&rbrObl=6, accessed December 3, 2019).

	Crimes against sexual freedom and sexual morality			*Rape*			*Sexual assault upon a child under the age of 14*			*Mediation in conducting prostitution*			*Other crimes against sexual freedom and sexual morality*		
	2017	2018	2019	2017	2018	2019	2017	2018	2019	2017	2018	2019	2017	2018	2019
Total accused persons	45	53	23	13	21	12	12	20	3	3	1	-	17	11	8
Conviction verdict	38	40	15	13	16	9	9	16	1	3	-	-	13	8	5
Acquittal verdict	2	5	1	-	3	1	1	2	-	-	-	-	1	-	-
Rejection verdict	1	-	2	-	-	1	1	-	1	-	-	-	-	-	-
Judgment based on a draft plea agreement	-	-	1	-	-	-	-	-	1	-	-	-	-	-	-
Judgment for issuing a penal warrant	-	-	1	-	-	-	-	-	-	-	-	-	-	-	1
Judgment based on a guilty plea	-	4	3	-	1	1	-	1	-	-	-	-	-	2	2
Investigation terminated	1	4	-	-	1	-	-	1	-	-	1	-	1	1	-
Security measures	3	-	5	-	-	-	1	-	1	-	-	-	2	-	4

Table 3.7. Accused Adult Perpetrators of Crimes against Sexual Freedom and Sexual Morality and Detention, by Year. Source: State Statistical Office (https://www.stat.gov.mk/PublikaciiPoOblast.aspx?id=43&rbrObl=6, accessed December 3, 2021).

Crimes against sexual freedom and sexual morality	*2017*	*2018*	*2019*	*Average*
Total	3	12	2	5.7
Up to 3 days	-	1	-	0.3
Over 3–15 days	-	-	-	-
Over 15 days-1 month	-	-	-	-
Over 1–2 months	-	3	-	1.0
Over 2–3 months	2	1	-	1.0
Over 3 months	1	7	2	3.3

In most of the cases, the crimes against sexual freedom and sexual morality were committed by a single perpetrator (on average per year 31.7), then, on average per year in 2 cases there were accomplices (mostly two perpetrators, although in 2017 there was a case of five or more perpetrators), and 0.3 were instigators (see table 3.11).

Regarding the age of the convicted adult perpetrators, most of them are age 30 to 39 (20.6 percent), next is the age group 50–59 years (18.5 percent), then, perpetrators age 25–29 years and 40–49 years (14.7 percent). Perpetrators that are age 21–24 years account with 9.7 percent, and those that are age 18–20 years and 60 and over account with 8.8 percent (see table 3.12). This type of crime follows the age pattern that applies to the crime in general.

Most of the convicted perpetrators of sexual offenses have completed upper secondary school (about 32 percent), about 30 percent have completed primary and lower secondary school, about 12 percent are without education, and 5.5% have an incomplete education. Only 2.2 percent have completed higher education, and about 21 percent are with unknown educational attainment (see table 3.2). To conclude, perpetrators of sexual offences have a low level of education (as perpetrators of crime in general).

Regarding their occupation most of the perpetrators are unemployed (32.4 percent), 7.9 percent are craft and related trades workers, and 6.1 percent are

Table 3.8. Convicted Adult Perpetrators of Crimes against Sexual Freedom and Sexual Morality and Type of Sentence, by Year. Source: State Statistical Office (https://www.stat.gov.mk/PublikaciiPoOblast.aspx?id=43&rbrObl=6, accessed December 3, 2021).

Crimes against sexual freedom and sexual morality	*2017*	*2018*	*2019*	*Average*	*%*
Convicted	38	44	20	34	
Punishments—Total	29	34	15	26	76.5
Alternative measures—Total	9	10	5	8	23.5
Convicted but no penal sentence	-	-	-	-	-

Table 3.9. Convicted Adult Perpetrators of Crimes against Sexual Freedom and Sexual Morality and Applied Main Sentence - Imprisonment and Fine, by Year. Source: State Statistical Office (https://www.stat.gov.mk/PublikaciiPoOblast.aspx?id=43&rbrObl=6, accessed 3 December 2021).

	Crimes against sexual freedom and sexual morality				*Rape*				*Sexual assault upon a child under the age of 14*				*Mediation in conducting prostitution*				*Other crimes against sexual freedom and sexual morality*			
	2017	2018	2019	Average	2017	2018	2019	Average	2017	2018	2019	Average	2017	2018	2019	Average	2017	2018	2019	Average
Total imprisonment	28	32	13	24.3	11	12	8	10.3	8	15	2	8.3	1	-	-	0.3	8	5	3	5.3
life	-	-	-	-	-	-	-	-	-	-	-	-	-	-	-	-	-	-	-	-
20 years	-	1	-	0.3	-	-	-	-	-	1	-	0.3	-	-	-	-	-	-	-	-
10-15 years	4	6	2	4	-	-	-	-	3	6	2	3.7	-	-	-	-	1	-	-	0.3
5-10 years	6	4	4	4.7	1	1	2	1.3	2	3	-	1.7	-	-	-	-	3	-	2	1.7
3-5 years	5	10	1	5.3	-	3	1	1.3	3	3	-	2	1	-	-		1	4	-	1.7
2-3 years	3	3	1	2.3	2	3	1	2	-	-	-	-	-	-	-	-	1	-	-	0.3
1-2 years	2	1	1	1.3	1	1	1	1	-	-	-	-	-	-	-	-	1	-	-	0.3
6-12 months	4	5	4	4.3	3	2	3	2.7	-	2	-	0.7	-	-	-	-	1	1	1	1
up to 6 months	4	2	-	2.0	4	2	-	2	-	-	-	-	-	-	-	-	-	-	-	-
Total fine	1	1	-	0.7	-	-	-	-	-	-	-	-	-	-	-	-	1	1	-	

Table 3.10. Convicted Adult Perpetrators of Crimes against Sexual Freedom and Sexual Morality and by Types of Applied Alternative Measures, by Year. Source: State Statistical Office.

	2017					*2018*					*2019*					*Average*				
	Chapter 19	Art. 186	Art. 188	Art. 191	Other	Chapter 19	Art. 186	Art. 188	Art. 191	Other	Chapter 19	Art. 186	Art. 188	Art. 191	Other	Chapter 19	Art. 186	Art. 188	Art. 191	Other
Alternative measures-Total	9	2	1	2	4	10	5	2	-	3	5	2	-	-	3	8	3	1	0.7	3.3
Probation Imprisonment	9	2	1	2	4	10	5	2	-	3	5	2	-	-	3	8	3	1	0.7	3.3

Table 3.11. Convicted Adult Perpetrators of Crimes against Sexual Freedom and Sexual Morality and Complicity, by Year. Source: State Statistical Office (https://www.stat.gov.mk/PublikaciiPoOblast.aspx?id=43&rbrObl=6, accessed December 3, 2021).

	Total	Alone/perpetrator	Accomplice	Instigator	Accessory
2017	38	36	2	-	-
2018	44	43	-	1	-
2019	20	16	4	-	-
Average	34	31.7	2	0.3	-

Table 3.12. Convicted Adult Perpetrators of Crimes against Sexual Freedom and Sexual Morality and Age, by Year. Source: State Statistical Office (https://www.stat.gov.mk/PublikaciiPoOblast.aspx?id=43&rbrObl=6, accessed December 3, 2021).

	Total	*18-20 years*	*21-24 years*	*25-29 years*	*30-39 years*	*40-49 years*	*50-59 years*	*60 and over*
2017	38	6	-	5	7	5	8	3
2018	44	3	7	4	9	7	9	5
2019	20	-	3	6	5	3	2	1
Average	34	3	3.3	5	7	5	6.3	3
%		8.8	9.7	14.7	20.6	14.7	18.5	8.8

professionals. For a high percentage of the perpetrators, the occupation is unknown (41.2 percent) This confirms also the general pattern of criminals.[73]

To conclude, there is a difference in the data provided by the police and the SSO that influence the figures and conviction ratios. Crimes against sexual freedom and sexual morality account in the total number of crimes with, on average, 0.3 percent reported, and 0.6 percent accused and convicted adult perpetrators. It can be noted that there was a decrease in the number of

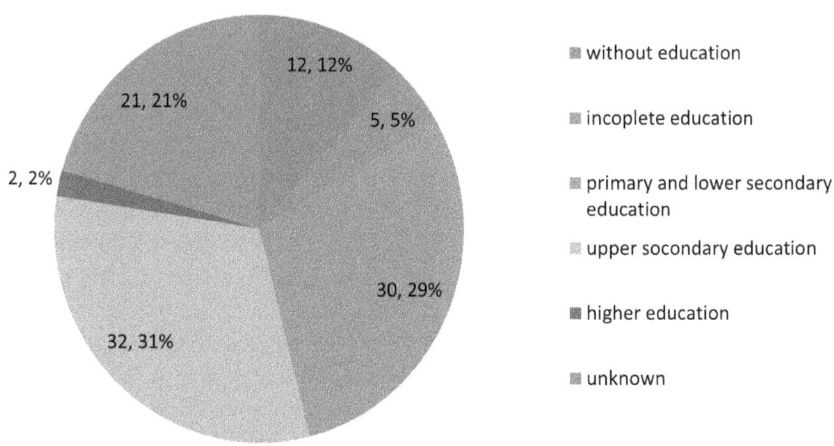

Figure 3.2. Convicted Adult Perpetrators' Education.

reported, accused, and convicted over the years, with slight fluctuations. In 2019, there was a sharp decrease of the numbers. More than 70 percent of the convicted perpetrators of *delicta carnis* were sentenced to imprisonment. In most of the cases, they were committed by a single perpetrator and the victim knew the perpetrator. The profile of perpetrator of crimes against sexual freedom and sexual morality is Macedonian, a male, age thirty to thirty-nine, with a low level of education and unemployed. The sexual exploitation is also the main objective of the trafficking in persons and trafficking in children which are within the chapter of the Penal Code "Crimes against the Humanity and the International Law." Those crimes account on average 0.9 percent of the total number of accused persons, 1.1 percent of the convicted, and 0.2 percent of the total number of persons that are not convicted. Over the last three years, there were only one convicted perpetrator for human trafficking in 2017 sentenced to imprisonment for one to two years, six in 2018 (one sentenced to imprisonment for three to five years and to five sentenced to probation), and none in 2019.

CONCLUDING REMARKS

Sexual offenses have their own place in the systematics of the Macedonian criminal legislation, but the provisions in the Criminal Code and the elements of the crimes have not provided adequate protection of victims of sexual violence in practice. The concept of rape is problematic, as includes the coercion as a formal element and has no special approach toward appropriate protection of children from sexual abuse from legislative point has been made.

From a procedural view, there are no significant shortcomings, that is, modern methods, special investigative measures, and special measures for protection of victims of sexual violence, especially children—victims are applied in practice without major problems. However, the official figures for reported, accused, and convicted perpetrators of sexual offenses presented in the statistical analyses show that nearly 59 percent of the reported perpetrators for *delicta carnis* are convicted. Hence, the attrition of sexual offenses is relatively high in North Macedonia. This is a pattern that follows the crime in general, a trend described in the criminology as "loss of crime." The attrition of sexual offenses and the "dark figure" *lato sensu*—the latter consisting of cases that have never been reported in North Macedonia can be summarized from several aspects: first, the weaknesses in the legislative framework; second, the rigidity of the case law in many situations, but also the inadequate attitude of the police towards the victims in certain cases; third, the "slow" justice, distrust in the institutions and the social stigma experienced by the victims; fourth, the mentality and traditions, which still greatly contributes to instances of sexual violence, especially in the family, is treated as a "taboo" and issue that should be resolved within the family; fifth, the inefficiency of the criminal justice system, and so on.

The first step for overcoming the abovementioned reasons is facing the obvious flaws of the current legislation. While the provisions on rape from comparative aspect are nowadays considerably different, in MCC the coercion is still a constitutive element of the crime. This leaves many perpetrators of unwanted sexual acts unprosecuted and they are formally legal, but essentially, they constitute sexual abuse. We believe that criminalizing every nonconsensual sexual action would make victims of these acts to be finally recognized as victims and the perpetrators of these acts to be put on trial.

Another aspect that seeks immediate attention is the sexual abuse of children. Even the formal title of the relevant provision in the positive legislation ("sexual assault of a child under the age of 14") is not adequate. In line with some comparative examples, the offenses of sexual abuse of children should be systematized in a separate chapter of the Criminal Code, giving special emphasis to the essentially different object of protection in these cases from the one of the sexual offenses perpetrated against adults.

Whereas the free decision for willful engagement in sexual act is relevant when it comes to an adult, the consent for intercourse when it comes to a child is irrelevant and therefore no exculpating. The age of consent should be elevated from fourteen to fifteen years.

The wide range for the prison sentence in many provisions (for example, prescribed frames from one to ten or from four to twenty years of imprisonment) is another issue that needs to be addressed by the legislator. It might lead to situations that perpetrators of similar cases and under similar circumstances to be sentenced very dissimilarly by different courts (uneven sentencing policy) that would further harm the frail confidence that citizens have in the judiciary.

Faced with challenges of the forthcoming legislative reforms and the need for sensitizing institutions, it is necessary to have into consideration the necessity for subsequent capacity building of the institutions for adequate implementation of the new provisions and concepts, followed by intensive awareness rising campaigns. It will be a long time before we see substantial changes in this area, but the first step to be done is of utmost importance.

REFERENCES

Literature

Arnaudovski, L., *Kriminologija* (2 Avgust S-Štip, Skopje 2007).

Deanoska, Trendafilova A., and Mujoska, E., *Istanbulskata (CAHVIO) konvencija i zastitata na decata od seksualno nasilstvo* (MRKK, Skopje 2013) 180.

Gruevska, Drakulevski A., *Semejnoto nasilstvo vo Republika Makedonija* (MRKK, Skopje 2013).

Jehle, J. M., "Attrition and Conviction Rates of Sexual Offences in Europe: Definitions and Criminal Justice Responses," *European Journal on Criminal Policy and Research* 18 (2012), https://doi.org/10.1007/s10610-011-9163-x. Accessed December 3, 2021.

Kalajdziev, G., Lazhetikj, G., Nedelkova, L., Denkovska, M., Trombeva, M., Vitlarov, T., Jankulovska, P., Kadiev, D., *Komentar na Zakonot za krivicnata postapka* (OSCE, Skopje 2018).

Kambovski, V., *Komentar na Krivicniot zakonik* (Matica, Skopje 2015).

Kambovski, V., Buzarovska-Lazetik, G., Nanev, L., Kosevaliska, O., Arifi, B., and Saiti, D., *Komentar na Zakonot za pravda za decata*, (UNICEF i SPPMD Kavadarci, 2018).

Kambovski, V., and Tupanceski, N., *Kazneno pravo—poseben del* (V-to izmeneto i dopolneto izdanie, Praven fakultet, Skopje 2011).

Kanevcev, M., *Praktikum za krivicno pravo—poseben del* (Praven fakultet, Skopje 2003).

Lazetik, G., "Procedural Measures for Witness Protection in Comparative and Domestic Law," in *Protection of Witnesses, Collaborators of Justice and Victims in Domestic and International Law* (International Organization for Migration—IOM and Swiss Agency for Development and Cooperation—SDC Skopje 2006).

Lazetik, G., Nanev, L., and Kosevaliska, O., *Postapuvanje so deca vo rizik i deca vo sudir so zakonot* (Praven fakultet, Skopje 2015).

Lazetik, G., and Zdravkova, I., "Pravata na žrtvite na trgovijata so luģe vo sudskite postapki," in *Sprečuvanje i borba protiv trgovija so luģevo Severna Makedonija horizontalen instrument za Zapaden Balkan i Turcija—Vtora faza* (Sovet na Evropa, Skopje 2020).

Lazhetikj-Buzharovska, G., Kalajdziev, G., Misoski, B., and Ilikj, Dimoski D., *Kazneno procesno pravo—uchebno pomagalo* (Praven fakultet "Justinijan Prvi," Skopje 2015).

Marjanovic, G., and Kanevchev, M., *Makedonsko krivicno pravo* (VIII-mo izmeneto i dopolneto izdanie, Praven fakultet, Skopje 2016).

Sulejmanov, Z., *Kriminologija* (Grafos, Skopje 2007).

Legislation and Other Resources

Council of Europe, Convention on preventing and combating violence against women and domestic violence [2011].

Criminal Code of Republic of North Macedonia, Official Gazette no. 37/96, 80/1999, 4/2002, 43/2003, 19/2004, 81/2005, 60/2006, 73/2006, 7/2008, 139/2008, 114/2009, 51/11, 135/11, 185/11, 142/12, 166/12, 55/13, 82/13, 14/14, 27/14, 28/14, 115/14, 196/15, 226/15, 97/17 and 248/18.

Criminal Procedure Code, Official Gazette, no. 150/2010, 100/2012, 142/2016 and 198/2018.
Law on justice for children, Official Gazette of the RNM, nos. 148/2013, 152/2019 and 275/2019.
Law on witness protection, Official Gazette of the RM, no. 38/05, 58/05 and 71/18.
Makstat Base, Convicted Adult Persons, http://makstat.stat.gov.mk/PXWeb/pxweb/mk/MakStat/MakStat__Sudstvo__ObvinetiOsudeniStoriteli/275_SK2_Mk_T13_ml.px/table/tableViewLayout2/?rxid=46ee0f64-2992-4b45-a2d9-cb4e5f7ec5ef, accessed December 21, 2021, http://makstat.stat.gov.mk, accessed December 21, 2021.
Ministry of Justice of Republic of North Macedonia, *Annual Operation Plan for 2021,* https://www.pravda.gov.mk/Upload/Documents/MP%20Operativen%20Plan%20za%202021%20%20R%2013%2025%20R.PDF, accessed December 3, 2021.
Ministry of Interior, *Summary analysis of the total crime in the Republic of North Macedonia in the period from 2010 to 2019,* https://mvr.gov.mk/analiza/kriminal/31, accessed December 3, 2021.
National Commission for Combating Trafficking in Human Beings and Illegal Migration, *Annual Reports,* http://nacionalnakomisija.gov.mk/mk/, accessed November 12, 2021.
State Statistical Office of Republic of Macedonia, *Perpetrators of Criminal Offences* (2008–2019), stat.gov.mk, accessed December 3, 2021.

Cases

Supreme Court of Macedonia, *Collection of Judicial Decisions 1980–1984, Book III* (Skopje 1985).
Supreme Court of Macedonia, *Collection of Judicial Decisions, Book II* (Skopje 1980).
Supreme Court of Macedonia, *Collection of Judicial Decisions, Book VII* (Skopje 1999).

NOTES

1. Public Prosecution Gostivar Public Relations, Announcements 12.23.2021, https://jorm.gov.mk/obvinenie-za-siluvane-vo-gostivar/, accessed December 23, 2021.
2. Public Prosecution Gostivar Public Relations, Announcements 7.12.2021, https://jorm.gov.mk/lazhen-odha-od-kochani-i-negovi-sorabotniczi-osomnicheni-za-polov-napad-vrz-dete-i-za-izmami-vo-gostivar/, accessed December 20, 2021.
3. Public Prosecution Prilep Public Relations, Announcements 7.12.2021, https://jorm.gov.mk/obvinenie-za-trenerot-po-%d1%9fudo-zaradi-polovi-de%d1%98stvi%d1%98a-vrz-decza/, accessed December 21, 2021.
4. Ljupco Arnaudovski, *Kriminologija* (2 Avgust S-Štip, Skopje 2007); Zoran Sulejmanov, *Kriminologija* (Grafos, Skopje 2007).

5. Aleksandra Gruevska Drakulevski, *Semejnoto nasilstvo vo Republika Makedonija (*MRKK Skopje 2013), 109–162.

6. Obviously, this illustrates best that the Macedonian legal system in respect to sexual offenses is still very traditional. For additional explanation, see n. 30.

7. Criminal Code of Republic of North Macedonia, Official Gazette no. 37/96, 80/1999, 4/2002, 43/2003, 19/2004, 81/2005, 60/2006, 73/2006, 7/2008, 139/2008, 114/2009, 51/11, 135/11, 185/11, 142/12, 166/12, 55/13, 82/13, 14/14, 27/14, 28/14, 115/14, 196/15, 226/15, 97/17 and 248/18.

8. Council of Europe Convention on preventing and combating violence against women and domestic violence [2011].

9. Vlado Kambovski and Nikola Tupanceski, *Kazneno pravo—poseben del* (prosvetno delo 2011), 189.

10. Ibid., 190.

11. Kambovski and Tupanceski (n. 9), 190.

12. Aleksandra Deanoska Trendafilova and Elena Mujoska, *Istanbulskata (CAHVIO) konvencija i zastitata na decata od seksualno nasilstvo* (MRKK Skopje 2013), 180.

13. MCC, article 418-a human trafficking and article 418-d, child trafficking.

14. Annual Reports of the National Commission for Combating Trafficking in Human Beings and Illegal Migration, http://nacionalnakomisija.gov.mk/mk/, accessed November 12, 2021.

15. Kambovski and Tupanceski (n. 9), 190.

16. Ibid.,191.

17. Ibid.

18. Ibid., 190.

19. MCC, Article 186.

20. MCC, Article 186, para. 1.

21. Complex criminal acts are offenses that consist of several actions. For example, rape is considered a crime consisting of coercion plus sexual intercourse. See Gjogji Marjanovic and Metodija Kanevchev, *Makedonsko krivicno pravo* (VIII-mo izmeneto i dopolneto izdanie, Praven fakultet, Skopje 2016), 128.

22. Judgment of the Supreme court of Macedonia, KZh, No. 372/74, *Collection of Judicial Decisions, Book II* (Skopje 1980).

23. Metodija Kanevcev, *Praktikum za krivicno pravo—poseben del* (Praven fakultet, Skopje 2003), 95.

24. MCC, Article 188.

25. Parliament of Republic of North Macedonia, Draft Law on Amendments of the Criminal Code, https://sobranie.mk//materialdetails.nspx?materialId=4448d2a8-7fc4-4fdc-9c2a-b43443de38c2, accessed December 21, 2021.

26. For example, if the victim is a prostitute, see Kambovski and Tupanceski (n 9), 193.

27. Collection of Judicial Decisions, Book III (Skopje 1985), Judgment of the Supreme court of Macedonia, KZ, No. 22/83.

28. Ibid., Judgment of the Supreme court of Macedonia, KZ, No. 109/84.

29. Ibid., Article 188, paras. 2–5.

30. Ibid., Article 187.

31. Kambovski and Tupanceski (n. 9), 198–199.
32. MCC, Article 187, paras. 2–4.
33. Ibid. Article 188.
34. Vlado Kambovski, *Komentar na Krivicniot zakonik* (Matica 2015), 817.
35. *Collection of Judicial Decisions, Book VII* (Skopje 1999), Judgment of the Supreme court of Macedonia, KVP, No. 80/98.
36. Kambovski and Tupanceski (n. 9), 201.
37. Ibid., 202.
38. See Decision of the Supreme Court of Macedonia, KZh br. 166/83, *Collection of Judicial Decisions 1980–1984, Book III* (Skopje 1985).
39. MCC, Article 189.
40. Kambovski (n 34), 819.
41. MCC, Article 190.
42. Ibid., Articles 191–194. For statistical data, see http://makstat.stat.gov.mk, accessed December 21, 2021.
43. For statistical data, see Makstat Base, Convicted Adult Persons, http://makstat.stat.gov.mk/PXWeb/pxweb/mk/MakStat/MakStat__Sudstvo__ObvinetiOsudeniStoriteli/275_SK2_Mk_T13_ml.px/table/tableViewLayout2/?rxid=46ee0f64-2992-4b45-a2d9-cb4e5f7ec5ef, accessed December 21, 2021.
44. Ibid., Article 418-a.
45. In the Macedonian language and in the Criminal Code, it is marked as 418-г, where "г" from the Macedonian (Cyrillic) alphabet equals to "d" in the Latin (Roman) alphabet.
46. Chart of signatures and ratifications of Treaty 210 https://www.coe.int/en/web/conventions/full-list?module=signatures-by-treaty&treatynum=210 accessed December 21, 2021.
47. This is envisaged in the Annual Operation Plan of the Ministry of Justice of Republic of North Macedonia for 2021. See https://www.pravda.gov.mk/Upload/Documents/MP%20Operativen%20Plan%20za%202021%20%20R%2013%2025%20R.PDF, accessed December 3, 2021.
48. CoE, GREVIO Baseline Evaluation Timeline https://rm.coe.int/icinf-2016-2rev5-timetable-baseline-evaluation-procedure/1680a39958, accessed December 21, 2021.
49. Professors Nikola Tupanceski and Aleksandra Deanoska Trendafilova are appointed members in the Ministry of Justice Working Group on drafting the new Macedonian Criminal Code.
50. Official Gazette of the RNM, no. 150/2010, 100/2012, 142/2016, and 198/2018.
51. Gordana Lazetik and others, *Kazneno procesno pravo - ucebno pomagalo* (Praven fakultet "Justinijan Prvi," Skopje 2015) 201–204; Gordan Kalajdziev and others, *Komentar na Zakonot za krivicnata postapka* (OSCE, Skopje 2018), 556–576.
52. Differences regarding personal characteristics of the victims, their relation to the perpetrator and consequences from the criminal offence, CPC, Article 54.
53. CPC, Article 44.
54. Ibid., Article 18: The public prosecutor is obliged to undertake criminal prosecution if there is evidence that a criminal offence that should be ex officio prosecuted has been committed, unless otherwise provided by this Law.

55. Ibid., Article 44 para. 1/3 of the CPC.

56. Official Gazette of the RNM, no. 38/05, 58/05, and 71/18.

57. Gordana Lazetik and others (n. 51) 150–152; Kalajdziev and others (n. 51) 520–530.

58. CPC, Article 226.

59. Ibid., Article 229.

60. Ibid., Article 53.

61. Gordana Lazetik and Irena Zdravkova, "Pravata na žrtvite na trgovijata so luģe vo sudskite postapki," in *Sprečuvanje i borba protiv trgovija so luģevo Severna Makedonija horizontalen instrument za Zapaden Balkan i Turcija—Vtora faza* (Sovet na Evropa, Skopje 2020).

62. CPC, Article 53 para 3.

63. Ibid., Article 54.

64. Ibid., Article 54 para. 4 and Article 146 para 2.

65. Ibid., Article 55 of the CPC.

66. LJC, Article 79 para. 4.

67. Gordana Lazetik, Nanev, and Kosevaliska: *Postapuvanje so deca vo rizik i deca vo sudir so zakonot* (Praven fakultet, Skopje 2015).

68. Official Gazette of the RNM, nos. 148/2013, 152/2019, and 275/2019.

69. Vlado Kambovski and others, *Komentar na Zakonot za pravda za decata* (UNICEF i SPPMD Kavadarci, 2018).

70. https://www.stat.gov.mk/Default_en.aspx, accessed December 3, 2021.

71. Jörg-Martin Jehle, "Attrition and Conviction Rates of Sexual Offences in Europe: Definitions and Criminal Justice Responses," *European Journal on Criminal Policy and Research* 18 (2012): 145, https://doi.org/10.1007/s10610-011-9163-x, accessed December 3, 2021.

72. For details, see stat.gov.mk, accessed December 3, 2021.

73. Ibid.

Chapter 4

A Perspective on the Evolution of the Legal Framework of Sexual Offenses in Romania

Cristian Dumitru Miheș and
Carmen Adriana Domocoș

Romania is considered, still, a traditional state regarding aspects of everyday life.[1] This feature is more visible when we draw our attention to family relations as well as sex crimes. First of all, the premise from which we start is the heterogeneity of Europe's space, the multitude of populations, religions, ethnicities, cultures, economic systems, and their permanent interaction,[2] more or less violent over the millennia,[3] the growing influence of the East on the West[4]—aspects found and well known to any European intellectual. This chapter is based on the proposition that discussing sexual offenses, titled as "offences against sexual freedom and integrity" in the Romanian Penal Code, can only be possible in the following context: the psychosocial traits of the Romanian people, the social evolution of the family, the legislative evolution, and the trends for the future manifested in the present.

From a social point of view, the input of other sciences may be important, which is why we will appeal to sociology and psychology. In this context, two points are to be considered. A sociological picture of the family in Romania at the level of 2009 shows, in essence, that "without diminishing its importance as a social institution, the family is no longer a conservative institution, but one increasingly adapted to transformations in society, democracy and open."[5] At the same time, it is concluded that the family is part of the social dynamics, being "conditioned" more and more by economic and social changes.[6]

As for a psychological perspective, some individualities[7] are identified in the category "how we think we are": "welcoming / friendly / tolerant (warm),"[8] "indifferent/careless (cynical/skeptical),"[9] "emotional (angry),"[10] "intelligent,"[11] "religious,"[12] "gregarious,"[13] "with undisciplined behavior often determined by context—but with a positive personality, so with the potential for good and competitive behavior in the right context (for example, at work)."[14] Obviously, these traits should not be absolutized because "the human mind, like human biology, is not defined nationally!"[15]

A current issue, intensely debated in Romanian society is that of sex education.[16] We appreciate that this aspect is relevant for the present topic because the lack of education or the deficiencies in education represent one of the determining factors of crime, and of sexual offences, in particular. There were extensive debates in society, even in Parliament, within the Ministry of National Education, the Orthodox Church intervening in this dispute.[17] Opinions were diverse, from the total elimination of the term "sex education," the replacement with the term "health education," or the integration of specific notions of sex education in other disciplines and not the establishment of a new discipline in the curriculum. Also, parental consent was in question as condition to attend sex education classes, and whether or not this agreement constitutes a barrier to access to education. What is certain is that the debate has not ended yet, the law (amending provisions) was challenged, without success, at the Constitutional Court, sent back to Parliament for re-examination by the President of Romania,[18] not having completed the legislative process a year after the adoption of the initial amendments. Practically, now there is no sex education in Romania.

Considering the European member states that followed the manifest tendencies of re-defining the notions of family by including in them any two persons in relations of the nature of those resulting from marriage, regardless of their sex, there was actually no surprise in the ECJ's decision passed in the case C-490/20.[19]

In Romania, however, the situation remains unchanged, although a referendum to amend the Romanian Constitution took place on October 6 and 7, 2018.[20] The approach was based on a citizens' initiative and was actively supported by the Orthodox Church and the Roman Catholic Church. The initiative aimed at replacing the phrase *"between spouses"* in Art. 48, para. (1) of the Constitution with a more restrictive one, "between a man and a woman." According to the explanatory memorandum of the draft law, it aims to remove any ambiguity that the use of the term "spouses" (. . .) "could bring in shaping the notion of 'family,' of the relationship between 'family' and the fundamental right of a man and a woman to marry and start a family"[21]. Marriage is already regulated in Art. 277 of the Civil Code, which prohibits other forms of cohabitation equivalent to it (same-sex marriages and civil partnerships). The referendum aimed at the constitutional prohibition of same-sex marriages, because the Civil Code can be changed without consulting the population. One of the positive effects of the referendum was the update of the legislation concerning domestic violence. In particular, the Law no. 217 from 2003[22] was amended and a new instrument—temporary protection order was regulated. The provisional protection order is issued by the police officers who, in the exercise of their duties, find that there is an imminent risk that the life, physical integrity or freedom of a person may be endangered by an act of domestic violence, in order to reduce this risk.

This chapter aims to present the evolution of legislative changes in the field of sexual offenses and their effects, as well as to highlight and analyze the main features of the report prepared by the Judicial Review for the Supreme Judicial Council. The chapter provides the Romanian insight into sexual offences, their certain challenges for investigating, and as such comes up with some proposals.

In this regard, firstly, from a cultural background standpoint, this chapter describes the current perception of sexual offences in Romania. Indeed, just two years ago, there was a referendum on the proposed change of the Constitution regarding the definition of marriage. That referendum brought attention of the public issues regarding traditional families and domestic violence, protection of victims in family violence, police and procedural measures necessary, and so on. Although the modification of Constitution was not approved, it encouraged an intense discussion about domestic violence raised from public debates during the referendum campaign. Police procedures were improved as immediate measures allowed to be imposed by the police officers directly, court procedures on issuing and enforcing a restraining order were set, and so on. Secondly, it discusses the data from a report of the Superior Council of Magistracy, Plenum, Decision no. 127 of 27.07.2021 on the approval of the Joint Thematic Report no. 20–2770 / 20–2771 of the Judicial Inspection, Report on the practice of courts and prosecutor's offices next to them, in investigating and resolving cases of sexual offences perpetrated against minor victims.[23] Finally, the chapter provides *de lege ferenda* proposal as regarding sexual offenses.

MAIN CHANGES IN THE LEGAL FRAMEWORK OF SEXUAL OFFENCES: FROM 1968 TO 2014

During the communist period, a new penal code was adopted which entered into force on January 1, 1969[24] and which was meant to regulate important aspects of criminal law respecting the then vision of the legislature. The then adopted Penal Code enjoyed stability, a desideratum that (politics) the criminal legislation after the Revolution of December 1989 did not reach. The field of sexual offenses was one that did not change significantly, remaining in the same form (almost) until after the 1989 regime change.[25]

From a historical perspective, we appreciate that some clarifications and delimitations between the old regulation[26] and the one adopted in 1968 would be welcome. In short, the 1968 Penal Code was adopted to ensure the enforcement of "Socialist Law" in opposition with the royal regime legislation.[27] Because an aspect of interest is that this Penal Code, adopted in 1968, includes in the texts a series of new aggravating circumstances: the fact that the victim committed suicide, or that the rape resulted in injury to the victim's bodily integrity or health.[28] At the same time, it was no longer provided as an aggravating circumstance as "the pregnancy of the victim and the transmission of a venereal disease,"[29] as these circumstances were considered not necessary by the new legislator.[30]

Special attention should be paid to the provisions regarding the incidence of the institution of removal of criminal liability in the case of the perpetrator's marriage to the victim of the crime—even if it was found in the old regulations. The Penal Code of 1968 extended the effects of the application of this institution, in the sense that the criminal liability for all co-perpetrators or participants would be removed if any of the participants marries the victim.[31] The reason for this provision as it was identified by the doctrine of those times lay in the fact that marriage repairs the moral damage caused to the victim, "and in some cases avoids the birth of an illegitimate child,"[32] respectively in the fact that by discontinuing the criminal process "strengthens the family recently formed."[33]

On this last point, from our point of view, the above view was wrong and detrimental to many victims. The very existence of this alternative added pressure to the victims (all of them women) in order "to accept" this so-called marriage. On the other hand, most of the rape offenses are perpetrated among persons who previously know each other and not strangers, and there was a rather widespread belief that the women were inventing complaints about rape, and that this was an issue that should be solved within the family.[34]

Another crime that has undergone significant changes in the incriminating text is seduction.[35] In the Penal Code of 1968, the text has a more permissive form, the material act not being limited to "formal promises," which leads to the conclusion that any promises made for the purpose required by the text of the law can attract criminal liability.[36] Through symmetry, the parties can reconcile not only through marriage, but also in the situation where they do not marry.

As for homosexual acts,[37] they were incriminated both in the old regulation, which used the formula of "sexual inversion,"[38] and in Art. 200 of the Penal Code 1968 as "Same-sex sexual relation."[39] In this case, both the number of the article and its content remained virtually unchanged until the repeal of these provisions after the 1989 Revolution. It includes—as was the previous text—also acts of "sexual inversion" between relatives in a direct line, considering that they fall either to acts of sexual perversion or to sexual relations between persons of the same sex.[40]

It is worth mentioning the elimination from the provisions of the criminal law of two offenses[41]: the attack on decency through abuse of power[42] and sexual inversion with animals.

A turning point in the approach to sexual offenses was the change of regime following the Revolution of December 1989. The effect of the change in approach and penal policy was a quite frequent modification of texts relating to sexual offenses, especially rape and mainly in the first decade between 1990 and 2000.[43] Given the number of changes and the substance of these changes, as it will be presented in the following paragraphs, it was rightly said that "the rule criminalizing rape was one of the most frequently amended rules in the Special Part of the Penal Code."[44]

The first important change took place by Law no. 140 of 1996[45] as a result of which the crime of rape had modified in terms of its content. One of the main features of modification was that the passive subject can only be a female person. In terms of the material element, the law mentioned of sexual intercourse—a formulation that limits the commission of rape only through sexual intercourse (natural sexual act). The incidence of the cause of impunity that would intervene through the marriage of the victim with the perpetrator was limited to the circumstance that it intervenes before the decision has become final, respectively this cause of impunity was incident in all situations, except the one regulated by letter "a"—the act was committed by two or more persons together.[46]

Considering the last aspect, the exception was introduced due to the fact if the rape was perpetrated by two or more persons together, than the (eventual) agree to sexual intercourse was not likely granted to both (or more) offenders. After all, the victim cannot marry both, or more than one offender.

At the same time, through these changes the sanctioning regime became more severe, with the minimum and maximum sentence being raised.[47] The legislator considered at that moment that the solution to deal with this kind of sexual offenses is to toughen the sanctions. The same law amends the incriminating text of same-sex sexual relations.[48] One of the amendments was that the existence of the offense was conditioned by the commission of the act in public or the occurrence of a public scandal.[49] Further, a number of aggravating circumstances such as the commission of an act by an adult against a minor, without specifying the age of the minor and without being conditioned by the commission of the act in public or the occurrence of a public scandal were introduced. As an effect of the modifications, the rape between persons of the same sex was practically included in Art. 200 of the Penal Code as an aggravated form of crime. The aggravating circumstances were reinforced in case of significant consequences for the victim's life, health, or integrity. The last paragraph provided for an assimilated form of offense consisting in inciting or enticing a person to engage in same-sex sexual intercourse, as well as propaganda or association or any other act of proselytizing committed for the same purpose. We consider that the modified provision criminalizing homosexual sexual relationships was restrictive and "ensured" effective legislative and social conservatism and practically and legally limits sexual life.[50]

What's more, the substantial modifications of the provisions regarding sexual offenses were introduced through the provisions of Law no. 197 of 2000.[51] Basically, this regulation brings substantial progress in terms of the awareness of the importance and the accomplishment of the protection of the family members, being an important landmark in the concretization of the criminal policy update in Romania regarding the family members. In particular, the commission of many of the offenses against the person against family members is an aggravating circumstance. Further, from a procedural point of view, a new security measure was introduced: "g) the prohibition to return to the family home for a certain period," applicable especially in the case of crimes committed against family members. In the absence of such a provision, the family member who committed a crime—including sexual offenses against a family member, could not return to the family home for a period of time ordered by the court.[52] Meantime, the notion of the family member was introduced into the Penal Code through Law no. 197 of 2000.[53]

With regard to legal texts relating to sexual offenses, perhaps the most important change was in the case of rape[54]:

(a) instead of the expression "sexual intercourse with a female person" the formula "sexual act of any kind, with another person." As a consequence, the victim is no longer just a woman, it can also be a man, and the law no longer objectively limits the act of sexual intercourse, but includes any sexual act, of any nature. This amendment put an end to the dispute over whether a woman can be a co-perpetrator of the crime of rape (by coercion, for example), that is, this form of the text will make other provisions in this chapter irrelevant (for example, sexual relations between persons of same-sex committed by coercion).[55]

In relation to the other two issues, we can see that they support the protection of the family as an institution and of family members. What's more, the modification did end the dispute whether the spouse can be a victim of rape by the other spouse.[56]

(b) the rape of the family member has been introduced as an aggravating circumstance; from our point of view, the rape committed against the family member is extremely serious and can negatively affect, major the subsequent evolution of the family members. From this perspective, the institution of aggravation is justified.

(c) the cause of impunity which may arise as a result of the marriage between the perpetrator and the victim has been repealed. The family is not the place where the rape charges should be solved (as mentioned above), but the place of safety and protection and development for all its members. In this line of thoughts, the marriage between the sex offender and the victim is out of the question.

The last two changes mentioned above, indicate a paradigm shift from the legislator`s point of view in the direction of reassessing the family relations.

The next stage of modifications was generated by the Emergency Ordinance no. 89 of June 21, 2001,[57] for the amendment and completion of some provisions of the Penal Code regarding crimes related to sexual life. Thus, rape was redefined[58] (again)—as sexual intercourse of any kind with a person of the opposite sex or of the same sex, including in the text the express formula that also covers situations between people of the same sex and increased the punishment for forms aggravated from the second paragraph, respectively the incident age for the situation of the aggravating circumstance in the third paragraph was raised to fifteen years (compared to fourteen years previously).

The expression sexual act of any kind was interpreted by the High Court of Cassation and Justice in the sense that it represents: "any way of obtaining sexual satisfaction by using sex or acting on sex, between persons of different sex or the same sex."[59] The decision was made since there were two trends as mentioned in the findings of the decision: "Some courts have ruled that *sexual intercourse, of any kind, with a person of the opposite sex or of the same sex* means any means of obtaining sexual satisfaction, both by sexual intercourse with a person of the opposite sex or by sexual intercourse with a person of the same sex, as well as by any other act, likely to be considered even sexual perversion, if it was committed by coercing a person or taking advantage of his inability to defend himself or to express the will. Other courts, on the contrary, have ruled in the sense that by *sexual intercourse, of any nature, with a person of the opposite sex or of the same sex*, within the meaning of the provisions of Art. 197 para. 1 (rape) and Art. 198 of the Penal Code (sexual act with a minor), means any way of obtaining sexual satisfaction by using or acting on sex, between persons of the opposite sex or of the same sex, obviously by coercion or taking advantage of the person's inability to defend or and expressed the will."[60] At the same time, this normative act repeals the provisions of Art. 200 Penal Code which criminalized same-sex sexual relations. Only from this moment, we can say that same-sex relationships, freely consented to, are no longer considered a criminal offence under Romanian law.

Then followed the Emergency Ordinance no. 143 of 2002[61] which had as object the amendment and completion of some provisions of the Penal Code and some special laws, in order to protect minors against sexual abuse and which aggravated the sanction for the situation in which rape was committed on a minor under fifteen years of age or resulted in the death of the victim.

Subsequently, considering it necessary to draft a new Penal Code, the Romanian Parliament adopted the Penal Code of 2004 (Law no. 301 of 2004[62]), which did not enter into force even for one day and which, after successive postponements was repealed by Law no. 286 of July 17, 2009. We consider of relevance to include into this chapter the reference to this Code because it was distinguished by increasing sanctions, especially by increasing the minimum and maximum number of years in prison for a very large number of crimes. The same thing happened in the case of sexual offenses, an eloquent example being the first paragraph, which contained aggravated forms of rape and which remained virtually unchanged in the content of the offenses, instead the punishment limits for these aggravating circumstances were increased from five to eighteen years in severe detention from ten to twenty years. It can be noted that this general approach might be wrong, since the toughen of punishments cannot, solely, determine a decrease of the criminal phenomenon.[63] On the other hand, maybe there were isolated cases where the increase was needed, but there was no actual debate on this matter,[64] and no supportive point of view for this idea, neither form the doctrine, nor the practitioners, and as a consequence this code.[65]

THE CURRENT LEGISLATIVE FRAMEWORK: AFTER 2014

The new Penal Code[66] which entered into force, on February 1, 2014, and the implementation of this important normative act was achieved through the provisions of Law no. 187/2012 for the implementation of Law no. 286/2009 regarding the Penal Code.[67] In Romania, crimes against sexual life are regulated, and as such, punished according to the provisions of the Penal Code, Chapter VIII—*Crimes against sexual freedom and integrity.*[68] It provides six categories of crimes against sexual life, including rape and sexual intercourse with a minor.

Although the doctrine, prior to the adoption of the new Penal Code,[69] emphasized the importance of changes that would eliminate differences in interpretation that could have resulted from the application of the 1969 Penal Code text, the legislator seems to have fallen to the other extreme of overregulation.[70] The observation is justified by the presence in the text of the law of the first two paragraphs, which reformulates (again) the definition of the crime of rape, resulting in two forms of the same crime, including other hypotheses of committing the act.

Art. 218 of the Penal Code, thus, criminalizes "rape" in the basic form of the crime, under the following conditions: "(1) Sexual intercourse, oral or anal intercourse with a person, committed by coercion, making it impossible to defend or to express his will or taking advantage of this condition is punished with imprisonment from 5 to 10 years and a ban on exercising certain rights; (2) With the same punishment shall be sanctioned any other acts of vaginal or anal penetration committed under the conditions of par. (1)"

Firstly, there is an allocation of two paragraphs to define the same act, provided that the situation described in the second sub-paragraph could be included directly in the first subparagraph, all the more so as the conditions for sanction are identical. Secondly, it is to be emphasized the increase in the severity of the sanction from a minimum of three years to a minimum of five years in prison.

Concerning the aggravated forms,[71] it should be noted that remain the aggravating circumstances from the former regulation within the new Penal Code: (a) the victim is in the care, protection, education, guarding or treatment of the perpetrator; (b) the deed was committed by a family member[72]—the situation being added "or by a person living with the victim"; (e) the act resulted in bodily injury—being added the situation "or endangered the life of the victim in any other way"; (f) the deed was committed by two or more persons together. On the other hand, we also have new aggravating circumstances: "(c) the victim is a minor[73]; (d) the act was committed for the purpose of producing pornographic materials."

At the same time, within Paragraph 3, index 1 of Art. 218 of the Penal Code, by Law no. 217 of 2020,[74] a new aggravating circumstance was introduced which is meant to protect minor victims: "The punishment is imprisonment from 7 to 15 years and the prohibition of exercising certain rights when the deeds provided in par. (1) and (2) were committed against a minor in the circumstances provided in par. (3) lit. a), b) and d)-f) or by a person who has previously committed a crime against sexual freedom and integrity against a minor, a crime of child pornography or pimping against a minor." There is an aggravating circumstance not only in relation to the actual sexual offenses, but also to those that may be related to them, such as child pornography or pimping. If the rape resulted in the death of the victim, the penalty is imprisonment from 9 to 18 years and a ban on exercising certain rights.[75]

For the basic forms of the crime of rape, the criminal action is initiated upon the prior complaint of the injured person, which means that for all other forms the criminal investigation is initiated *ex officio* and the reconciliation of the parties cannot be questioned. As for the attempts, it is explicitly sanctioned as well, according to the Romanian legal system (Art. 33 of Penal Code)[76] with half of the punishment limits for the crime in consummated form.

The idea behind the last modifications is to protect the minors that are more often victims of sexual offences. However, to criminalize certain acts will not improve the protection of minors if this is the only measure the state (legislator) will take. In this regard, we should mention the provision of art. 222 index 1 of Penal Code "Acts committed in aggravating circumstances": If the facts provided in Article 220—Sexual intercourse with a minor; Article 221—Sexual corruption of minors; Article 222—Recruitment of minors for sexual purposes—"are committed by two or more persons together or by a person who has previously committed a crime against the freedom and sexual integrity of a minor, a crime of child pornography or pimping against a minor, the special limits of punishment are increased by a third."

More recently, the law eliminated the statute of limitation in cases of sexual offenses such as: rape, sexual aggression, a sexual act with a minor.[77] As regarding the last two laws, some scholars rightfully did criticize the modality of "populist" regulation, especially when it is about penal regulation.[78]

OVERVIEW OF THE PRESENT SITUATION AND ITS REFLECTION IN CIVIL SOCIETY

The remarkable statistical data should be indicated: Regarding the number and categories of crimes against sexual life committed in Romania, according to statistical data registered by the Supreme Council of Magistracy,[79] in the last nine years there were 8,543 cases of rape and 2927 cases of sexual intercourse with a minor. The increase in the number of crimes in sexual life determined the reaction of the legislator in the sense of increasing the punishments.

On the other hand, professionals working with children reported, according to data collected by the Directorates-General for Social Assistance and Child Protection, about 570 cases of sexual abuse with child victims in 2018. Reporting cases of sexual violence is a very serious problem in Romania, as in other countries, because most of the time the victims are afraid that they will not be believed, that they will be ashamed, they are afraid of the consequences of the threats they receive from the aggressors or they are afraid that they will be blamed for the situations they went through.[80] Due to these causes, a large part of this category of crimes are unknown to the authorities, the reservation in denouncing the facts may have a genesis in the mentality of the victims, lacking the minimum legal education.[81] Often, the negative pressures coming from the victim's family in the sense of not denouncing the deed constitute impediments in discovering[82] these deeds. The absence of psychological counseling may be another plausible explanation.[83]

According to the data provided by the reports of the High Court of Cassation and Justice, in the period 2016–2018, 553 final convictions were passed for cases of sexual intercourse with a minor and another 962 for rape.[84] An important fact[85] acknowledged is that many courts changed the charge of rape to sexual intercourse with a minor, stating that there is no evidence to prove the constrain of the child (minor) to sexual act.[86]

These situations occur when the minor victims, often under the age of fifteen, do not have the opportunity to resist or are afraid to ask for help and under the threats of aggressors are influenced not to notify parents or legal representatives about what happens to them. Thus, these inactions of the victims are considered to be the value of consent, and thus the legal frameworks of sexual acts are changed. In 2017, out of the total number of cases of sexual intercourse with a minor, pending before the courts, only 42.17 percent of cases ended in final convictions. Of these, 50 percent were suspended executions and only 25.77 percent of cases ended with executions in detention. Of those sentenced to prison, about 88 percent received sentences of less than five years.[87]

Another aspect identified as relevant in terms of cases of sexual abuse of minors is the age difference between perpetrators and victims. In the current form of the Penal Code, the age difference between the victim and the aggressor is only taken into account in para. (5) in Art. 220 of Law no. 286/2009 regarding the Penal Code. This aspect is worth discussing because in many cases, the aggressors are at least twice the age of the victims, this fact being completely "ignored" by the judges when pronouncing the sentences. Moreover, there are cases where victims are considered to have misbehavior or inappropriate clothing and are found guilty of abuse.[88]

LAW IN PRACTICE ON SEXUAL OFFENCES AND THE CIVIL SOCIETY

The multitude of regulations and their more or less logical succession has created a direct effect in jurisprudence and a mediated (indirect) one in society. First of all, we have faced different approaches in judicial practice, both in terms of investigating sex crimes and in terms of judging cases and solutions. The more different approaches we see the more questions can arise in the mind of individuals, the press, or civil society in general. From this perspective, the judiciary body must assume its fundamental role within the state and self-regulate or unify its practice. At the same time, greater openness to the general public, especially in sensitive cases, would help to ensure a more effective administration of justice.

On the other hand, the right to freedom of expression of individuals is a fundamental right and it must be respected. However, the views and positions adopted by civil society on the lack of efficiency of judicial bodies in discovering and investigating such acts are not always well informed and sometimes they prove a lack of understanding the judicial procedures. In a society in which values such as family, child, freely consented intimate life, religion, good morals, to categorize the acts or decisions of the courts as "abuses," or "ignorance" the individuals, civil society and even the press should be aware of the legal framework of the criminal procedures and make statements accordingly, in order not to exceed the limits of this fundamental right.

The approach is not accidental if we consider the purpose pursued by "informing" in this way the public opinion on the activity of justice as a public service in the service of the citizen, knowing that manipulating the recipient of the legal norm is much easier when they are "supported" by court decisions that prove the "negligence" and "indifference" of those judges who leave such slips "unsanctioned," thus reaching the point of proposing the sanctioning of "guilty" magistrates.

Although we must not fall into the trap of the media and let the judicial file be trialed by the public, especially given the fact that the elements of the file and the circumstances of the deed are not known to the general public, still situations in which the suspects were not applied severe preventive measures, although it seems that there were indications in the sense of their application, either the consideration of the victim as the main trigger of the crime, or the court held that it is not necessary to order the measure of pre-trial detention because the deed did not trigger public scandal in the sense that the world was not revolted, given that the defendant acknowledged the commission of the act[89]—put under question the hard work of the courts to identify, investigate and prosecute sexual offenses. Unfortunately, this generates a lack of faith in the judiciary coming from the large scale of the population. Also, other reasons for the lack of trust in the judicial decision can be found in the insufficient legal education and also in the ineffective communication between the judicial system through its branches and the large public.

That is why the Superior Council of Magistracy remarked the problem and ordered through the Judicial Inspection the elaboration of a thorough report. Thus, in a recent report prepared by the Judicial Inspection and approved by the Superior Council of Magistracy on July 27, 2021,[90] *Report on the practice of courts and prosecutor's offices attached to them in investigating and resolving cases of crimes against sexual life with minor victims* relevant aspects regarding the investigation of these crimes, the protection and psychological counselling of minor victims in the case of crimes against sexual life in Romania, the legislative gaps were identified.

Since it is a very recent report, we consider important to extract and highlight two important sets of aspects related to the topic of our chapter, as follows[91]:

> First, I would have to underline aspects that are related to the judicial system: *how the victims are examined; the whereabouts of the hearing; the attitude of the judicial officials; the role of the public defender.*

It was concluded that in some cases, minors were examined in a non-proper manner. The law regulates the presence of a parent, tutor, or lawyer and a psychologist or representative of the Social and Children Protection Divisions.[92] Meantime, we have to bear in mind that examination of a sexual offence victim should be examined with finesse, paying attention to all the signs and the behavioral aspects of the person examined. From the statements taken by the criminal investigation bodies to the minor victims it results that none of them was recorded audio-video, the motivation retained regarding the lack of technical means.

The role of the judges was emphasized by underlining that a preponderant adoption of a formal, cold, distant behavior, totally circumscribed to the procedural norms, is undesirable: "It is the judge's attitude that makes its mark on the entire interaction."[93] As the role of the public defender, it was advocated the specialization of the lawyers in the field of juvenile justice, more or less as asked in the case of judges.

Practically, the person conducting the hearing (judge, prosecutor, investigator, lawyer) using "skills in communicating with children, both verbally and nonverbally,"[94] should create a comfortable personal space to obtain reliable and useful information.

> Secondly, aspects related to the (minor) victims of sexual offences: *The problem of victim's consent, and the establishing the validity of that consent; the problem of reporting the sexual offence; the level of education of the victim.*

The report stated that the consent of the victims was assessed "usually on a case-by-case basis, not only by reference exclusively to his age but, depending on the specific data of the case, by corroborating all the evidence administered," and aspects as the age of the injured person, the physical constitution of the injured person, the report of psychological assessment/psychiatric expertise of the injured person, which shows signs of psycho-emotional trauma, specific symptoms of depression, suicidal ideation post-traumatic stress disorder, the moral constraint of the victim by the perpetrator/the quality of the perpetrator—author's moral ascendancy over the victim, witness statements, relevant content of the social networks. That means if there is a (formal) consent expressed by the victim or there is a high probability that the consent will be invalidated by the rest of the proofs. The problem of reporting any sexual offence was and still is a sensitive issue. And, further, "if they overlap with the lack of practical experience of the person conducting the hearing, with the emotion generated by the unfriendly environments in which it takes place, it will lead to obtaining a misled statement, at most."

Following the analysis and adoption of this report, The Superior Council of Magistracy decided to initiate some concrete measures to remedy the deficiencies found in the management of the investigation and trial of crimes against sexual life and submitted to the Minister of Justice specific proposals to amend criminal law and criminal procedure, to improve it with regard to sexual offenses with minor victims. The followings appear as relevant and justified from the perspective of the topic we are analyzing[95]:

1. Modification of the provisions of the Code of Criminal Procedure, respectively Art.111 paragraph (6) Code of Criminal Procedure, in the sense that the measures regarding the conduct of hearings in premises designed or adapted for this purpose and, respectively, through or in the presence of a psychologist or another specialist in victim counselling to acquire binding force.
2. Legal regulation of the obligation to perform a psychological evaluation of the minor injured person in cases involving crimes against liberty and sexual integrity.
3. Legal regulation of the obligation to carry out the procedure with juveniles' victims in cases involving offenses against liberty and integrity sexual harassment, in court, in a non-public hearing.
4. Elimination of the legislative non-correlation between the provisions of Art.93 paragraph (4) and Art.281 paragraph (1) letter f) Code of Criminal Procedure, in the sense of regulating the sanction of nullity absolute and if the injured person is heard in the absence of a lawyer.
5. Development and application at national level of a mandatory methodology of hearing of minor victims of crime, in particular victims of crime sexual abuse, adopted after consulting all the factors involved.

What's more, the Ministry of Justice established "The Working Group on Victim Issues" that gives priority to the practice of courts and prosecutor's offices in cases of sexual offenses with minor victims. One of the solutions supported by the Ministry of Justice is the establishment of investigation chambers for minors at the level of each prosecutor's office. Another decision already adopted at the level of the working group is the update of the framework methodology for multidisciplinary team intervention in situations of violence against children and domestic violence. Following these aspects, the working group identified solutions for the involvement of community assistants in the territory to collaborate with employees of child protection departments, the involvement of academia in organizing training courses on the psychological component and solutions for a methodology, at the National Institute for Forensic Medicine level, on the collection of serological and DNA samples.[96]

CONCLUDING REMARKS

Until this moment, it seems that the present legal frame did not generate good results in fighting sexual offences in Romania. That is why the law faces constant changes, and it became a national problem as resulting from the report described above. The report clearly addresses and states the problem in fighting sexual offenses especially involving minor victims, but its finding is valid for the whole phenomenon. On the other hand, we have to underline a rather ineffective/wrong approach. Our legislator did choose to tighten of punishments for certain categories of crimes and to provide the non-statutory limitation of criminal liability (imprescriptible) for new categories of crimes, including sex offenses. In our opinion, the first choice was not proved to be effective since there were no significant positive effects registered. The second choice is debatable from a constitutional point of view since one can argue that it ignores the constitutional principle of non-retroactivity of the law by introducing the imprescriptible feature also for crimes committed under the old regulation. Also, the second choice proves the ineffectiveness of the administration of justice regarding sex crimes. Beyond this vice of constitutionality, the transition to the sphere of imprescriptible of criminal liability in the case of more and more crimes finally betrays the inefficiency of criminal courts in discovering, investigating and prosecuting crimes, which is neither desirable nor admirable.

The reactions of the criminal law specialists to the populist and popular legislative changes in the mentioned field did not delay to appear,[97] being noticed the tendency of the legislator to "give satisfaction" to the general public demanding an eye for an eye and a tooth for a tooth, "fair justice" or "fair measure," even at the cost of sacrificing the classical principles of criminal law, such as the humanism of criminal law, the preventive purpose (not only educational-retributive) of criminal punishment, the proportionality of the sanction.

The above-mentioned numerous changes in law and problems in practice denote the indecision of the legislature, of the decisive political factors. Being in indecision derives both from the insufficient preparation and analysis of sensitive topics still for our society, and from the failure to assume a coherent policy[98]—being necessary a real “paradigm shift.”[99]

REFERENCES

Literature

Antoniu, G., et al., *Explanations of the New Criminal Code, vol. III articles 188–256* (Universul Juridic Publishing House 2015).

Augustin, Stoica O., *Criminal Law, Special Part* (Didactic and Pedagogical Publishing House 1976).

Basarab, M., et al., *Commented Criminal Code, Special Part, vol. 2* (Hamangiu Publishing House 2008).

Bodea, R., and Bodea, B., *Criminal Law, Special Part* (Hamangiu Publishing House 2018).

Butler, S. M., “Violence and Murder in Europe” in Matthew S Gordon, Richard W Kaeuper and Harriet Zurndorfer (eds), *The Cambridge World History of Violence*, vol. 2 (Cambridge University Press 2020).

Cioclei, V., “3P, Un ‘virus’ reactivat, care amenință sănătatea justiției penale” (2020) 2 Analele Univeristății Bucureşti—Forum Juridic 1, https://drept.unibuc.ro/dyn_img/aubd/Cioclei%203P,%20un%20%E2%80%9Evirus%E2%80%9D%20reactivat,%20care%20amenin%C8%9B%C4%83%20s%C4%83n%C4%83tatea%20justi%C8%9Biei%20penale.pdf,. accessed August 1, 2021.

Cioclei, V., “Violența în familie, o nouă țintă a politicii penale,” *Analele Univeristății Bucureşti—Forum Juridic 2 (2020)*, https://drept.unibuc.ro/dyn_img/aubd/Valerian%20Cioclei%20Violen%C8%9Ba%20%C3%AEn%20familie.pdf, August 1, 2021.

Cotorobau, A., “Aspecte teoretice şi practice referitoare la infracţiunea de viol,” *Universul Juridic Review* 21, no. 5 (2019).

David, D., *The psychology of the Romanian people, The psychosociological profile of the Romanian people in an experimental cognitive monograph / Psihologia poporului român, Profilul psihosociologic al poporului român într-o monografie cognitive experimental* (Polirom Publishing House 2015).

Dongoroz, V., et al., *The New Criminal Code and the Previous Criminal Code, Comparative Presentation* (Politica Publishing House 1968).

Georgescu, A. B., “Despre importanța contextului unei fapte pentru încadrarea ei juridică în infracțiunea de viol sau în cea de act sexual cu un minor,” (June 25, 2021) https://www.juridice.ro/738118/despre-importanta-contextului-unei-fapte-pentru-incadrarea-ei-juridica-in-infractiunea-de-viol-sau-in-cea-de-act-sexual-cu-un-minor.html, accessed January 25, 2022.

Gherasim-Proca, O., “Mobilization and political conflicts in Romania. A competition between populisms?,” in Bogdan Ștefanachi and Alexandru Muraru (eds), *România—de la Marea Unire la Integrarea Europeană. Dezbateri, provocări,* perspective (Editura Universităţii “Alexandru Ioan Cuza” din Iaşi 2020).

Mahon, R. Mc, Eibach, J., and Roth, R., "Making Sense of Violence? Reflections on the History of Interpersonal Violence in Europe," *Crime, Histoire & Sociétés / Crime, History & Societies* 2, no. 17 (2013): 5, http://journals.openedition.org/chs/1423, accessed January 23, 2022.

Mihes, C., "The Safety Measure of the Ban on Returning to the Family Home for a Determined Period," *Revista Facultății de Drept Oradea* 1 (2000).

Mirişan, V., and Domocoş, C. A., *Criminal Law General Part* (Universul Juridic Publishing House 2019).

Mite, L. M., "Incriminarea şi dezincriminarea homosexualitatii. Articolul 200 din Codul penal Românesc," *Noua Revistă de Drepturile Omului* 2 (2016), http://www.revistadrepturileomului.ro/assets/docs/2016_2/NRDO%202016_2_documentar.pdf, accessed January 25, 2022.

Papadopol, V., "Criminal Law, Special Part," in *Principles of Law, Ministry of Justice* (Scientific Publishing House 1959).

Popescu, R., *Introduction to Family Sociology. The Romanian Family in Contemporary Society* (*Introducere în sociologia familiei. Familia Românească în societatea contemporană*) (Polirom Publishing House 2009).

Predescu, O., "Populism şi naţionalism versus valorile şi obiectivele Uniunii Europene," *Universul Juridic Review* 1 (2017).

Sălăjan, L. C., "The Political Psychologies of 'Eastern' and 'Western' Europe: Insights from Ontological Security," *Eurolimes* 29 (2020).

Streteanu, F., and Nitu, D., *Criminal Law General Part, vol. I* (Universul Juridic Publishing House 2018).

Legislation and Others

European Parliament, "The Rights of LGBTI People in the European Union" (PE 651.911, November 2020), https://www.europarl.europa.eu/RegData/etudes/BRIE/2020/651911/EPRS_BRI(2020)651911_EN.pdf, accessed January 24, 2022.

Peticilă, M., Introducerea educației sexuale în şcoli ca disciplină obligatorie sub denumirea de Educație sexuală, susținută de ministrul Educației, care spune că este nevoie şi de educație parentală' (June 18, 2021), https://www.edupedu.ro/introducerea-educatiei-sexuale-in-scoli-ca-disciplina-obligatorie-sub-denumirea-de-educatie-sexuala-sustintuta-de-ministrul-educatiei-care-spune-ca-este-nevoie-si-de-educatie-parentala/, accessed January 24, 2022.

Pintilie, C., "Actul sexual cu un minor—dilema socială a contemporaneității" (July 24, 2020), https://cezarpintilie.ro/blog/actul-sexual-cu-un-minor/, accessed January 25, 2022.

The motives of adopting the PL-x no.101 / 09.03.2020 - Draft Law for amending and supplementing Law no.286 / 2009 on the Criminal Code, as well as for amending art. 223 paragraph (2) of Law no.135 / 2010 on the Criminal Code criminal procedure, http://www.cdep.ro/proiecte/2020/100/00/1/em131.pdf, accessed July 30, 2021.

The Working Group on Victim Issues, https://www.just.ro/grupul-de-lucru-privind-problematica-victimelor-analizeaza-cu-prioritate-practica-instantelor-si-a

-parchetelor-in-cauzele-privind-infractiuni-sexuale-cu-victime-, accessed January 24, 2022, http://www.cdep.ro/proiecte/2019/400/50/7/creex457_2019.pdf> accessed January 24, 2022, https://www.edupedu.ro/iohannis-cere-reexaminarea-legii-care-prevede-inlocuirea-notiunii-de-educatie-sexuala-cu-cea-de-educatie-sanitara-si-introducerea-obligativitatii-acordului-scris-a/, accessed January 24, 2022.

Cases

High Court of Cassation and Justice, *Casefile no. 3/2005*, decision no. III/2005 available at http://www.cab1864.eu/upload/Decizia%20nr%20III%202005.pdf, accessed July 29, 2021.

Case 490/20 *V.M.A. v Stolichna obshtina, rayon "Pancharevo"* [2021] ECJ, https://curia.europa.eu/jcms/upload/docs/application/pdf/2021-12/cp210221en.pdf, accessed January 25, 2022.

The Superior Council of Magistracy, Plenum, Decision no. 127, July 27, 2021 on the approval of the Joint Thematic Report no. 20–2770 / 20–2771 of the Judicial Inspection, *Report on the practice of courts and prosecutor's offices attached to them in investigating and resolving cases of crimes against sexual life with minor victims,* https://www.csm1909.ro/ViewFile.ashx?guid=1c656a33-bd25-4118-85f1-6411fdeb1c4f-InfoCSM, accessed July 27, 2021.

Decision no. 327/2020 of the Brăila Court, http://www.rolii.ro/hotarari/5fe5544ee49009a81f000046.

NOTES

1. See Daniel David, *The Psychology of the Romanian People, The Psychosociological Profile of the Romanian People in an Experimental Cognitive Monograph* (Polirom Publishing House 2015), 27–44; Raluca Popescu, *Introduction to family sociology. The Romanian family in contemporary society* (Polirom Publishing House 2009), 101 and 102.

2. Petr Rozmahel, Ludek Kouba, Ladislava Grochová and Nikola Najman, "Integration of Central and Eastern European Countries: Increasing EU Heterogeneity?," *WWWforEurope Working Paper* 9 (2013), https://www.econstor.eu/bitstream/10419/125664/1/WWWforEurope_WPS_no009_MS77.pdf, accessed January 23, 2022.

3. Sara M Butler, "Violence and Murder in Europe," in Matthew S Gordon, Richard W Kaeuper, and Harriet Zurndorfer (eds), *The Cambridge World History of Violence, vol. 2* (Cambridge University Press 2020), 331–346; Richard McMahon, Joachim Eibach and Randolph Roth, "Making Sense of Violence? Reflections on the History of Interpersonal Violence in Europe," *Crime, Histoire & Sociétés / Crime, History & Societies* 17, no. 2 (2013): 5, http://journals.openedition.org/chs/1423, accessed January 23, 2022.

4. Loretta C. Sălăjan, "The Political Psychologies of 'Eastern' and 'Western' Europe: Insights from Ontological Security," *Eurolimes* 29 (2020): 65.

5. Popescu (n. 1), 101.
6. Ibid.
7. David (n. 1), 317 and 318.
8. Ibid., 322.
9. Ibid.
10. Ibid., 330.
11. Ibid., 331.
12. In relation to one of the features identified above, religiosity, it should be noted that at the same time the author of the monograph draws attention to the need for "catechesis" regarding the proper promotion of religion and the diminution of the importance of superstitions. Ibid., 330.
13. Ibid., 327.
14. Ibid., 328.
15. Ibid., 19.
16. Mihai Peticilă, "Introducerea educației sexuale în școli ca disciplină obligatorie sub denumirea de Educație sexuală, susținută de ministrul Educației, care spune că este nevoie și de educație parentală" (June 18, 2021), https://www.edupedu.ro/introducerea-educatiei-sexuale-in-scoli-ca-disciplina-obligatorie-sub-denumirea-de-educatie-sexuala-sustintuta-de-ministrul-educatiei-care-spune-ca-este-nevoie-si-de-educatie-parentala/, accessed January 24, 2022.
17. Maria Taga, "BOR [abbrevation of Romanian Ortodox Church] se opune obligativităţii Educaţiei sexuale în şcoli. 'Are un conţinut inadecvat copiilor'" (July 22, 2021), https://adevarul.ro/educatie/scoala/bor-opune-obligativitatii-educatiei-sexuale-scoli-educatia-sexuala-continut-inadecvat-copiilor-1_60f928245163ec42715418c5/index.html, accessed January 24, 2022.
18. The president's request for re-examination called for replacing the notion of "sexual education" with "education for health" and to waive the request for parents written consent in order for the child to take part in these classes. See https://www.edupedu.ro/iohannis-cere-reexaminarea-legii-care-prevede-inlocuirea-notiunii-de-educatie-sexuala-cu-cea-de-educatie-sanitara-si-introducerea-obligativitatii-acordului-scris-a/, accessed January 24, 2022. For the request, see http://www.cdep.ro/proiecte/2019/400/50/7/creex457_2019.pdf, accessed January 24, 2022.
19. "Child, being a minor and a Union citizen, whose birth certificate was drawn up by the host Member State and designates as parents two persons of the same sex: the Member State of which the child is a national is obliged to issue an identity card or a passport to that child without requiring a birth certificate to be drawn up beforehand by its national authorities" (Case 490/20 *V.M.A. v Stolichna obshtina, rayon "Pancharevo"* [2021] ECJ, https://curia.europa.eu/jcms/upload/docs/application/pdf/2021-12/cp210221en.pdf, accessed January 25, 2022.
20. Ovidiu Gherasim-Proca, "Mobilization and Political Conflicts in Romania. A Competition between Populisms?," in Bogdan Ștefanachi and Alexandru Muraru (eds), *România—de la Marea Unire la Integrarea Europeană. Dezbateri, provocări, perspective* (Editura Universităţii "Alexandru Ioan Cuza" din Iaşi 2020), 71 and 72.
21. Explanatory memorandum of the draft law, 6, http://www.cdep.ro/proiecte/2017/100/20/7/em34.pdf, accessed January 26, 2022.

22. Republished after several amendments in Official Gazette no. 1012, October 30, 2020.

23. The Superior Council of Magistracy, Plenum, Decision no. 127 of 27 July 2021, https://www.csm1909.ro/ViewFile.ashx?guid=1c656a33-bd25-4118-85f1-6411fdeb1c4f-InfoCSM, accessed July 29, 2021.

24. The Criminal Code of the Socialist Republic of Romania was adopted on June 21, 1968, by the Great National Assembly.

25. Vintilă Dongoroz and others, *The New Criminal Code and the previous Criminal Code, comparative presentation* (Politica Publishing House 1968), 126; Oliviu Augustin Stoica, *Criminal Law, Special Part* (Didactic and Pedagogical Publishing House 1976), 128; Radu Bodea and Bogdan Bodea, *Criminal Law, Special Part* (Hamangiu Publishing House 2018), 143.

26. The Criminal Code of 1936, Named Criminal Code "Carol II" according to the law titled: "Name of the Unification Codes of Legislation," decreed under No. 577 /1936 and published in the Official Gazette, part I, No. 73 of March 27, 1936.

27. "Inspired by the principles of our socialist law, respecting the provisions of the Constitution, the norms contained in the penal code are intended to defend the revolutionary conquests of the people, the social and state order, the sovereignty and independence of the country, national wealth, fundamental rights and freedoms of all citizens. Considering that the crimes against the socialist order, against what our people have won through hard and long struggles, are the most serious crimes against the people, the penal code provides harsh punishments against those who commit actions against the security of the state or its capacity defense" (Explanatory Statements of the 1968 Penal Code, in Dongoroz and others (n. 25), 5–7.

28. Ibid., 124.

29. Idem.

30. Idem.

31. According to Art. 197 para. 3 from 1968 Penal Code (Law no. of June 15, 21, 1968 regarding the adoption of the Criminal Code of Romania): "The acts provided in paras. 1 and 2 *(rape and aggravated rape—completion added)* shall not be punished if the marriage between the perpetrator and the victim took place before the decision became final, and in case of participation, if the marriage between the victim and any of the participants occurred. This cause of impunity has an effect on all participants."

32. Dongoroz and others (n. 25), 125.

33. Dongoroz and others (n. 25), 125; Vasile Papadopol, "Criminal Law, Special Part" in *Principles of Law, Ministry of Justice* (Scientific Publishing House 1959), 654 and 655.

34. See European Commission (Eurobarometer), "Gender-based Violence," https://europa.eu/eurobarometer/surveys/detail/2115, accessed on January 24, 2022.

35. According to Art. 199 from 1968 Penal Code, Seduction was criminalized as: "The act of a person who, by means of marriage vows, causes a female person under the age of 18 to have sexual intercourse with him, is punishable by imprisonment from one to five years. Reconciliation of the parties removed the criminal liability."

36. Dongoroz and others (n. 25), 126; Stoica (n. 25), 128.

37. Homosexual relations included sexual relations among the persons of the same sex. Further, to this crime were assimilated the Encouraging or enticing a person to practice homosexual relations. In the same time, if the act was committed on a minor, or did results serious injury to bodily integrity of health, or death or suicide of the victim—then the acts were criminalized as aggravating circumstances of homosexual relations (Art. 200 of the Penal Code from 1968).

38. The legal doctrine explained the abandonment of the formula "sexual inversion" motivating that "this expression should be avoided in the texts of criminal law, it having different meanings in medical science" (Dongoroz and others [n. 25], 127).

39. Stoica (n, 25), 133.

40. Dongoroz and others (n, 25), 128–129.

41. Ibid., 130.

42. From our point of view, this deed is practically the precursor of sexual harassment, especially in the context of subordination relationships, a fact that will be found in future regulations of the Penal Code.

43. Cezar Pintilie, "Actul sexual cu un minor—dilema socială a contemporaneității" (July 24, 2020), https://cezarpintilie.ro/blog/actul-sexual-cu-un-minor/, accessed January 25, 2022.

44. Matei Basarab and others, *Commented Criminal Code, Special Part, vol. 2* (Hamangiu Publishing House 2008), 271.

45. Official Gazette no. 289, November 14, 1996.

46. Basarab and others (n. 44), 271.

47. Ibid.

48. Art. 200 reads as follows: "Sexual intercourse between persons of the same sex, committed in public or if they have caused a public scandal, shall be punished by imprisonment from one to 5 years. The act of having an adult having sex with a minor of the same sex is punishable by imprisonment from 2 to 7 years and the prohibition of certain rights. Sexual intercourse with a person of the same sex unable to defend himself or to express his will or by coercion is punishable by imprisonment from 3 to 10 years and the prohibition of certain rights. If the deed provided in par. 2 and 3 result in serious injury to bodily integrity or health, the penalty is imprisonment from 5 to 15 years and the prohibition of certain rights, and if it results in the death or suicide of the victim, the penalty is imprisonment from 15 to 25 years and prohibition of certain rights. Encouraging or enticing a person to have sexual relations between persons of the same sex, as well as propaganda or association or any other acts of proselytize committed for the same purpose shall be punished by imprisonment from one to five years."

49. Committing the act in public or producing a public scandal are quite imprecise rules at that time, which could have given rise to abuses. For example, if the act reached the knowledge of a group of persons, by any means then it was considered to have been committed in public.

50. Liviu Marius Mite, "Incriminarea și dezincriminarea homosexualitatii. Articolul 200 din Codul penal Românesc," *Noua Revistă de Drepturile Omului* 2 (2016): 56, http://www.revistadrepturileomului.ro/assets/docs/2016_2/NRDO%202016_2_documentar.pdf, accessed January 25, 2022.

51. Published in the Official Gazette no. 289, November 14, 1996.

52. Cristian Mihes, "The Safety Measure of the Ban on Returning to the Family Home for a Determined Period," *Revista Facultății de Drept Oradea* 1 (2000): 105, 110.

53. "A family member means a spouse or close relative, if the latter lives and manages with the perpetrator."

54. Basarab and others (n. 44), 271.

55. George Antoniu and others, *Explanations of the New Criminal Code, vol. III articles 188–256* (Universul Juridic Publishing House 2015), 199; Basarab and others (n. 44), 273.

56. Obviously, the conservative doctrine, even of Civil Law, claimed that rape between spouses is not possible, with the main motivation that there is a presumption of consent to sexual intercourse once the marriage is concluded. We have argued the opposite, even before this express change, based on the idea that if the law does not distinguish between the perpetrator and the victim, then we should not make this distinction either as in the Latin expression, ubi lex non distinguit, nec nos distinguere debemus.

57. Official Gazette no. 338, June 26, 2001.

58. "Sexual intercourse, of any nature, with a person of the opposite sex or of the same sex, by coercing him or taking advantage of his impossibility to defend himself or to express his will, shall be punished by imprisonment from 3 to 10 years and prohibition of certain rights. The punishment is imprisonment from 5 to 18 years and the prohibition of certain rights, if: a) the deed was committed by two or more persons together; b) the victim is in the care, protection, education, guard or treatment of the perpetrator; b ^ 1) the victim is a member of the family; c) the victim has been seriously injured in bodily integrity or health. The penalty is imprisonment from 10 to 20 years and the prohibition of certain rights if the victim has not reached the age of 15, and if the act resulted in the death or suicide of the victim, the punishment is imprisonment from 15 to 25 years and the prohibition of certain rights."

59. High Court of Cassation and Justice, decision no. III/2005, http://www.cab1864.eu/upload/Decizia%20nr%20III%202005.pdf, accessed July 29, 2021.

60. Basarab and others (n. 44) 275. See also High Court of Cassation and Justice Decision No. III of May 23, 2005 regarding the meaning to be attributed to the acts referred to in art. 197 para. 1 and Art. 198, as well as Art. 201 of the Penal Code (case-file no. 3/2005), http://legislatie.just.ro/Public/DetaliiDocumentAfis/65296, accessed December 5, 2021.

61. Official Gazette no. 804, November 5, 2002.

62. Official Gazette no. 575, June 28, 2004.

63. Andriana Cotorobau, "Aspecte teoretice şi practice referitoare la infracţiunea de viol," (2019) 21 (5) Universul Juridic Review 52. On the other hand, since in case of sexual offenses, 50 percent of convictions were suspended executions, and only 25.77 percent of cases ended with executions in detention, one of the solutions proposed was not to give the possibility for the courts to decide suspension of the imprisonment for sex offenders—The motives of adopting the PL-x no.101 / 09.03.2020 - Draft Law for amending and supplementing Law no.286 / 2009 on the Criminal Code, as well as

for amending Art. 223 paragraph (2) of Law no.135 / 2010 on the Code of Criminal Procedure, http://www.cdep.ro/proiecte/2020/100/00/1/em131.pdf, accessed July 30, 2021.

64. Valerian Cioclei, "Violența în familie, o nouă țintă a politicii penale," (2020) 2 Analele Univeristății București—Forum Juridic 1, https://drept.unibuc.ro/dyn_img/aubd/Valerian%20Cioclei%20Violen%C8%9Ba%20%C3%AEn%20familie.pdf, August 1, 2021.

65. For more details on the motives for adopting the new Penal Code, https://sintact.ro/get/scanlex/pdf/mof_pdf/2009/2009cp.pdf, accessed December 5, 2021.

66. Law no. 286 of July 17, Official Gazette no. 510, June 24, 2009.

67. Official Gazette no. 757, November 12, 2012.

68. As early as 1865, the Penal Code provided for sexual offenses as crimes and offenses against individuals. See Cotorobau (n 63), 52.

69. Basarab and others (n. 44), 276.

70. Antoniu and others (n. 55), 182.

71. Within the third paragraph of Art. 218 of the Penal Code: "the punishment is imprisonment from 7 to 12 years and the prohibition of exercising certain rights when: a) the victim is in the care, protection, education, guarding or treatment of the perpetrator; b) the deed was committed by a family member or by a person living with the victim; c) the victim is a minor; d) the deed was committed for the purpose of producing pornographic materials; e) the deed resulted in bodily injury or endangered the life of the victim in any other way; f) the deed was committed by two or more persons together."

72. In an initial regulation of the new Penal Code, which was subsequently amended by Law no. 217 of 2020, mentioned below.

73. In an initial regulation of the new Penal Code, which was subsequently amended (emergency ordinance no. 18 of 2016, published in the Official Gazette no. 389 of May 23, 2016), this circumstance referred to a sixteen-year-old victim, given that the minor under Romanian law lasts up to eighteen years.

74. Official Gazette no. 1012, October 30, 2020.

75. According to Art. 65 of the Penal Code, "the accessory punishment consists in the prohibition of exercising the rights provided in art. 66 para. (1) lit. a), b) and d)-o), the exercise of which was prohibited by the court as a complementary punishment: a) the right to be elected to public office or to any other public office; b) the right to hold a position involving the exercise of state authority; d) the right to choose; e) parental rights; f) the right to be a guardian or curator; g) the right to hold office, to exercise the profession or trade or to carry out the activity used for the commission of the crime; h) the right to possess, carry and use any category of weapon; i) the right to drive certain categories of vehicles established by the court; j) the right to leave the territory of Romania; k) the right to hold a management position within a legal person governed by public law; l) the right to be in certain localities established by the court; m) the right to be in certain places or at certain sporting, cultural or other public gatherings, established by the court; n) the right to communicate with the victim or with his/ her family members, with the persons with whom he/ she committed the crime or with other persons, established by the court, or to approach them; o) the

right to approach the home, workplace, school or other places where the victim carries out social activities, under the conditions established by the court."

76. Florin Streteanu and Daniel Nitu, *Criminal Law General Part, vol. I* (Universul Juridic Publishing House 2018), 181; Valentin Mirişan and Carmen Adriana Domocoş, *Criminal Law General Part* (Universul Juridic Publishing House 2019), 169 and 170.

77. Law no. 186, 1st July 2021, Official Gazette no. 6570, July 2, 2021.

78. Cioclei (n 64); Ovidiu Predescu, "Populism şi naţionalism versus valorile şi obiectivele Uniunii Europene," *Universul Juridic Review* no. 1 (2017): 6; Gherasim-Proca (n. 20), 67–70.

79. These aspects are extracted from The motives of adopting the PL-x no.101 / 09.03.2020 - Draft Law for amending and supplementing Law no.286 / 2009 on the Penal Code, as well as for amending Art. 223 paragraph (2) of Law no.135 / 2010 on the Code of Criminal Procedure, http://www.cdep.ro/proiecte/2020/100/00/1/em131.pdf, accessed July 30, 2021.

80. Ibid.

81. Ibid.

82. Ibid.

83. Ibid.

84. Ibid.

85. Alexandru Bogdan Georgescu, "Despre importanţa contextului unei fapte pentru încadrarea ei juridică în infracţiunea de viol sau în cea de act sexual cu un minor" (June 29, 2021), https://www.juridice.ro/738118/despre-importanta-contextului-unei-fapte-pentru-incadrarea-ei-juridica-in-infractiunea-de-viol-sau-in-cea-de-act-sexual-cu-un-minor.html, accessed January 15, 2022.

86. These aspects are extracted from The motives of adopting the PL-x no.101 / 09.03.2020 - Draft Law for amending and supplementing Law no.286 / 2009 on the Criminal Code, as well as for amending Art. 223 paragraph (2) of Law no.135 / 2010 on the Code of Criminal Procedure, http://www.cdep.ro/proiecte/2020/100/00/1/em131.pdf, accessed July 30, 2021.

87. Ibid.

88. Ibid.

89. From the content of decision no. 327/2020 of the Brăila Court, which reformed the decision of the Braila Court which allowed the replacement of pre-trial detention with house arrest, http://www.rolii.ro/hotarari/5fe5544ee49009a81f000046, accessed July 25, 2021, some paragraphs are at least intriguing and inexplicable: "The defendant's actions, although reprehensible, are not so serious as to have generated a widespread social rumor. There were no outings, protests in the press"; "In this regard, the court of first instance considered that in this case a preventive measure is required, but by no means the most difficult, because in the case of crimes of genocide, terrorist attack, aggravated murder, crimes against humanity there would be no basis for taking any preventive measure, killing those guilty remaining the only sanction, but not regulated by law. As the defendant cannot be killed, cannot be stoned in the public square, the court of first instance considered that he can be placed under house arrest for 60 days from 22.12.2020 to 20.02.2021 inclusive."

90. The Superior Council of Magistracy, Plenum, Decision no. 127, July 27, 2021, on the approval of the Joint Thematic Report no. 20–2770 / 20–2771 of the Judicial Inspection, Report on the practice of courts and prosecutor's offices attached to them in investigating and resolving cases of crimes against sexual life with minor victims, https://www.csm1909.ro/ViewFile.ashx?guid=1c656a33-bd25-4118-85f1-6411fdeb1c4f-InfoCSM, accessed July 27, 2021.

91. The following points are extracted from: The Superior Council of Magistracy, Plenum, Decision no. 127, July 27, 2021, on the approval of the Joint Thematic Report no. 20–2770 / 20–2771 of the Judicial Inspection, Report on the practice of courts and prosecutor's offices attached to them in investigating and resolving cases of crimes against sexual life with minor victims, https://www.csm1909.ro/ViewFile.ashx?guid=1c656a33-bd25-4118-85f1-6411fdeb1c4f-InfoCSM, accessed July 26, 2021.

92. Article 124 para 1 of The Code of Criminal Procedure.

93. Report on the practice of courts and prosecutor's offices attached to them in investigating and resolving cases of crimes against sexual life with minor victims, 295, https://www.csm1909.ro/ViewFile.ashx?guid=1c656a33-bd25-4118-85f1-6411fdeb1c4f-InfoCSM, accessed July 26, 2021.

94. Ibid.

95. These proposals were filed by Legislation, documentation and litigation Department of CSM. See https://www.csm1909.ro/ViewFile.ashx?guid=204ed70b-2393-4eb1-ad76-6fcb50fb2683-InfoCSM, accessed January 24, 2022.

96. The Working Group on Victim Issues, https://www.just.ro/grupul-de-lucru-privind-problematica-victimelor-analizeaza-cu-prioritate-practica-instantelor-si-a-parchetelor-in-cauzele-privind-infractiuni-sexuale-cu-victime-minore/, accessed August 2, 2021.

97. Cioclei (n 64); Valerian Cioclei, "3P, Un 'virus' reactivat, care amenință sănătatea justiției penale," (2020) 2 Analele Univeristății București—Forum Juridic 1, https://drept.unibuc.ro/dyn_img/aubd/Cioclei%203P,%20un%20%E2%80%9Evirus%E2%80%9D%20reactivat,%20care%20amenin%C8%9B%C4%83%20s%C4%83n%C4%83tatea%20justi%C8%9Biei%20penale.pdf, accessed August 1, 2021.

98. The author's conclusion: "The Romanian Parliament is practically a miniature Romania that cannot change on its own!," in David (n 1), 331.

99. This paradigm shift should include, "in the polytrophic" component of Romanian culture, the component of scientifically validated knowledge (evidence-based knowledge), meaning a culture based on knowledge, absolutely mandatory in a globalized world, driven by knowledge (knowledge-based) society)" in ibid., 330.

Chapter 5

Grooming Re-Examined

The Protection of Children from Sexual Abuse in the Republic of Croatia

Barbara Herceg Pakšić

Traditional policing and legislative framework opportunities include acceptance of the indisputable fact[1]—various abuse forms more often than not leave life-long consequences.[2] Children victims are the most vulnerable society members. If criminal law protection wants to address the proper issues, it needs appropriately formed incriminations, high-standard criminal proceedings and educated persons skilled in communicating with children. Child sexual abuse exists as both a disposition pathology and a form of criminality.[3]

The proclamation of the right to protection from all forms of violence[4] was followed by the first global public recognition of the existence of sexual violence against children that took place two and a half decades ago, in 1996, at the First World Congress in Stockholm with the participation of 122 countries.[5,6] In the meantime, the (criminal) law protection scope was improving with the most recent need focused on technology challenges, the digital age and virtual environments. This is a time of online victimization. Internet sexual abuse of young people is recognized as an international crime without geographical boundaries[7] acknowledging that the Internet has undoubtfully contributed to the increased prevalence of grooming.[8] The notion *cyber-paedophilia* is used[9] as well as *sexting*, *grooming*, *cyberbullying,* and so on. Children spend a significant amount of time on the internet so without adequate supervision they represent a primary group of victims of cyber violence. Information and communication technology (ICT) has increased the abusers accessibility to children and the exploitation possibilities; facilitated sexual abuse, image and video sharing; reinforced the impact of long-lasting harmful abuse and contributed to commercial gains.[10] Even though these behaviors and consequences occurred in an offline environment beyond technology (schools, clubs, or families), in online environments children are less inhibited, more vulnerable[11] and risk-taking.[12] A child's social vulnerability is a strong victimization indication, which is related to a socially and emotionally poor background and should be viewed in relation to the degree of parental supervision of the child's online communication.[13] The child sexual abuse model includes four preconditions: motivation for sexual abuse, overcoming the individual's inhibitions, surmounting of external obstacles and overcoming the child's resistance, where grooming facilitates all except the first precondition.[14]

Statistics are not a reliable indicator of real cases and the dark figure is estimated to be from 1:6 to 1:20.[15] Data from twenty-five years ago revealed there were 300,000 abused children in Germany.[16] According to recent data, in Europe one in five children is a victim of some form of sexual violence[17] and around 5 percent of UK children will suffer contact sexual abuse at some point during childhood.[18] The estimates are generally based on self-reports by children.[19] A considerable discrepancy between the reported and actual cases[20] is a sad state of affairs. Low report willingness complicates getting an impression on the incidence of digital contacts with potential offenders resulting in sexual abuse.[21] An effective response requires interstate co-operation, often hampered by national criminal (substantive or procedural) law inconsistencies (due to the double criminality requirement or norm identity) with difficulties in legal assistance and/or extradition, e.g. for child pornography.[22] Normative uniformity becomes a necessary precondition in the fast-growing and transnational occurrence of the sexual abuse of children, facilitated by the ICT use. Inasmuch, the European harmonization policy is on board with planning and implementing effective child protection.

Croatian media reports on sexual abuse cases in Croatia were primarily sensational with the goal to attract an audience and "condemn the sex offender," followed with public proposals for stern repression of such acts and rigorous solutions.[23] This maintains the legislative need for re-examination of the number of incriminations and their content, the penal frameworks, and case law practice regarding sentencing. The current Croatian Criminal Code[24] was being created in time close to Croatia's accession to the European Union (EU). During the drafting time (before 2011), the obligation to comply with European standards was taken into consideration-Croatia was a member of the Council of Europe (CoE) and became a member of the EU on July 1, 2013 (shortly after the CC became effective in January 2013). In addition, considering the solutions of the comparative criminal justice systems, an evident effort was made to improve the criminal law protection of children. Criminal acts pertaining to the sexual abuse of children and their exploitation have been substantially amended in relation to the previous CC, dating from 1997. The legislator opted for a new chapter of offenses whose content was made introducing some existing but amended incriminations, and some new ones.

SOLICITATION OF CHILDREN—DEFINITION AND THE INTERNATIONAL, EUROPEAN AND COMPARATIVE PERSPECTIVE

Solicitation of children for sexual purposes is more commonly known as "grooming,"[25] however notions like "online enticement of children," "internet luring of children," "sexual grooming," and "internet seduction of children" are also used which indicates a lack of terminology consistency. The term grooming has gained attention in the last two decades.[26] Ken Lanning was probably the first to use the term, conceptualizing grooming as "the process whereby some sex offenders non-violently access and control their child victims to facilitate sexual victimization."[27] Online grooming is a form of cyber violence. In broad strokes, this violence is characterized by a lack of consistent definitions and there is no stable lexicon or typology of offenses[28] so, "no static definition of online grooming is possible."[29] It can be described as the practice where an adult "befriends" a child with the intention of sexual abuse.[30]

The abuse itself is more likely to occur following the grooming[31] during which the perpetrator may try to normalize the suggested behavior to a child.[32] Klimek writes that online sexual grooming primarily consists of pedophiles using personal websites to target children who meet their age, gender and looks inclinations.[33] Befriending a child with the desire for sexual gratification sings the same tune as an adult pretending to be another young person. This includes discussing intimate matters by gradually exposing the child to sexually explicit materials to reduce resistance or inhibitions about sex.[34] A "predatory act"[35] of skillful and strategic manipulation (of a child and the community) facilitates sexual abuse: it is more easily committed, interferes detection and hides intention.[36] Longer lasting and single victim grooming still occurs, but the dynamics have changed: over the last few years, the time between initial contact and the offending outcome has significantly shortened and perpetrators contact a large number of victims.[37] Adults send a sexual text and media via social platforms aimed at approaching a victim (minor) in person.[38]

The grooming behavior stages are (vulnerable) victim selection, obtaining access to a child, trust development and desensitizing the child to touch.[39] There is no universal model: Offenders use various technology types and often set up their victims and put their plan in motion months before arranging a physical meeting.[40] The high variance level depends on the individuals involved, with impossibility to pinpoint the beginning and ending point.[41] Detection more likely comes out ahead in retrospective behavior analysis, than in prospective identification.[42]

Online grooming has been widely researched from a social and psychological perspective[43] whereas (criminal) law analyses are not that common due to the fact that grooming incrimination itself is of a relatively recent date. As an "important part of the offence chain"[44] it has contributed to awareness that this pre-offense behavior should be criminalized, since its prevention is a prevention of contact sexual abuse. It is followed by a complex tangle of harm that includes self-blaming, fear from personal consequences, shame and embarrassment, fear of disbelief and being left without protection.[45] Not only the abuse itself, but also the grooming experience governs the severity of trauma symptoms. Threatening or violent grooming is most likely to cause harm: "anxiety, depression, sleep problems, dissociative issues, and overall trauma symptoms."[46]

Thorough-paced criminal liability encompasses the European level grooming ban. Opposed to other acts prohibiting the CSAM, reports show that grooming related acts have a lower implementation level, seemingly due to a lack of understanding of this concept.[47] The impression is that grooming has a generally agreed-upon legal meaning (as solicitation of children for sexual purposes), in a manner defined in two legally binding instruments—the CoE Lanzarote Convention of 2007 and the EU Directive 2011/93,[48] both of which advocate for the incrimination obligation.

The CoE Lanzarote Convention[49] is the first instrument to establish specific CSAM forms as criminal offences,[50] and the first international instrument to criminalize the solicitation of children for sexual purposes through ICTs.[51] Mainly reflecting the worrying phenomenon of children being sexually harmed by adults initially encountered in cyberspace—Internet, chat rooms, or game sites,[52] offline grooming types (real contacts or non-electronic communications) are outside the provision scope. Danger inherent to technology use is amplified by monitoring difficulties, so the focus is on the Internet and mobile phones.[53] According to Art. 23, a deliberate proposal to meet expressed by an adult to a child who has not reached a certain age (age is defined depending on each national system) should be criminalized if made through ICTs, with the purpose of sexual exploitation followed by acts that lead to such an encounter.[54]

There are three necessary constitutive elements: the sexual solicitation of a child (often manifested as online chatting), the intentional proposal to meet (in order to commit a sexual offence) and "material" acts leading to such a meeting (i.e., the perpetrator arriving at the meeting place). Sexual chatting with a child in itself is insufficient to set forth criminal responsibility.[55]

The Convention on Cybercrime[56] that focuses on possible cyber abuse types is mostly directed at child pornography, but stipulates the connection between ICTs and specific criminal offences. It is the basis of the Lanzarote Convention. The crossover between child pornography and grooming exists, meaning that perpetrators are not just passively viewing or trading images, but engaging in grooming. As there is a clear overlap, some authors indicated the need of further research to estimate the potential risk of crossing-over from online to offline offenses.[57]

The EU explicitly recognized protection of children's rights in the Charter of Fundamental Rights of the EU.[58] The protection level is visible through the minimum rules concerning the definition of criminal offences and sanctions in the area of sexual exploitation of children.[59] In 2012, in *the Infusino case,*[60] the European Court of Justice connected the severity of criminal acts of sexual assault, sexual coercion and rape of a minor with the concept of "imperative grounds of public security," reasoning that a Member State can expel the perpetrator from their territory, in accordance with Article 28(3)(a) of Directive 2004/38/EC.[61] Despite the fact that a previous criminal conviction does not in itself constitute ground for cross-border movement limitations, the Court relied on Art. 83 (1) TFEU which labels the sexual exploitation of children as a serious crime with a cross-border dimension, highlighting the security constellation of offence as a first-order question.[62]

The protection cornerstone was the Council Framework Decision 2004/68/JHA on combating the sexual exploitation of children and child pornography[63] but it had its relevant shortcomings.[64] The need to harmonize resulted in the EU Directive 2011/93[65] listing behaviors that Member States should criminalize and setting forth attention for an adequate legal solution for offline grooming too (Recital 19). The national legislator selects the incrimination modality: preparatory offence, offence attempt or particular sexual abuse offence. The directive stipulates at least one year of imprisonment for a proposal of intended sexual activities with a child or child pornography production, made through ICT by an adult to a child under the age of sexual consent, if followed by material acts leading to a meeting. An ICT attempt to commit the offences of child pornography access, possession, and acquisition through child solicitation is also punishable[66] as well as inciting, aiding and abetting to any of the listed offenses. Most of the member states have in place legislation that transposes this obligation.[67] However, given the complexity and the variety of the measures to be transposed in domestic laws, challenges have risen showing that further efforts are needed to fully apply the directive.[68]

Under the United Nations Convention on the Rights of the Child, states are obliged to all necessary measures to protect children from all forms of violence, including sexual abuse and to prevent the abuse, coercion, and exploitation of a child for the purpose of unlawful sexual activity.[69] Some necessary incriminations are related to offering, extraditing, or accepting a child for the purpose of sexual exploitation, transfer of organs of a child for profit, involvement of a child in forced labor or child pornography,[70] and there is a recognized link between sexual exploitation and transnational organized crime.[71] Procedures involving children should be urgent,[72] understanding that the child's position includes a high consideration standard (appropriate access to justice, reparation, compensation, and social assistance) where direct contact with the perpetrator due to procedural issues is to be avoided as much as possible.

Considering the extreme expansion of ICTs and online criminality forms, the appropriateness of the incrimination scope limit where a proposal to meet has been made is questionable—in terms of successful abuse suppression, a demand of (material) acts leading to a meeting to occur can be squaring a circle. Taking into account that most offending outcomes happen online (i.e., deceiving children into pornography production or chat or webcam activities[73]), it is not likely that a physical meeting will occur or the intention or need for it exists: "screen to screen" can be the only modality form. Online sexual perpetrators are focused more on web-based actions, that is, sexual conversations and coercing into taking indecent photos or video chats.[74] Despite the possibility of online contact leading to (offline) meeting(s) for sexual purposes, reports show that this number is relatively low and is decreasing, that is, in the UK there was a reduction from 11.7 percent in 2011 to 6.8 percent in 2012.[75] In these types of cases of complete online abuse, the lack of a constitutive element of the criminal offense will leave the abuse unpunished and victims without protection. Related to this issue, half a decade ago the Lanzarote Committee expressed the opinion that online grooming does not necessarily result in a meeting in person and nonetheless causes serious harm to the child.[76] Taking into consideration the evolving and dynamic nature of conditions, interpretation and understanding, unlimited to Convention notions, grooming should follow up-to-date circumstances and be open to extending criminalization not involving an offline meeting.[77] Online grooming victims face "shame and guilt for having, to some extent, contributed to their own exploitation (e.g., because initially they agreed to turn on their webcams and/or take photos), as well as the anxiety of permanently losing control of the images and not knowing who has seen them."[78] Therefore, it seems needed and necessary to extend the legal interpretation in ways to cover online "meetings" or to have the meeting demand removed from the incrimination requests.

Another scope limitation tackles the incrimination obligation only when directed at children who have not reached the age of sexual consent. Depending on the national legislator, this commonly means the age of fourteen or fifteen. This is a slippery slope: Children above that age are not sufficiently protected. They can still be lured or manipulated into an exploitative situation.[79] Children who groom other children with sexual intent are not covered by the incrimination scope. The growing trend of society's over-sexualization certainly contributes to children's impression of the acceptability of sharing sexual images (sexting) or explicit online conversations, with little or no consideration of related risks. The age difference in contact persons is sometimes used to describe the discrepancy in notions of online grooming—where contact is made between an older adult and a child—and online solicitation—where contact is made between young adults and a child[80] and is visible in European legislation depending on legislator intention to provide a state reaction. In England, the offender must be eighteen years, but in the Netherlands, there is no age limit. The Dutch legislator has chosen to have the ability to react to a wider range of sexual manipulations, between children as well—"taking sexual pictures using mobile telephones and subsequent blackmail, resulting in actual sexual contact."[81]

SELECTED CRIMINAL LAW SYSTEMS AND SUPPRESSION ISSUES

Tackled at the European level with an expected quick and serious effect on national legislations, grooming has challenged criminal law systems in capacity and ability in successful compliance to incrimination obligation. However, evaluations of this obligation as "not well prepared"[82] have risen to the surface. The role of criminal law in contemporary society is in general gaining in importance. The classic paradigm has shifted in the direction of social value design, scanning for potential dangers, and consequently extending its boundaries. Grooming incrimination, even though a step forward, can well relate with precautionary criminal law[83] as well as the broader challenges of proving harmful intent in a "thought" crime and "pre-emptive" police strike.[84] Given that CSAM prevention is at the forefront of social and state concern, specific forms of civic activism are not uncommon (adults present themselves as minors and enter chat rooms and platforms) which can also lead to challenges (i.e., abetting in offence). When a conversation involves sexual solicitation, the volunteers report this to the prosecution authorities.[85] Despite the significant number of existing offences related to CSAM, only relatively recently have acts specifically targeted online grooming, criminalizing such behavior.[86] Normative strategies vary: adoption of specific regulations or acts, interpretation of existing acts or provisions, or, what is most common, adoption of specific criminal law provision.[87]

The United Kingdom was one of the first states initiating a strong legislative path of illegal child contact and grooming with the intent of committing a sexual offence. This was followed by other countries in Europe (i.e., Norway in 2007 and the Netherlands in 2010) and outside, that is, in Australia, Canada, Singapore, New Zealand.[88] Some countries lacking this incrimination are still relying on existing acts to exercise the leading role in these matters. Examples are Belgium or Italy.[89] In England, the grooming incrimination decision was a part of the changes in the "decency legislation" (the Sexual Offence Act dating from 1956) and was conditioned by the increased concern about the danger of sexual abuse of children.[90] Nowadays it is a part of the Sexual Offences Act of 2003 (Art. 15, Meeting a child following sexual grooming) and the number of registered cases and convictions has gradually increased.[91] It is intended to protect children under sixteen from adults who communicate with them (not restricted to online communications and can take place anywhere in the world) and then arrange a meeting with the purpose of sexual abuse, either at that meeting or subsequently. When the offender meets the child, travels with this intention, arranges to meet, or the child travels with the intention of meeting the offender, the offence is completed.[92] It is stipulated as "a preparatory act, made concrete by two previous contacts and a subsequent act towards committing the offence." There is no requirement that the concrete meeting is intended to include sexual contact, and "it is sufficient to establish that this meeting is part of a communication process serving the suspect's intention to have sexual contact."[93] It is triable by Magistrates' or the Crown Courts with the majority of cases being settled by plea bargaining.[94]

In the German Criminal Code (germ. *Strafgesetzbuch, StGB*), grooming is placed among Criminal offences against sexual self-determination (germ. *Straftaten gegen die sexuelle Selbstbestimmung*). These offences have been recently amended a few times.[95]. The basic incrimination regarding the protection of children from sexual abuse refers to § 176 StGB, Sexual abuse of children (germ. *Sexueller Mißbrauch von Kindern*), stating that a perpetrator who commits sexual acts against a person under fourteen years of age (a child) will be punished by imprisonment from six months to ten years. The grooming is not separately regulated but is part of this incrimination (§ 176/4 p. 3. StGB), stating that imprisonment from three months to five years will be imposed on anyone who acts on a child through letters (germ. *Schriften*) or ICT for the purpose of sexual acts by the perpetrator or a third party or child pornography. The notion of letters is interpreted extensively in accordance with §11/3 StGB, which includes sound carriers (germ. *Tonträger*), images (germ. *Bildträger*), data stored in a computer system (germ. *Datenspeicher*), illustrations (germ. *Abbildungen*), recordings and other displays. Furthermore, the same sentence shall be imposed on anyone who acts on a child by showing pornographic images or depictions, recordings of pornographic content through ICT or by speech, in accordance with § 176/4 p. 4. StGB. This communication type is one between the perpetrator and potential victim, structurally fundamentally different from the communication between like-minded people.[96] The last sharpening of the criminal law blade took place in 2015. In order to harmonize the legislation with the Directive 2011/93 / EU, § 176/4 p. 3 of StGB was modified in a way that includes child pornography and covers ICT related modality.[97]

In the Netherlands, grooming became a criminal offence in 2010 in Art. 248e[98] as a result of concern about the increasing digitalization as an option for the manipulation of children.[99] It is directed only at online grooming incrimination[100]: any person that uses a computerized work environment or communication service to suggest a meeting with a person under sixteen and takes action to achieve it, with the intention of an indecent act or sexual act image is punishable by maximum two years' imprisonment or a fine. The provision is described as "open nature" but with foreseeable challenges regarding enforcement.[101]

Under section § 2422 of the United States Criminal Code (the federal enticement statute), it is a crime to knowingly persuade, induce, entice, or coerce any individual under the age of eighteen to engage in prostitution or any sexual activity for which any individual can be charged with a criminal offence. In *United States v. Chambers,* appealing to his grooming attempt conviction by the district court, Chambers argued that there was no substantial step toward offence completion since he did not travel to meet the victim. His fourteen months of online chatting with (what he believed was) a fourteen-year-old girl was labelled by him as just "a bunch of talk," denying that intention existed. Affirming conviction, the Court of Appeals recognized that plans to meet never culminated in a meeting, but in light of all circumstances (sexual chat, formulated plan, invited victim to travel at his expense to meet him, confirming victim was taking birth control, obtained a web camera to send to her), the incrimination line was crossed.[102]

Legislative review of grooming incrimination in 196 countries shows the multifarious global picture.[103] Even without a tailor-made provision, existing case law interpretations can enable online grooming prosecution, as in Belgium with the Electronic Communications Act.[104]

INCRIMINATION OF CHILD GROOMING IN THE REPUBLIC OF CROATIA

Due to omission of thorough discussions on the notion and meaning of grooming, its understanding in Croatia is still at the rudimentary level.[105]

With regards to the Republic of Croatia, the Lanzarote Convention entered into force on January 1, 2012.[106] The Croatian CC was already half a year in effect when the EU Directive became obligatory. The grooming offence had largely corresponded to European solutions adopted in the Convention and the Directive, but with room for improvement. General research interest in child sexual abuse in Croatia was at the peak in the period 2005–2009 but then declined, due to interest in other topics such as peer violence and cyber-bullying, thus sexual abuse is more researched as a form of child abuse in general.[107] One reflection on this is the possible "reluctance among Croatian researchers and professionals to conduct research on the most serious and tabooed abuse forms burdened by a series of ethical and methodological considerations."[108] The existing research belongs to the fields of psychology, social work, education and health, and rarely law.

The inability to identify predatory behaviors is potentially connected with the lack of awareness or what classifies as sexual grooming.[109] Even in countries with the same criminal law tradition (such as Croatia, Slovenia, and Germany), related sexual offenses against children are differently handled, which includes different penal frameworks.[110] The CC entered into force on January 1, 2013, driven by the will of the Croatian legislator to improve child protection. Previously regulated within general sexual offenses, offences related to children were singled out, supplemented with new or improved incriminations, and separately regulated in Chapter XVII, titled *Criminal Offences of Child Sexual Abuse and Exploitation.* This comprehensive approach raised the age limit for consensual sexual relations from fourteen to fifteen[111] and opened the door for a novelty that was not a part of the legislative scope of the previous CC: Solicitation of children for satisfaction of sexual needs (Art. 161 of CC). The incrimination name was criticized for its linguistic inconsistency.[112] It incriminates intentional conduct where an adult (person over eighteen) proposes a meeting to a child (persons under fifteen) through ICT or in other manner, with the intention of committing sexual abuse of a child under fifteen or exploiting for pornography or pornographic performances and takes action to achieve this meeting. The punishment is imprisonment from six months to five years. The provision has clear specification of the victim's and perpetrator's age.

The CC does not contain the definition of the ICT term. Instead, Art. 87 (in paragraphs 18–20), defines three terms. Computer system (as any device or group of interconnected or connected devices, one or more of which automatically process data on the basis of a program, as well as computer data stored, processed, loaded, or transmitted for the purposes of its operation, use, protection, and maintenance). Computer data (any expression of facts, information, or ideas in a form suitable for processing in a computer system) and a computer program (a set of computer data can cause a computer system to perform a particular function). Contact with a child with the aim of sexual abuse does not suffice; it is necessary for the adult to take measures to bring about an encounter, that is, after soliciting a child using ICT or other manner and takes any action to achieve the agreed meeting. The manner of the realization of the meeting is not specified so the activities can vary: the perpetrator's departure to the agreed location, obtaining a description of the location of meeting the victim, purchasing a train ticket or tickets in connection with the intended meeting, or booking a hotel room.[113] Up to three years imprisonment is punishment for the preparatory act that includes collecting, giving or transmitting data on children under the age of fifteen.

The second offense version has been effective since January 1, 2020. The major deficiencies of the first version (effective from January 1, 2013) include not referring to grooming for the purpose of child pornography and the punishment was significantly less severe—up to three years for grooming and up to one year for data manipulation.[114] This less severe punishment should be critically observed especially in view of the (optional) general possibility of Croatian courts to impose a fine as the main punishment for the criminal offences for which a prison sentence of up to three years is prescribed (Art. 40 / 4 CC). Even though this option may be suitable in the context of other criminal offences, the Croatian legislator was on the right track raising the punishment as well as making other improvements since the first version was not fully in compliance with the Lanzarote Convention demands. Due to the directive's specifically formed provision on minimal maximum penalty ("maximum term of imprisonment of at least one year"), some Croatian reflections were directed at the wish to respect state sovereignty in penal norms as the scope limit of supranational European legal solutions.[115]

In comparison with European standards, the Croatian incrimination of grooming goes beyond the minimum responsibility scope. First, besides online grooming (ICT perpetration modality), it incriminates also offline grooming. This is not unfamiliar among European solutions: that is, the UK Sexual Offences Act of 2003 has the same form. However, the linguistic expression could be better since the Croatian provision states that the meeting suggestion is made *through ICT or in other manner*. The latter is a general clause (normally used in other provisions) but here, it seems to be unnecessarily overburdening the legal text. It suffices to incriminate (any) *proposal for a meeting* so that all situations are covered. Second, the convention and the directive have set the sanctioning standard of the perpetrator who would engage in online grooming with a child with the purpose of sexual exploitation or child pornography. The Croatian solution accepts a scope of wider responsibility including the activities that are part of arranging a meeting with a person who is not the perpetrator, so that the other person participates in the sexual exploitation of a child or child pornography. Some authors have expressed their disagreement, considering that the purposefulness and ratio of expansion is questionable, as this is an unnecessary liability extension beyond demands of European acts.[116]

During the criminal law procedure, the prosecution must prove, beyond all reasonable doubt, that the meeting was arranged with a sexual purpose in mind, which will be related to *in concreto* circumstances regarding grooming. Comparative reflections from police and probation officers have pointed out the difficulties regarding this issue, that is, that it may be impossible to confirm needed intent, especially where the perpetrator has no previous CSAM convictions.[117] Going beyond the purely legislative level, according to data from the Croatian Bureau of Statistics[118], this provision in reality is hitting the skids. The number of convicted perpetrators as well as the number of reports is rather low.

The years taken into analysis were from the CC's entry into force until the most recent published data. It is visible that altogether eleven perpetrators during the period of eight years ended up convicted. The percentage of grooming convictions within this group ranges from 0–4 percent. All convictions concern proposing a meeting and taking measures to make it happen, with the intention of committing sexual abuse, or exploiting a child for pornography, while the punishable act of data collecting was not recognized in practice at all.

In Croatia, the court practice accessibility is hampered due to only partially published judgments. However, in five collected decisions on pre-trial detention, dating from 2019 and 2020,[119] it was visible that the accused were male, all same kind of recidivists—previously convicted for CSAM. All of them were accused of simultaneously committing several criminal offenses in this area (sexual abuse of a child under fifteen, grooming, introducing a child to pornography and exploiting a child for pornography). Pre-trial detention was determined for all of them based on the likelihood of repeated offence. Therefore, the Supreme Court decisions were all regarding rejection of an applicant's appeal against a lower court's decision imposing pre-trial

Table 5.1. Overview of Reports, Accusations and Convictions in Croatia 2013-2019. Source: Croatian Bureau of Statistics.

Year	*2019*	*2018*	*2017*	*2016*	*2015*	*2014*	*2013*
CSAM*	103	97	104	94	99	97	73
Grooming** Convictions	2	4	3	0	0	2	0
Grooming Reports	5	4	5	9	8	1	5
Grooming Accusations	3	5	3	0	0	2	0

* Number of perpetrators convicted for criminal offenses including child sexual abuse and exploitation (CSAM). ** Solicitation of children for satisfaction of sexual needs

detention. Similarly, the decision of the Constitutional Court was regarding extending the duration of a pre-trial detention measure. In reaching a decision on pre-trial detention, this court resonates through the principle of proportionality, that is, whether reasons of public interest prevail over the applicant's right to personal liberty and the presumption of innocence. In the mentioned case, it was decided that the applicant's constitutional rights had not been violated and that the pre-trial detention was reasonably imposed.

CONCLUDING REMARKS

Effective child protection from (any) violence is an imperative in the contemporary world. In times of striving for maximum, holistic, and comprehensive protection, it is necessary to ensure that international standards are adequately and effectively fitted into the national legal regulation framework. Despite the requirements of the Directive 2011/93/EU, the Budapest and the Lanzarote Conventions, and the legislation modification that followed, legal solutions in the specific CSAM area have plenty of room for improvement. Adapting the criminal law tools in view of the changing nature of contemporary (cyber) crime (advanced approach to ICT technologies, protection from inappropriate content and contacts as well as personal data privacy) sometimes suffers objections claiming prevention has overshadowed other objectives of criminal law. The importance of traditional criminal law requirements is starting to be conditioned by their flexibility—the possibility of adapting to contemporary requirements challenging criminal law. The grooming incrimination reflects the role of penal policy and the possibility of appropriate preventive action: manner of effective provisions to offer protection prior to the occurrence of the physical sexual abuse.

Exception from the general rule of preparatory actions impunity is a way of seeking possibilities in earlier temporal intervention aimed at enhancing prevention. Without it, the attempt stage of a classic contact sexual offence would remain, leaving the child in greater danger. Even without a static definition, grooming seems to have an agreed legal meaning according to European standards. The evolving interpretation could be open to thoughts on extending criminalization to cases not involving an offline meeting and extending protection by increasing the age limit of a child.

A comparative perspective has shown that states have recognized the need and relatively recently targeted (online) grooming, criminalizing such behavior, with variations in normative strategies: from tailor-made incriminations to extensive interpretation of existing provisions. The Croatian current policy revealed a rapid readiness for the implementation of European standards, but the fast pace resulted in shortcomings that needed improvement. Bringing the legislative level in order even with a wider responsibility scope, did not result in visible suppression of the prohibited behavior, as is seen in the insignificant practical effect as well as the rather low number of convictions. This means that the Croatian legislator's aspiration to increase protection in this area has not yet resulted in the desired efficiency. Despite of the mentioned rarity, practice insight resulted in some information regarding the perpetrator's profile, the offence characteristics and the procedural measure of pre-trial detention. In conclusion, legislative changes are an easier part of the story, but without effort in educating and preparing the relevant competent authorities in recognizing, investigating and prosecuting child grooming, the real results are left hanging in the air.

REFERENCES

Literature

Beech, A. R., Elliott, I. A., Birgden, A., and Findlater, D., "The Internet and Child Sexual Offending: A Criminological Review,"" *Aggression and Violent Behaviour* 13 (2008).

Burgess, A. W., and Hartman, C. R., "On the Origin of Grooming," *Journal of Interpersonal Violence* 33 (2018).

Bock, S., and Harrendorf, S,, "Strafbarkeit und Strafwürdigkeit Tatvorbereitender Computervermittelter Kommunikation," *Zeitschrift für die gesamte Strafrechtswissenschaft* 126 (2014).

Cano, A. E., Fernandez, M., and Alani, H., "Detecting Child Grooming Behaviour Patterns on Social Media," in L. M. Aiello and D. McFarland (eds), *Lecture Notes in Computer Science (including subseries Lecture Notes in Artificial Intelligence and Lecture Notes in Bioinformatics)*, vol. 8851 (Springer Verlag 2014), 412.

Canter, D., Hughes, D., and Kirby, S., "Paedophilia: Pathology, Criminality, or Both? The Development of a Multivariate Model of Offence Behaviour in Child Sexual Abuse," *The Journal of Forensic Psychiatry* 9 (1998).

Choo, K. K. R., "Online Child Grooming: A Literature Review on the Misuse of Social Networking Sites for Grooming Children for Sexual Offences" (2009) xii, www.aic.gov.au, accessed September 18, 2020.

Derenčinović, D., "Dječja pornografija na internetu-o kažnjivosti posjedovanja i virtualnoj dječjoj pornografiji," *Hrvatski ljetopis za kazneno pravo i praksu* 10 (2003).

Eisele, J., "Vorbemerkungen zu den §§ 174 ff," in *Schönke/Schröder Strafgesetzbuch Kommentar* (30th ed, C. H. Beck 2019), 1757–1759, rn. 9–14.

Endres, J., and Scholz, B., "Sexueller Kindesmißbrauch Aus Psychologischer Sicht," *Neue Zeitschrift für Strafrecht* 14 (1994).

Herceg, Pakšić B., "Virtualna komunikacija i izazovi kaznenog prava novog doba," in Tena Velki and Krešimir Šolić (eds), *Izazovi digitalnog svijeta* (I, Fakultet za odgojne i obrazovne znanosti, Sveučilište Josipa Jurja Strossmayera Osijek 2019).

Klimek, L., "Solicitation of Children for Sexual Purposes: The New Offence in the EU (Under The Directive 2011/92/EU)," *International and Comparative Law Review* 12 (2018).

Kool, R., "Prevention by All Means? A Legal Comparison of the Criminalization of Online Grooming and Its Enforcement," *Utrecht Law Review* 7 (2011).

Kostakopoulou, T., and Ferreira, N., "Testing Liberal Norms: The Public Policy and Public Security Derogations and the Cracks in European Union Citizenship," [2013] Legal Studies Research Paper No. 2013–18, Warwick School of Law 1, https://papers.ssrn.com/sol3/papers.cfm?abstract_id=2271722, accessed October 10, 2020.

Lalor, K., and McElvaney, R., "Overview of the Nature and Extent of Child Sexual Abuse in Overview of the Nature and Extent of Child Sexual Abuse in Europe" (2010), https://arrow.tudublin.ie/aaschsslbk, accessed September 29, 2020.

Ost, S., "Getting to Grips with Sexual Grooming? The New Offence under the Sexual Offences Act 2003," *Journal of Social Welfare and Family Law* 26 (2004).

——, *Child Pornography and Sexual Grooming: Legal and Societal Responses* (Cambridge University Press 2009).

Popović, S., "Child Sexual Abuse in Croatia: A Systematic Review of Research," *Ljetopis Socijalnog Rada* 25 (2018).

Radford, L., et al., "Child Abuse and Neglect in the UK Today" (2011) 117, https://learning.nspcc.org.uk/media/1042/child-abuse-neglect-uk-today-research-report.pdf, accessed September 8, 2020.

Rittossa, D., "Seksualni delikti na štetu djece-hrvatski kaznenopravni okvir kroz prizmu zahtjeva iz direktive 2011/93/EU," *Hrvatski ljetopis za kaznene znanosti i praksu* 25 (2018).

Scherrer, A., and Van Ballegooij, W., "Combating Sexual Abuse of Children-Study" (2017) 13, www.europarl.europa.eu/thinktank, accessed September 28, 2020.

Schulman, C., "Global Project on Cybercrime Protecting Children against Sexual Violence: The Criminal Law Benchmarks of the Budapest and Lanzarote Conventions" (2012) 69, www.coe.int/cybercrimewww.coe.int/cybercrime, accessed September 30, 2020.

Škrtić, D., "Mamljenje djeteta za zadovoljenje spolnih potreba uporabom informacijsko-komunikacijske tehnologije," *Zbornik Pravnog fakulteta Sveučilišta u Rijeci* 34 (2013).

Webster, S., et al., "European Online Grooming Project - Final Report" (2012) 5, https://www.academia.edu/23987615/European_Online_Grooming_Project_Final_Report, accessed September 8, 2020.

Williams, A., "Child Sexual Victimisation: Ethnographic Stories of Stranger and Acquaintance Grooming," *Journal of Sexual Aggression* 21 (2015), https://www.tandfonline.com/doi/abs/10.1080/13552600.2014.948085, accessed September 17, 2020.

Winters, G. M., and Jeglic, E. L., “Stages of Sexual Grooming: Recognizing Potentially Predatory Behaviors of Child Molesters,” *Deviant Behaviour* 38 (2017).

Wolak, J., David Finkelhor, and Kimberly Mitchell, “Internet-Initiated Sex Crimes against Minors: Implications for Prevention Based on Findings from a National Study Internet Adolescence Sexual Assault,” *Journal of Adolescent Health* 35 (2004), http://unh.edu/ccrc/pdf/CV71.pdf, accessed September 9, 2020.

Legislation and others

Charter of Fundamental Rights of the European Union OJ C 83/389, 2010.

Child Exploitation and Online Protection Centre, “Threat Assessment of Child Sexual Exploitation and Abuse” (2013), https://www.norfolklscb.org/wp-content/uploads/2015/03/CEOP_Threat-Assessment_CSE_JUN2013.pdf2013, accessed August 3, 2020.

Council Framework Decision 2004/68/JHA of December 22, 2003, on combating the sexual exploitation of children and child pornography. OJ L 13/44 2004.

Council of Europe CETS 201 - Explanatory Report to the Council of Europe Convention on the Protection of Children against Sexual Exploitation and Sexual Abuse, 2007.

Council of Europe Mapping Study on Cyberviolence, 2018.

Council of Europe Convention on Cybercrime, 2001.

Council of Europe Convention on the Protection of Children against Sexual Exploitation and Sexual Abuse, 2007.

Croatian Criminal Code, Official Gazette 125/2011, 144/2012, 56/2015, 61/2015, 101/2017, 118/2018, 126/2019, 84/2021.

Crown Prosecution Service, Rape and Sexual Offences—Chapter 2: Sexual Offences Act 2003—Principal Offences, and Sexual Offences Act 1956 - Most Commonly Charged Offences.

Directive 2004/38/EC of the European Parliament and of the Council of April 29, 2004, on the right of citizens of the Union and their family members to move and reside freely within the territory of the Member States.

Directive 2011/92/EU of the European Parliament and of the Council of 13 December 2011 on combating the sexual abuse and sexual exploitation of children and child pornography, and replacing Council Framework Decision 2004/68/JHA.

Državni zavod za statistiku, Punoljetni počinitelji kaznenih djela-prijave, optužbe i osude (za razdoblje 2013–2019) [*Adult perpetrators of Criminal Offences, Reports, Accusations and Convictions, statistical reports for the years 2013–2019*], https://www.dzs.hr/, accessed August 3, 2020.

ECPAT International, “Global Monitoring, Status of Action Against Commercial Sexual Exploitation of Children Germany, 2nd edition” (2012) 5, www.ecpat.net, accessed July 31, 2020.

International Centre for Missing & Exploited Children, The Koons Family Institute on International Law & Policy “Online Grooming of Children for Sexual Purposes: Model Legislation & Global Review” (2017), 14.

Interagency Working Group ECPAT International, "Terminology Guidelines for the Protection of Children from Sexual Exploitation and Sexual Abuse" (2016) 49, http://luxembourgguidelines.org/english-version/, accessed August 3, 2020.

Netherlands Criminal Code (Wetboek van Strafrecht).

Lanzarotte Committee, Opinion on Article 23 of the Lanzarote Convention and its Explanatory Note, 2016.

Report from the Commision to the European Parliament and the Council Assessing the Extent to Which the Member States Have Taken the Necessary Measures in Order to Comply with Directive 2011/93/EU of 13 December 2011 on Combating the Sexual Abuse and Sexual Exploitation of Children and Child Pornography, 2016.

Resolution 2011/33 adopted in 2011 by the Economic and Social Council on Prevention, Protection and International Cooperation against the Use of New Information Technologies to Abuse and/or Exploit Children.

Treaty on the Functioning of the European Union OJ C 326, December 26, 2012.

United Kingdom, Sexual Offences Act, 2003.

United Nations, Convention on the Rights of the Child, 1989.

United Nations, Convention against Transnational Organized Crime, 2000.

United Nations Guidelines for Action on Children in the Criminal Justice System, 1997.

United Nations Optional Protocol to the Convention on the Rights of the Child on the Sale of Children, Child Prostitution and Child Pornography, 2000.

Zakon o potvrđivanju Konvencije Vijeća Europe o zaštiti djece od seksualnog iskorištavanja i seksualnog zlostavljanja), Official Gazette-International Contracts 11/11, 13/11.

Cases

II Kž 271/2020–4 [2020] Supreme Court of the Republic of Croatia

II Kž 276/2020–4 [2020] Supreme Court of the Republic of Croatia

II Kž 416/2019–4 [2019] Supreme Court of the Republic of Croatia

II Kž 63/2019–5 [2019] Supreme Court of the Republic of Croatia

P.I. v Oberbürgermeisterin der Stadt Remscheid [2012] C 348/09, ECLI:EU :C:2012:300.

U-III/5295/2019 [2020] Constitutional Court of the Republic of Croatia

United States v Chambers, 642 F.3d 588 (7th Cir. 2011)

NOTES

1. This paper is a product of work that has been fully supported by the Faculty of Law, Josip Juraj Strossmayer University of Osijek under the project no. IP-PRAVOS-18 "Artificial Intelligence and Criminal Law."

2. Barbara Herceg Pakšić, "Virtualna komunikacija i izazovi kaznenog prava novog doba," in Tena Velki and Krešimir Šolić (eds), *Izazovi digitalnog svijeta* (I,

Fakultet za odgojne i obrazovne znanosti, Sveučilište Josipa Jurja Strossmayera Osijek 2019), 161.

3. David Canter, Derek Hughes, and Stuart Kirby, "Paedophilia: Pathology, criminality, or both? The development of a multivariate model of offence behaviour in child sexual abuse," *The Journal of Forensic Psychiatry* 9 (1998): 532, 550.

4. United Nations, Convention on the Rights of the Child, 1989, Article 19.

5. ECPAT International, "Global Monitoring, Status of Action Against Commercial Sexual Exploitation of Children Germany, 2nd edition" (2012) 5, www.ecpat.net, accessed July 31, 2020.

6. The second congress was held in Yokohama, Japan, in 2001, and it took the position that sexually exploited children were in fact victims of a type of terrorism. The third congress was held in 2008 in Brazil, and the sexual exploitation of children was then rated as the worst kind of power demonstration.

7. Stephen Webster and others, "European Online Grooming Project—Final Report" (2012) 5, https://www.academia.edu/23987615/European_Online_Grooming_Project_Final_Report, accessed September 8, 2020.

8. Suzanne Ost, *Child Pornography and Sexual Grooming: Legal and Societal Responses* (Cambridge University Press 2009), 26.

9. Amparo Elizabeth Cano, Miriam Fernandez, and Harith Alani, "Detecting Child Grooming Behaviour Patterns on Social Media," in LM Aiello and D McFarland (eds), *Lecture Notes in Computer Science (including subseries Lecture Notes in Artificial Intelligence and Lecture Notes in Bioinformatics)*, vol. 8851 (Springer Verlag 2014), 412.

10. Council of Europe, "Mapping Study on Cyberviolence" (2018) 12, www.coe.int/cybercrime, accessed August 3, 2020.

11. Herceg Pakšić (n. 2), 162.

12. Webster and others (n. 7), 15.

13. Renée Kool, "Prevention by All Means? A Legal Comparison of the Criminalization of Online Grooming and Its Enforcement," *Utrecht Law Review* 7 (2011): 69, 50.

14. Ost (n 8), 32–33.

15. Johann Endres and Berndt Scholz, "Sexueller Kindesmißbrauch Aus Psychologischer Sicht," *Neue Zeitschrift für Strafrecht* 14 (1994): 466, 468.

16. *Ibid.*

17. Kevin Lalor and Rosaleen McElvaney, "Overview of the Nature and Extent of Child Sexual Abuse in Overview of the Nature and Extent of Child Sexual Abuse in Europe" (2010), https://arrow.tudublin.ie/aaschsslbk, accessed September 29, 2020; Amandine Scherrer and Wouter van Ballegooij, "Combating Sexual Abuse of Children-Study" (2017) 13, www.europarl.europa.eu/thinktank, accessed September 28, 2020.

18. Lorraine Radford and others, "Child Abuse and Neglect in the UK Today" (2011) 117, https://learning.nspcc.org.uk/media/1042/child-abuse-neglect-uk-today-research-report.pdf, accessed September 8, 2020.

19. Janis Wolak, David Finkelhor, and Kimberly Mitchell, "Internet-Initiated Sex Crimes against Minors: Implications for Prevention Based on Findings from a

National Study Internet Adolescence Sexual Assault," *Journal of Adolescent Health* 35 (2004): 424e11, http://unh.edu/ccrc/pdf/CV71.pdf, accessed September 9, 2020.

20. Council of Europe, "CETS 201—Explanatory Report to the Council of Europe Convention on the Protection of Children against Sexual Exploitation and Sexual Abuse" (2007), 1.

21. Kool (n. 13), 48.

22. Davor Derenčinović, "Dječja pornografija na internetu-o kažnjivosti posjedovanja i virtualnoj dječjoj pornografij," *Hrvatski ljetopis za kazneno pravo i praksu* 10 (2003): 3, 6.

23. Dalida Rittossa, "Seksualni delikti na štetu djece-hrvatski kaznenopravni okvir kroz prizmu zahtjeva iz direktive 2011/93/EU," *Hrvatski ljetopis za kaznene znanosti i praksu* 25 (2018): 29, 30–31.

24. Official Gazette 125/2011, 144/2012, 56/2015, 61/2015, 101/2017, 118/2018, 126/2019, 84/2021 (further in text CC).

25. Council of Europe (n. 20), 23.

26. Ann Wolbert Burgess and Carol R. Hartman, "On the Origin of Grooming," *Journal of Interpersonal Violence* 33 (2018): 17.

27. *Ibid.*, 20.

28. Council of Europe (n. 10), 6.

29. Lanzarotte Committee, "Opinion on Article 23 of the Lanzarote Convention and Its Explanatory Note" (2016) 7, para. 20, https://edoc.coe.int/en/children-s-rights/7064-lanzarote-committee-opinion-on-article-23-of-the-lanzarote-convention-and-its-explanatory-note.html, accessed September 8, 2020.

30. Interagency Working Group ECPAT International, "Terminology Guidelines for the Protection of Children from Sexual Exploitation and Sexual Abuse" (2016) 49, http://luxembourgguidelines.org/english-version/, accessed August 3, 2020.

31. Ost (n. 8), 32.

32. Suzanne Ost, "Getting to Grips with Sexual Grooming? The New Offence under the Sexual Offences Act 2003," *Journal of Social Welfare and Family Law* 26 (2004): 147, 148.

33. Libor Klimek, "Solicitation of Children for Sexual Purposes: The New Offence in the EU (Under The Directive 2011/92/EU)," *International and Comparative Law Review* 12 (2018): 141, 144.

34. Council of Europe (n. 20), 23.

35. Ost (n. 32), 32.

36. Georgia M. Winters and Elizabeth L. Jeglic, "Stages of Sexual Grooming: Recognizing Potentially Predatory Behaviors of Child Molesters," *Deviant Behaviour* 38 (2017): 724.

37. Child Exploitation and Online Protection Centre, "Threat Assessment of Child Sexual Exploitation and Abuse" (2013), https://www.norfolklscb.org/wp-content/uploads/2015/03/CEOP_Threat-Assessment_CSE_JUN2013.pdf2013, accessed August 3, 2020, 10, para 35 and 36

38. Cano, Fernandez, and Alani (n. 9), 412.

39. Winters and Jeglic (n. 36), 725–727.

40. Kim-Kwang Raymond Choo, "Online Child Grooming: A Literature Review on the Misuse of Social Networking Sites for Grooming Children for Sexual Offences," (2009) xii, www.aic.gov.au, accessed September 18, 2020.

41. Winters and Jeglic (n. 36), 725.

42. Andy Williams, "Child Sexual Victimisation: Ethnographic Stories of Stranger and Acquaintance Grooming," *Journal of Sexual Aggression* 21 (2015): 28, 29, and 39, https://www.tandfonline.com/doi/abs/10.1080/13552600.2014.948085, accessed September 17, 2020.

43. Cano, Fernandez, and Alani (n. 9), 414.

44. Williams (n. 42), 29 and 31.

45. Molly R. Wolf and Doyle K. Pruitt, "Grooming Hurts Too: The Effects of Types of Perpetrator Grooming on Trauma Symptoms in Adult Survivors of Child Sexual Abuse," *Journal of Child Sexual Abuse* 28, no. 3 (2019): 345, 348.

46. Ibid., 353.

47. Cristina Schulman, "Global Project on Cybercrime Protecting Children against Sexual Violence: The Criminal Law Benchmarks of the Budapest and Lanzarote Conventions" (2012) 69, www.coe.int/cybercrimewww.coe.int/cybercrime, accessed September 30, 2020.

48. It is also used in non-binding instruments such as Resolution 2011/33 adopted in 2011 by the Economic and Social Council on Prevention, Protection and International Cooperation against the Use of New Information Technologies to Abuse and/or Exploit Children. The CRC Committee, in General Comment No. 13 of 2011, mentions that "in contact with others through ICT, children may be bullied, harassed or stalked (child 'luring') and/or coerced, tricked or persuaded into meeting strangers off-line, being 'groomed' for involvement in sexual activities and/or providing personal information."

49. Convention on the Protection of Children against Sexual Exploitation and Sexual Abuse, 2007.

50. All forty-seven Council of Europe member states have signed, and forty-five states have ratified the convention.

51. Lanzarotte Committee (n. 29), 9, para 1.

52. Council of Europe (n. 20), 23.

53. Ibid.

54. Article 23—Solicitation of children for sexual purposes.

55. Council of Europe (n. 20), 23.

56. Council of Europe, Convention on Cybercrime, 2001. Also known as Budapest Convention. It is the first international treaty on crimes committed via the Internet and other computer networks.

57. Anthony R Beech, Ian A Elliott, Astrid Birgden, Donald Findlater, "The Internet and Child Sexual Offending: A Criminological Review," *Aggression and Violent Behaviour* 13 (2008): 216, 222, and 226.

58. OJ, C 83/389 of March 30, 2010. See Article 24 of the Charter—The rights of the child.

59. Articles 67 and 83 of the Treaty on the Functioning of the EU (as amended by the Treaty of Lisbon). OJ, C 83/47 of March 30, 2010. Article 83(1) TFEU provides

that the sexual exploitation of children is one of the areas of particularly serious crime with a cross-border dimension.

60. Judgment of the Court (Grand Chamber), May 22, 2012., *P.I. v Oberbürgermeisterin der Stadt Remscheid*, Case C-348/09, ECLI:EU:C:2012:300.

61. Directive 2004/38/EC of the European Parliament and of the Council of April 29, 2004, on the right of citizens of the Union and their family members to move and reside freely within the territory of the member states.

62. Theodora Kostakopoulou and Nuno Ferreira, "Testing Liberal Norms: The Public Policy and Public Security Derogations and the Cracks in European Union Citizenship" [2013] Legal Studies Research Paper No. 2013–18, Warwick School of Law 1, 11–12, https://papers.ssrn.com/sol3/papers.cfm?abstract_id=2271722, accessed October 10, 2020.

63. Council Framework Decision 2004/68/JHA of December 22, 2003, on combating the sexual exploitation of children and child pornography. OJ, L 13/44 of January 20, 2004.

64. Klimek (n. 33), 147.

65. Directive 2011/93/EU of the European Parliament and of the Council of December 13, 2011, on combating the sexual abuse and sexual exploitation of children and child pornography, and replacing the Council Framework Decision 2004/68/JHA.

66. Directive 2011/93/EU, Art. 6.

67. Report from the Commission to the European Parliament and the Council assessing the extent to which the Member States have taken the necessary measures in order to comply with Directive 2011/93/EU of December 13, 2011 on combating the sexual abuse and sexual exploitation of children and child pornography, Brussels, December 16, 2016, COM (2016).

68. Scherrer and van Ballegooij (n. 17), 12 and 26.

69. United Nations, Convention on the Rights of the Child, 1990, Article 19, 34.

70. United Nations, Optional Protocol to the Convention on the Rights of the Child on the sale of children, child prostitution and child pornography, 2000, Art. 3. This protocol, as universal treaty specifically addressing the sexual exploitation of children, criminalizes certain acts in relation to the sale of children, child prostitution and child pornography, including attempt, complicity and participation. Explanatory Report to the Council of Europe Convention on the Protection of Children against Sexual Exploitation and Sexual Abuse, 2007, 2.

71. United Nations Convention against Transnational Organized Crime, 2000.

72. United Nations, Human Rights, Office of the High Commissioner, Guidelines for Action on Children in the Criminal Justice System 1997.

73. See n. 37.

74. International Centre for Missing & Exploited Children, The Koons Family Institute on International Law & Policy, "Online Grooming of Children for Sexual Purposes: Model Legislation & Global Review" (2017), 14.

75. Child Exploitation and Online Protection Centre (n. 73), 11, para. 43.

76. Lanzarotte Committee (n. 29), 6, para. 17.

77. Lanzarotte Committee (n. 29), 7, para 20.

78. ECPAT International (n. 30), 50.
79. Ibid.
80. Kool (n 13), 49.
81. Ibid., 63.
82. Ibid., 47.
83. Ibid., 46–47.
84. Ost (n. 32), 148 and 151.
85. Cano, Fernandez and Alani (n. 9), 414.
86. Klimek (n 33), 145.
87. Schulman (n. 47), 44.
88. Choo (n. 40).
89. Klimek (n. 33), 146.
90. Ost (n. 32).
91. Kool (n. 13), 47–48.
92. Sexual Offences Act (2003), https://www.cps.gov.uk/legal-guidance/rape-and-sexual-offences-chapter-2-sexual-offences-act-2003-principal-offences-and, accessed October 19, 2020
93. Kool (n. 12), 54–55.
94. Ibid., 54 and 56.
95. Jörg Eisele, "Vorbemerkungen zu den §§ 174 ff," in *Schönke/Schröder Strafgesetzbuch Kommentar* (30th edn, C. H. Beck 2019) 1757–1759, rn. 9–14.
96. Stephanie Bock and Stefan Harrendorf, "Strafbarkeit und Strafwürdigkeit Tatvorbereitender Computervermittelter Kommunikation," *Zeitschrift für die gesamte Strafrechtswissenschaft* 126 (2014): 337, 359.
97. Eisele (n. 95) 1758, rn. 12.
98.Dutch Criminal Code, Wetboek van Strafrecht, https://www.legislationline.org/download/id/6415/file/Netherlands_CC_am2012_en.pdf, accessed October 5, 2020.
99. Kool (n. 13), 61.
100. Offline grooming is punishable under art. 248a of Dutch CC.
101. Kool (n. 13), 67.
102. *United States v Chambers*, 642 F.3d 588 (7th Cir. 2011), https://www.courtlistener.com/opinion/218946/united-states-v-chambers/?q=&court_armfor=on&order_by=dateFiled+desc, accessed October 5, 2020.
103. International Centre for Missing & Exploited Children (n. 74), 39–55.
104. Schulman (n. 47), 41.
105. Herceg Pakšić (n. 2), 162.
106. Act ratifying the Council of Europe Convention on the Protection of Children against Sexual Exploitation and Sexual Abuse (Zakon o potvrđivanju Konvencije Vijeća Europe o zaštiti djece od seksualnog iskorištavanja i seksualnog zlostavljanja), Official Gazette-International Contracts 11/11, 13/11.
107. Stjepka Popović, "Child Sexual Abuse in Croatia: A Systematic Review of Research," *Ljetopis Socijalnog Rada* 25 (2018): 5, 11, and 20.
108. Ibid., 20.
109. Winters and Jeglic (n. 36), 731.
110. Rittossa (n. 23), 55–58.

111. Incriminations in which the offense constitutive element is that the person (child) is under eighteen years of age or under fifteen years of age are as follows: Sexual abuse of a child under fifteen years of age, sexual abuse of a child over fifteen years of age, satisfaction of lust in front of a child under the age of fifteen, solicitation of children to satisfy sexual needs, procuring a child, exploitation of a child for pornography, exploitation of children for pornographic performances, introduction of pornography to children, grave criminal offenses of sexual abuse and exploitation of a child.

112. Dražen Škrtić, "Mamljenje djeteta za zadovoljenje spolnih potreba uporabom informacijsko-komunikacijske tehnologije," *Zbornik Pravnog fakulteta Sveučilišta u Rijeci* 34 (2013): 1139, 1156.

113. Ibid., 1157.

114. In order to have complete criminal law protection, the old version had a separate provision regarding attempt, which in given time in accordance with the general part provisions of the CC would not be punishable. After CC was amended, this provision was omitted as unnecessary (with raising the punishment, attempt became punishable in accordance with general attempt provision).

115. Rittossa (n. 23), 36–37.

116. Škrtić (n. 112), 1157.

117. Ost (n. 32), 152.

118. Državni zavod za statistiku, Punoljetni počinitelji kaznenih djela-prijave, optužbe i osude (za razdoblje 2013–2019) [*Adult perpetrators of Criminal Offences, Reports, Accusations and Convictions, statistical reports for the years 2013–2019*], https://www.dzs.hr/, accessed August 3, 2020.

119. Four done by the Supreme Court of the Republic of Croatia and one by the Constitutional Court of the Republic of Croatia. Constitutional Court: U-III /5295/2019 of January 22, 2020; the Supreme Court of the Republic of Croatia: II Kž 416/2019–4 of 14 November 2019; II Kž 276/2020–4 of July 2, 2020; II Kž 63/2019–5 of March 1, 2019; II Kž 271/2020–4 of July 3, 2020. These are not finalized cases, but only decisions regarding pre-trial detention, so the conclusions are to be taken *cum grano salis*.

PART II

Sexual Crimes with the Dimensions of Gender-Based Discrimination

Chapter 6

Combating Sexual and Gender-Based Violence in Serbia

After the Istanbul Convention

Gordana Gasmi and Željko Nikač

Statistics on violence against women in Serbia are devastating, with more than 300 women killed in the last twenty years. In 2020 alone, 11,000 cases of gender-based violence were reported, and fifteen women were killed. Black statistics show that every third woman in Serbia is exposed to some kind of violence, mental and physical. Women often suffer violence for fear of abusers or condemnation of the environment in which they live, and often because they are economically dependent on the person who abuses them.[1] Thanks to the implementation of new legal solutions, the topic of gender equality and violence against women is no longer taboo in Serbia.

According to the World Health Organization at least one in three women worldwide experience one or more serious physical and/or sexual violent incidents during their lifetime, often from an intimate partner or ex-partner.[2] In Europe, according to recently conducted surveys,[3] 33 percent of women have experienced physical and/or sexual violence since the age of fifteen, which corresponds to 62 million women. Figures for all forms of violence, including stalking, are as high as 45 percent.[4] Nevertheless, most cases committed behind domestic walls, remain unreported.[5] This low reporting rate can be attributed in part to the cold, impersonal reporting process and the rape victim's fear of appearing at the trial of the suspect.[6] However, this sexual offence must be prevented and addressed from the very onset.[7] Harmful social norms and stereotypes across cultures and social classes are the root of gender-based violence that affects all societies with enormous cost for victims, their families, and economies.[8]

Every human being has the right to live free from all forms of violence. *Litke* notes that "The violence is intriguing. Universally doomed, and yet it is everywhere. Most of us are both fascinated and horrified by it. It is a fundamental ingredient of our entertainment (children's stories, world literature, film industry) and an essential addition to many of our social institutions. In most parts of the world, it is extremely common in family life, religious affairs, and political history."[9]

However, in reality, many forms of gender-based violence against women and girls, or violence that is directed against women do exist because she is a woman or that affects women disproportionally.[10] Among those forms of gender-based violence, rape is one of the most atrocious sexual offences and human rights violations, where the most prevalent victims are women and girls.[11] At the same time, it is very often under-reported.[12] When it comes to criminal proceedings, the impunity rate is rather high in most countries. Twenty years ago, the UN established the International Day for the Elimination of Violence against Women on November 25, and more than 1,700 organizations in more than one hundred countries around the world start the "16 Days of Activism" campaign on this day.[13] This fact speaks for itself on global character of the gender-based violence against women.

The Convention of the Council of Europe on Preventing and Combatting Violence against Women and Domestic Violence (Istanbul Convention, 2014), being the benchmark for international standards in this field, requires from its signatories to improve relevant national legislation.[14] Furthermore, the Istanbul Convention calls for more rigorous sanctions to be implemented against perpetrators.[15] "Council of Europe holds a significant role in the world with its 47 European member and non-European observer states, it functions as an anchor for ensuring human rights, notably the ones of women."[16]

Serbia has ratified this Convention in 2013 and as such was among the first states parties in which it entered into force on August 1, 2014. Transformative power of the norms of the Convention brought important improvements of national Criminal Code in Serbia in 2016 and fostered the launch of new pieces of legislation.

In the following text, relevant legislative framework and legal improvements in Serbia will be analyzed, as well as challenges and recommendations for further reform in this domain. Serbia received the first GREVIO Evaluation Report on legislative and other measures giving effect to the provisions of the Istanbul Convention, which was published in January 2020[17] and has identified further measures to be implemented, *inter alia*, in the area of combating sexual and gender-based violence. An open question is to what extent legal improvements in Serbia achieved more effective fight against sexual offenses, more specifically the phenomenon of rape. The chapter begins with the legal frameworks of sexual and gender based violence in

Serbia. The impact of the Istanbul Convention in Serbian law is analyzed. Relevant challenges and necessary reform measures in Serbia are presented. Finally, conclusions are formulated.

LEGAL FRAMEWORK OF SEXUAL AND GENDER-BASED VIOLENCE IN SERBIA

Serbia is part of the continental law system. Therefore, case law is not binding for the legal concept of sexual offences. In the Criminal Code (2005),[18] Chapter XVIII, rape is defined in Article 178 as follows:

1. "Whoever forces another to sexual intercourse or an equal act by use of force or threat of direct attack against the body of such or other person, shall be punished with imprisonment from three to twelve years.
2. If the offence specified in paragraph 1 of this Article is committed under threat of disclosure of information against such person or another that would discredit such person's reputation or honor, or by threat of other grave evil, the offender shall be punished with imprisonment from two to ten years.
3. If the offence specified in paragraphs 1 and 2 of this Article resulted in grievous bodily harm of the person against whom the offence is committed, or if the offence is committed by more than one person or in a particularly cruel or particularly humiliating manner or against a juvenile or the act resulted in pregnancy, the offender shall be punished with imprisonment from five to fifteen years.
4. If the offence specified in paragraphs 1 and 2 of this Article results in death of the person against whom it was committed or if committed against a child, the offender shall be punished with imprisonment of minimum ten years."

Chapter XVIII of the Criminal Code, titled: "Sexual offences," includes rape (Art. 178), Sexual Intercourse with a Helpless Person (Art. 179), Sexual Intercourse with a Child (Art. 180), Sexual Intercourse through Abuse of Position (Art. 181), Prohibited Sexual Acts (Art. 182), Sexual harassment (Art. 182a), Pimping and enabling sexual intercourse (Art. 183), Mediation in Prostitution (Art. 184), Showing, procuring and possession of Pornographic Material and exploiting a minor for pornography (Art. 185), Inducing a Minor to Attend Sexual Acts (Art. 185 a) and Abuse of Computer Networks and Other Methods of Electronic Communication To Commit Criminal Offences Against Sexual Freedom of Minors (Art. 185 b).

Unlike domestic violence and sexual harassment, rape has long been recognized as a serious legal offence. Penalties for rape range from two to fifteen years pursuant to the Serbian Criminal Code, and if a fatal consequence occurs, life imprisonment is envisaged. For domestic violence, the Criminal Code regulates the crime in the separate Chapter XIX, titled: "Offences relating to marriage and family," in the Art. 194, which is formulated in a gender-neutral manner.

Serbia made progress and has criminalized the different forms of violence against women covered by Articles 33 through 40 of the Istanbul Convention. Since 2016, the Criminal Code includes, among others, the offences of stalking, forced marriage, female genital mutilation, and sexual harassment.

However, the offence of rape is defined as forcing a person into sexual intercourse or an equal act by use of force or threat of direct attack against the body of such person, or another person (Article 178). In so doing, the traditional coercion model in regulating the consent in sexual offences is adopted. Consequently, rape is not defined as an act of sexual intercourse without consent of the victim, as required by the Istanbul Convention, but as an act committed with the use of coercion, force or threat. None of the sexual offences except the rape include this element of consent.

Taking into account that the concept of consent is rather new in many national legislations,[19] it is indicative to quote the Sexual Offences Act 2003 (SOA 2003) of England and Wales, which provided the definition of consent that includes "the freedom and capacity to make" such consent.[20] The burden of proof provisions has been altered as well. Section 75 introduced a number of "evidential presumptions" with regards to the consent. It defined circumstances under which the consent was presumed to not have been given. The burden of proof thus shifted from the complainant to the defendant. Such circumstances included for example, violence or threat of violence preceding the act, and the complainant being asleep or otherwise unconscious. Section 76 further provided circumstances for "conclusive presumptions about consent" including the deceit of the "nature or purpose of relevant act" or impersonation of a person previously known to the complainant.[21]

In contemporary circumstances, what is new is an understanding of such offences that reflects women's experience. Rape has traditionally been defined by male views of male sexuality.[22] However, in recent period, standpoints of the victim (mostly women and girls) in the form of the absence of consent, are being taken into consideration.

Starting from the point that the Istanbul Convention requires from states parties to provide for criminal legislation that encompasses the notion of lack of freely given consent to any of the sexual acts listed in Art. 36. of the Convention,[23] many nongovernmental organizations in Serbia conduct campaigns for amendments of the Criminal Code in this direction. The

Istanbul Convention specifies (Art. 36, par. 2) that consent must be given voluntarily as the result of the person's free will, as assessed in the context of the surrounding circumstances. More precisely, Autonomous Female Centre launched the initiative for change of the definition of the criminal offense of rape, so that every act of sexual penetration is punishable, regardless of the form and nature of the act, committed against a person who has not given his/her free consent, which will be taken into account in the context of each individual case.[24]

New Gender Equality Law of 2021[25] in its Art. 6 introduces legal concept of gender-based violence and defines violence against women as separate categories:

> Gender-based violence is any form of physical, sexual, psychological, economic and social violence committed against a person or groups of persons due to belonging to a certain gender or gender, as well as threats to such acts, regardless of whether they occur in public or private life, as well as any form of violence that mainly affects persons belonging to a certain gender;
>
> Violence against women means a violation of human rights and a form of discrimination against women and all acts of gender-based violence that cause or may lead to: physical, sexual, psychological or financial injury or suffering for women, including threats of such acts, coercion or arbitrary deprivation of liberty, either in public or in private life;

Those definitions of Gender Equality Law, that include also sexual violence, are harmonized with provisions of the Convention of the Istanbul Convention. Furthermore, this law contains Chapter VI, which is dedicated to prevention and suppression of gender-based violence.

The Law on the Prevention of Domestic Violence[26] in its Art. 4. refers to the criminal offence of domestic violence from the Criminal Code and furthermore other crimes defined in the Criminal Code: rape (Art. 178), stalking (Art. 138a), rape of helpless person (Art. 179), rape of a child (Art. 180), rape by misuse of official position (Art. 181), prohibited sexual acts (Art. 182); sexual harassment (Art. 182a), mediation in enabling sexual intercourse (Art. 183), mediation in prostitution (Art. 184), showing, obtaining and possessing pornographic material and exploiting minors for pornography (Art. 185), inducing the child to attend sexual activities (Art. 185a), incest (Art. 197), human trafficking (Art. 388) and neglect and abuse of the child (Art. 193).

This law has priority implementation regrading protection orders and risk assessment; therefore, the Law is completely harmonized with the Convention provisions, more precisely in relation to: The Article 50—Immediate response, prevention and protection, Article 51—Risk assessment and risk management, Article 52—Emergency barring orders, Article

53—Restraining or protection orders and Article 55—*Ex parte* and *ex officio* proceedings. It is the victim at the center of the risk assessment of domestic violence and violence against women, aimed at providing for security of the victim. The Law on the Prevention of Domestic Violence empowers prosecutors and police to have not only repressive, but also very important preventive roles in cases of domestic violence. Emergency protection orders are to be issued based solely on the risk assessment that there is possibility of violence and without the victim's consent. The authority for the issuance of emergency measures has been given only to specialized Domestic Violence police officers, who have eight hours to conduct all the interviews, gather evidence and assess the risk before issuing emergency order(s)—eviction from residence and restraining/no-contact order.[27]

This emergency police order last forty-eight hours, without the right to appeal. Within those forty-eight hours, prosecutors have twenty-four hours to request prolongation of the order from the court, and the court have twenty-four hours to decide on the prolongation, in an *ex-parte* proceeding, with the right to appeal. Once prolonged, the emergency protection order lasts for additional thirty days. The breach of the emergency protection orders is a misdemeanor offence punishable up to sixty days in prison. The law prescribes the possibility for initiating disciplinary proceeding for judges and prosecutors who fail to respect these short deadlines. Furthermore, this law provides for specialization of experts, exchange of information and coordinated response of services, obligations to report suspicion of domestic violence, informing victims, development of an individual plan of victim's protection and support, as well as better records of reports of measures, monitoring and reporting on the law enforcement.

All those norms are aimed at effective protection of the victim. Implementation period of this law that started since mid-2017 indicates the rise of emergency protection orders for the sake of victim safety. Consequently, this law bears not only modern legal significance, but furthermore it brought revolutionary novelties in practice of police and judiciary. During pandemic of COVID-19, police officers and deputy prosecutors and judges, treated the closure and ban on movement, due to the pandemic, as additional risk of gender based and domestic violence.[28] In 2020, an increase in violations of emergency measures by 5.9 percent was registered, as well as an overall increase of the number of perpetrators who repeat gender based violence by 10.5 percent compared to 2019 year. In 2020, the police registered 8.8 percent more "risky events" than in the previous year. A slightly larger number of orders were issued for both emergency measures, as well as a larger number of measures to remove the perpetrator from the apartment/house than in 2019.[29]

Under the Family Law[30] (Art. 197–200), domestic violence is defined as behavior by which one family member endangers the physical integrity, mental health, or tranquility of another family member. Domestic violence is considered to be, in particular, the infliction or attempted infliction of bodily injury; causing fear by threatening to kill or inflict bodily harm on a family member or a person close to him; coercion into sexual intercourse; inducing sexual intercourse or sexual intercourse with a person under the age of fourteen or an incapacitated person; restriction of freedom of movement or communication with third parties; insults, like any other insolent, reckless, and malicious behavior.[31]

This legal provision (Art. 197) defines violence through threatening behavior, and not through types of specific forms of violence (physical, sexual, psychological, and economic), while the circle of protected persons (family members) is prescribed in a special paragraph and corresponds to the definition in the Article 3 of the Istanbul Convention. Providing protection against domestic violence and the provisions of family law is especially important because it enables efficient and faster protection of the victim—the procedure is shorter, and the measures are aimed at preventing and preventing further violence. Article 198 of the Family Law regulates the following measures of protection against domestic violence: issuance of an eviction order from a family apartment or house, regardless of the right of ownership or lease of real estate; issuing orders for moving into a family apartment or house, regardless of the right of ownership or lease of real estate; ban on approaching a family member at a certain distance; ban on access to the area around the place of residence or work of a family member; prohibition of further harassment of a family member.

Much progress has been made in Serbia to criminalize the different forms of violence against women covered by Articles 33 through 40 of the Istanbul Convention. Since 2016, the Criminal Code includes, among others, the offences of stalking, forced marriage, female genital mutilation, and sexual harassment. Sexual harassment, legally defined as the imposition of unwelcome sexual demands or the creation of sexually offensive environments, has been a perennial problem.

When it comes to bylaws, which should provide a plan of measures and activities in relevant areas at the national and local level, it has been established since 2010, by adopting a national strategy, general and special protocols on the conduct of the competent services in protection of women from gender-based violence.[32] National gender equality strategy for the period from 2016–2020 and the accompanying two-year action plans contain specific measures related to the topic of violence against women and in mid-2021, a new Strategy for the Prevention and Combating of Gender-Based Violence and Domestic Violence was adopted.

THE IMPACT OF THE ISTANBUL CONVENTION IN SERBIAN LAW

An Overview of the Istanbul Convention: A Legal Breakthrough

The Council of Europe Convention on preventing and combating violence against women and domestic violence (Istanbul Convention, 2014) is the first legally binding instrument in Europe in this field, and in terms of scope, the most far-reaching international treaty to tackle this serious violation of human rights. It aims at zero tolerance for such violence and is a major step forward in making Europe and beyond a safer place.[33]

Ten years passed since signing of the Council of Europe Convention on Preventing and Combating Violence against Women and Domestic Violence in Istanbul.[34] By accepting the Istanbul Convention, governments are obliged to change their laws, introduce practical measures and allocate resources to effectively prevent and combat violence against women and domestic violence.[35] The convention is based on the principles of prevention, protection, punishment (concept of three "P") plus comprehensive and coordinated policies, which all represent four pillars of the Convention. Starting from empirical facts, the focus is primarily on violence against women, since nine of ten victims of domestic violence are women and girls.[36] This means that states are held responsible if they do not respond adequately to such violence. Under international law, a state is responsible for the commission of an intentionally wrongful act which is attributable to it, through the conduct of their agents such as the police, immigration officials and prison officers. A milestone born, *inter alia*, from the jurisprudence of the European Court for Human Rights (ECtHR) in Strasbourg, is more precisely one of the most known cases: *Opuz v Turkey* (2009)[37] as well as other cases.

> The whole course of criminal proceedings displays the vulnerability of the applicant and her mother in the process. Though, the criminal authorities sought a complaint by victim in assaults they are not serious enough to prosecute *ex officio*. The ECtHR considers that insisting in pursuance of complaint by victim where there is a life threating incidents using lethal weapons such as knife and shotguns is a failure of positive obligation to protect the right to life of the applicant's mother.[38]

Countries ratifying the convention have to establish services such as hotlines, shelters, medical services, counselling, and legal aid. Article 5 of the Convention, para. 1, addresses the state obligation to ensure that their authorities, officials, agents, institutions, and other actors acting on behalf of the state refrain from acts of violence against women, whereas paragraph 2 sets out Parties' obligation to exercise due diligence in relation to acts covered by the scope of this Convention perpetrated by non-state actors. In both cases, failure to do so will incur state responsibility. This principle is called: due diligence, stipulated in Art. 5 of the convention.

The Istanbul Convention was opened for signature in Istanbul in May 2011, and it entered into force in 2014, after ten states signatories had deposited their ratification instruments. Thirty-four member states of the Council of Europe have ratified it, twelve have signed it—along with the European Union (at the time of writing this paper). Turkey was the first CoE member state that ratified the Convention. Convention is titled as "Istanbul Convention" as a sign of gratitude for the support of Turkey in its ratification. Convention is open to accession also to other countries, non-members of the Council of Europe. However, it is historical paradox that we are witnessing the withdrawal of the Turkey from the Istanbul Convention notified in March 2021, which took effect on the July 1, 2021. This bears a huge negative impact for Turkey in terms of effective prevention of violence against women and domestic violence, as well as for victims' protection and prosecution of perpetrators.[39]

The Istanbul Convention's Approach to Sexual Offenses

The convention explicitly defines a series of acts that come under the umbrella of violence against women: psychological violence (Art. 33); stalking (Art. 34); physical violence (Art. 35); sexual violence, including rape (Article 36); forced marriage (Art. 37); female genital mutilation (Art. 38); forced abortion and forced sterilization (Art. 39); sexual harassment (Art. 40) and aiding or abetting and attempt (Art. 41) in all such acts. Although it does not define crimes in the name of so-called "honor," these are dealt with under Art.42. In the Art. 36 of the convention, rape is defined as follows:

Article 36—Sexual violence, including rape

1. Parties shall take the necessary legislative or other measures to ensure that the following intentional conducts are criminalized:
   a. engaging in nonconsensual vaginal, anal, or oral penetration of a sexual nature of the body of another person with any bodily part or object;
   b. engaging in other nonconsensual acts of a sexual nature with a person;
   c. causing another person to engage in nonconsensual acts of a sexual nature with a third person.
2. Consent must be given voluntarily as the result of the person's free will assessed in the context of the surrounding circumstances.

3. Parties shall take the necessary legislative or other measures to ensure that the provisions of paragraph 1 also apply to acts committed against former or current spouses or partners as recognised by internal law.[40]

> Paragraph 1 covers all forms of sexual acts which are performed on another person without her or his freely given consent and which are carried out intentionally. The interpretation of the word "intentionally" is left to domestic law, but the requirement for intentional conduct relates to all the elements of the offence. The penetration may be made with a bodily part or an object. The term "of a sexual nature" defines an act that has a sexual connotation. It does not apply to acts which lack such connotation.[41]

The case law of the European Court of Human Rights, such as *M.C. v. Bulgaria* judgment of December 4, 2003, guided the drafters of the Convention.[42] The court stated that it was

> persuaded that any rigid approach to the prosecution of sexual offences, such as requiring proof of physical resistance in all circumstances, risks leaving certain types of rape unpunished and thus jeopardizing the effective protection of the individual's sexual autonomy. In accordance with contemporary standards and trends in that area, the member states' positive obligations under Articles 3 and 8 of the Convention must be seen as requiring the penalization and effective prosecution of any non-consensual sexual act, including in the absence of physical resistance by the victim.[43]

The court also noted as follows:

> Regardless of the specific wording chosen by the legislature, in a number of countries the prosecution of non-consensual sexual acts in all circumstances is sought in practice by means of interpretation of the relevant statutory terms ("coercion," "violence," "duress," "threat," "ruse," "surprise" or others) and through a context-sensitive assessment of the evidence.[44]
>
> "Prosecution of this offence requires a context-sensitive assessment of the evidence in order to establish on a case-by-case basis whether the victim has freely consented to the sexual act performed. Such an assessment must recognize the wide range of behavioral responses to sexual violence and rape which victims exhibit and shall not be based on assumptions of typical behavior in such situations. It is equally important to ensure that interpretations of rape legislation and the prosecution of rape cases are not influenced by gender stereotypes and myths about male and female sexuality."[45]

The reason for this lies in the fact that predominant victims of the criminal offense of rape are women and girls. Therefore, is needed to eliminate negative gender stereotypes toward women during the prosecution of rape cases. In this context, it is necessary to take into account specificities of rape in relation to other crimes:

1. Rape is not just a physical attack, but a violation of personal, intimate and psychological boundaries.
2. It brings with it additional connotations and emotional impact, it is common related to the cultural context.
3. It is surrounded by hard-to-eradicate cultural myths and stereotypes.
4. It is predominantly a gender crime, predominantly committed by men against women and girls, but also against boys and other men.
5. The perpetrator is in most cases someone the victim knows, so the crime includes betrayal of trust.
6. Surviving rape often produces strong feelings in the victim guilt.
7. Rape carries specific health risks and consequences such as sexual intercourse communicable diseases, unwanted pregnancy, and HIV infection.
8. The crime reporting process and every trial is often perceived as a form of secondary victimization.[46]

The convention provides a definition of sexual harassment that is wider than the field of employment (Art. 40). As such, the convention recognizes that this type of conduct can also take place in formal and informal educational settings or for instance in leisure facilities.[47] At comparative law level, until the late 1970s, it was the one that the law did not regulate in an explicit manner.

The convention does not deal with trafficking or sexual exploitation, but covers many, if not all, of the forms of violence that women and girls in such situations may be faced with. This issue is dealt with in the Convention on Action against Trafficking in Human Beings the Convention on the Protection of Children against Sexual Exploitation and Sexual Abuse.

Implementation of the convention especially gains on relevance during the pandemic of COVID-19, since the increase of violence against women and domestic violence is evident at a global level, while access to specialized support services for victims is extremely hampered due to anti-pandemic measures.[48] Declaration of the Committee of the Parties to the Council of Europe Istanbul Convention (Convention on Preventing and Combating Violence against Women and Domestic Violence), on the tenth anniversary of the opening for signature of the Istanbul Convention of May 6, 2021, reiterates "the essential role of the Istanbul Convention in preventing and combating violence against women and domestic violence, as the most far-reaching and comprehensive set of standards to tackle this issue."[49] Furthermore, the declaration "acknowledges the major contribution of the Istanbul Convention monitoring mechanism in preventing and combating violence against women and domestic violence by providing tailored-made guidance as well as opportunities for states parties to learn from each other and exchange on best practices."[50]

THE RELEVANT CHALLENGES AND NECESSARY REFORM MEASURES IN SERBIA

The Relevant Challenges

In Serbia, a criminal offence is categorized as a rape only if it includes use of force or threat of use of force, which implies that the victim should physically resist. All other forms of penetration are not considered as a rape or coercion to sexual act, but as prohibited sexual acts, for whose basic form the foreseen penalty is a fine or a prison sentence of up to three years, even in cases where victims are children. The definition of rape in the Criminal Code is not completely harmonized with the provisions of Art. 36 of the Istanbul Convention, since it does not contain the lack of free consent, as one of the constituent elements of rape.

Under the current Criminal Code of Serbia, the reality that many women are unable to resist is ignored, either because they are overwhelmed by fear for their lives or are involuntarily drugged with narcotics. Furthermore, if the woman does not resist and cannot prove with evidence to her claim that she was raped, and if the bruises on her body do not speak in favor of the thesis that she defended herself and was against the sexual act, the legislator and a judge believe that she gave consent to rape, because it is in line with Criminal Code provisions. That is not the end of challenges that exist in the law of Serbia, because rape is considered only as a penetration with the male sexual organ, although in reality it often happens that women are raped with sharp objects, which cause serious injuries.

Rape, one of the most horrific crimes, still has a narrow definition in the Criminal Code of Serbia, which calls many of its types differently. While the reform of the understanding of rape has already taken place in European countries, Serbia is still hesitant to change.[51] Ireland, Great Britain, Belgium, Cyprus, Germany, Iceland, Luxembourg, and Sweden have reformed their laws so that it is clear that a lack of consent is enough to characterize sexual intercourse as rape.[52] These changes were mostly accelerated by cases from practice, such as the scandalous case in Germany where model *Gina-Lisa Lohfink* received a fine from the court for falsely reporting rape, although as evidence that she was raped, she had a recording of the intercourse, which clearly shows that she said "no." The sentence was later withdrawn.[53]

Other forms of sexual violence are covered by following provisions: sexual intercourse with an incapacitated person, sexual intercourse with abuse of official position and provisions on illicit sexual activity. The penalties for these crimes are as high as the penalties for rape, however what is actually a problem here is the insufficient level of respect for the victim.

In Serbia, the Criminal Procedure Code lacks of the notion of the victim,[54] but instead the notions of injured party and witness are applied. The rights of all injured parties are stated in Art. 50 of the Criminal Procedure Code. The court is obliged to inform the defendant and other participants in the proceedings about the rights they are entitled to. The Victims' Support Service has been established in higher courts and prosecutors' offices in four appellate areas of Serbia, but this does not meet the needs of the largest number of gender-based violence victims, whose proceedings are conducted in basic prosecutors' offices: BPO and courts. In accordance with Art. 50 CPC victims have the right to file a complaint to a higher prosecution office within eight days. This complaint mechanism was, at the beginning of the implementation of the CPC, very inefficient, while in recent years higher prosecution offices started returning cases ordering BPOs to continue investigation.

There are no fully established rape crisis or sexual violence referral centers in Serbia. European standard defined in the Istanbul Convention (Art. 25) requires specialized support by obliging states parties to provide for the setting-up of accessible rape crisis or sexual violence referral centers in sufficient numbers. Therefore, GREVIO urges the Serbian authorities to set up rape crisis and/or sexual violence referral centers, ensuring a sensitive response by trained and specialist staff, in sufficient numbers, recalling that one such center should be available for every 200,000 inhabitants and that their geographical spread should make them accessible to victims in rural areas as much as in cities. The gathering of relevant forensic documentation must not be subject to a charge.[55] GREVIO recommends free-of-charge documentation of forensic evidence adequate for the use by the criminal justice sector.

Victims of sexual violence, as well as other forms of violence, often experience secondary traumatization by repeating their testimony several times in front of different institutions. This is because in 99 percent of cases, the Higher Public Prosecutor's Offices in Serbia leave the first act of taking a statement from a rape victim to police officers, even though that statement is not evidence in the proceedings. For many victims, due to the procedure, which wastes time and timeliness of taking biological traces, it was later established in the court proceedings that some traces disappeared due to the passage of time.

In many other countries of the world, medical examination is carried out first, and only after that a statement is taken from the victim. Rape victims in Serbia, after a gynecological examination, are not examined by a forensic doctor in order to record other injuries on the body, nor are they tested for sexually transmitted diseases and do not receive a free pill for the day after. All three things, if someone instructs them that they should do it, they have to pay for it themselves. This situation signifies the obstacle for women's access to justice. In the absence of specialist support services for sexual violence, an adequate response by medical professionals is vital for a victim's physical and psychological well-being and her prospects of obtaining criminal justice. A number of training initiatives for health professionals on identifying and responding to gender-based and sexual violence have been initiated in 2019, mainly by the United Nations Population Fund (UNFPA) and other UN agencies.[56]

Another challenge is that the victims are forced to meet their rapists again, which is of course extremely traumatic. After they gave statements to the police and performed examinations ordered by the prosecution, and if the prosecution considers that there are grounds to initiate an investigation, the rape victims are called to the prosecution to testify before the suspect and his defense counsel. Art. 103 of the Criminal Procedure Code of Serbia defines the category of "particularly sensitive witness/injured party," which by definition includes all victims of sexual violence. However, in order for rape victims to be considered a particularly sensitive witness, the prosecution, and later the court, must issue a Decision granting them that status. After the rape victim is given the status of a particularly sensitive witness, the victim has the right to request to be heard without the presence of the suspect, and where it exists, in a special room, via a video link. A small number of senior public prosecutors in Serbia have a practice of immediately granting that status to rape victims.[57]

Necessary Reform Measures

Getting legal help is also complicated for the victim. Law on Free legal aid[58] was adopted in November 2018 but had started to apply in October 2019. According to the official Report of the Ministry of Justice on implementation of this law (March 2020), prevalent number of requests for free legal aid in criminal proceedings derive from situations of domestic violence and more specifically, violence against women. However, there were frequent cases of withdrawal of those requests due to victims' fear, who are mostly women and girls. Rape victims, if they do not have the funds to hire a lawyer themselves or are not granted free legal counsel in accordance with the Law on Free Legal Aid, usually testify before the prosecutor by being alone in a very small room with a deputy public prosecutor, defense counsel and suspect, and where they are asked for every little detail of the abuse they have survived while the abuser laughs in their face or insults them further. Unfortunately, often the deputy prosecutors who examine the victim, as well as the defense attorneys, can be rude and insensitive to the trauma that the victim had survived. Therefore, it should come as no surprise that a large number of victims have given up testifying.

Good news is that Serbia adopted a new Strategy for the Prevention and Combating of Gender-Based Violence and Domestic Violence in mid-2021. The Strategy envisages important improvements for suppression of secondary traumatization of rape victims. However, the Strategy does not provide for amendments to the Criminal Procedure Code in order to introduce the institution of a "trusted person," who would support the victim when giving testimony—in order not to be alone with the prosecutor, defense counsel and the abuser when giving testimony. Furthermore, in 99 percent of courts and prosecutor's offices in Serbia, there are no premises where victims can testify via video link.

One of the ambiguities of Serbian law is certainly the fact that marital rape is not prosecuted *ex officio*—a woman must file a private lawsuit against her husband. The rape in a double bed of marriage is not punishable at all in 127 countries of the world, which proves the imperfection of the justice at global level. Necessary measures to be pursued in Serbia:

- For increasing protection—it is needed to further support capacity building of law enforcement institutions, in line with international legal and policy frameworks[59];
- For comprehensive approach to dismantling violence against women and girls, it is necessary to address intersectionality and to support the most vulnerable groups;
- For prevention purposes and achieving zero tolerance, it is unavoidable to permanently undertake campaigns raising awareness and preventing gender-based and sexual violence through education;
- Continuation of prohibition of the introduction of a rape victim's reputation or sexual history at trial in order to enable the successful prosecution of rapists;
- Promoting prevention—by challenging harmful gender norms, working with all relevant stakeholders to ensure a victim-centered approach and measures that end recidivism by perpetrators, also engaging men and boys;

- Contributing to increasing prosecution of perpetrators, including those involved in human trafficking, by strengthening a victim-centered approach by the law-enforcement bodies[60];
- Increasing protection of survivors also by supporting access to life-saving social and justice services with a survivor-centered approach, particularly when survivors face intersecting discriminations;
- Support access to psycho-social support services and participation in economic and social life of victims of gender-based and sexual violence and victims of trafficking in human beings;
- Permanent strengthening of women's rights organizations and social movements as well as civil society organizations (CSOs) working on the intersectional dimension of gender-based and sexual violence and on conflict-related sexual violence.

CONCLUDING REMARKS

"Sexual violence and respectively rape are a common form of exerting power and control in abusive relationships and are likely to occur during and after break-up."[61] Therefore, criminalization and prosecution of such acts when committed against a current or former spouse or partner should be secured without exceptions. The legal future of these revolutionary laws hinges on a difficult question: how can courts protect victims without curtailing the rights of defendants? Bearing in mind this open question, the answer can be found in improving of cultural customs and social norms rather than exclusively in legal frameworks, because the essence of human rights violations lies, *inter alia*, in unequal distribution of power in society. Of course, modern legal frameworks are important for driving such social change toward the elimination of sexual violence, but only if legislation bears emancipatory implications. "But law is only a first step in transforming the social realities that it has so long ignored."[62]

Strategic legal significance of the Istanbul Convention is represented in the fact that it defines the violence against women as a severe discrimination and a violation of women's human rights. Although the convention was born under the auspices of the Council of Europe, it bears global importance through setting modern legal standards and by its openness for the accession to non-members of the Council of Europe. The special value of the convention legal standards in the area of fight against gender-based and sexual violence and domestic violence, is in its contribution to dismantling globally widespread negative gender stereotypes, which are one of the main causes of violence against women.[63] Convention represents a renewed aspiration towards establishing essential equality between women and men, aimed at removing deeply rooted unequal power relations between them. Its monitoring mechanism, GREVIO, proves to be *spiritus movens* in guiding governments to apply efficient measures and policies to respond to violence against women. Fulfilling the commitments taken under this Convention is crucial for it to reach its comprehensive potential. However, it is a long road, since more has to be achieved, such as in implementation of the Art. 36 related to definition of sexual violence based on the lack of consent.[64] Besides, in many countries referral centers for victims of sexual violence should be more present, as well as specialized services of support to those victims.

Serbian national policy measures against sexual and gender based violence are to be based on a greater research results on societal values toward intimate partner violence expressed through threats, intimidation and coercion in view of reporting, victim blaming, tolerance, and complete silence.[65] Finally, more resources are to be directed to permanent fight against gender based and sexual violence, in law enforcement, health settings, support programs for the victims and prevention measures, in line with the Convention standards.

In Serbia, difficulties in obtaining convictions for rape have stemmed from its traditional definition and its evidentiary requirements. Legal frameworks incorporate stereotypical views of gender differences and double standards of morality in many countries and in Serbia as well. There is a social atmosphere of blaming the victim—her (or his) clothes, decisions, life choices that are carefully monitored—all but the rapist himself. It is required from victims to respond with physical resistance, and thus to risk intensifying their injuries in order to prove them. These requirements have both limited the prosecution of sexual assaults and perpetuated sexual stereotypes.

According to some national surveys, physical force is absent in over half of all rapes; a third involves no weapons. Most sexual assaults occur through threats of force, and victims' most common response is verbal protest. Many are paralyzed with fear, while others decide not to risk provoking further brutality by a physical struggle. Such responses fail to satisfy resistance requirements defined by the law. In these cases, the law compounds the woman's injury by denying its existence. In addition to legal reforms, the culture of patriarchy must be abolished! Treating all people with dignity and respect is necessary. Only through promotion of gender equality and modernization of law is possible to achieve so needed trust of rape victims into judiciary. Modernization of relevant legal frameworks are aimed at validation of women's sense of violation and challenge of traditional rationalizations for sexual coercion. A central objective of contemporary feminists is to shift the blame from victims to aggressors.

This is even more important today, as the COVID-19 pandemic has taken a heavy toll with a substantial increase in femicide and gender-based and sexual violence, including domestic violence, in many parts of the world. The stigma and risk of retaliation that accompany criminal charges have kept rape the most underreported major felony. Consequently, efforts are necessary in every state to expand legal understandings of coercion. The crime of rape must be conceptualized as the product of power, which can be exercised in ways other than physical force. The injury of rape must be redefined to reflect the experience of fear, betrayal, and degradation that results from sexual coercion by social acquaintances as well as strangers.

Regional and cross-cultural comparisons suggest that sexual assault rates are lower in societies where women have gained greater influence, respect, and socioeconomic status. The challenge remaining is to redefine rape and, in long-term manner, to challenge and suppress the social understandings that legitimate it. In Serbia, as well as in other states, social response, and responsibility in issues of sexual and gender-based violence, together with effective implementation of the Istanbul Convention and national legislation, have a deterrent effect for perpetrators. The Council of Europe monitoring mechanism GREVIO has welcomed the clear policy commitment of Serbia to eliminate gender-based violence and the progress made in adapting its response to violence against women to international standards. With recent amendments to the Criminal Code (2016) and implementation of the new Law on Prevention of Domestic Violence (since 2017), it can be concluded that relevant Serbian legal system is prevalently harmonized with the prosperous provisions of the Istanbul Convention.

REFERENCES

Literature

Banks, M., "EU Leaders and MEPs Condemn Turkey's Decision to Withdraw from Istanbul Convention," https://www.theparliamentmagazine.eu/news/article/eu-leaders-and-meps-condemn-turkeys-decision-to-withdraw-from-istanbul-convention, accessed December 11, 2021.

Deborah, R., *Justice and Gender—Sex Discrimination and the Law* (Harvard University Press 1991).

Erbaş, R., "Effective Criminal Investigations in Combating Domestic Violence and the ECtHR: Prima Ratio v. Ultima Ratio?," in E. Stradella (ed), *Gender Based Approaches to the Law and Juris Dictio in Europe* (Pisa University Press 2020).

———, "Effective Criminal Investigations For Women Victims Of Domestic Violence: The Approach Of The ECtHR," *Women's Studies International Forum* 86 (2021), www.elsevier.com/locate/wsif, accessed December 16, 2021.

Gasmi, G., "Global Significance of European Standards of Women Human Rights Protection in Domain of Gender Based and Domestic Violence," *Fiat Iustitia* 1 (2019).

———, "New European Legal Standards in the Area of Women Human Rights," in Fodor E. M., Popovici P., Buzdugan C. (eds), *Efficiency of Legal Norms I* (Law Faculty, Cluj—Napoca, Romania 2012).

Gasmi, G., Prlja Dragan, and Jerotić Aleksandar, "European Leading Legal Principles of Combating Gender-based Violence—Istanbul Convention," in Lilić Stevan (ed), *Perspectives of Implementation of European Standards in Serbian Legal System* (Law Faculty, University of Belgrade 2017).

Gracia, E., "Unreported Cases of Domestic Violence against Women: Towards an Epidemiology of Social Silence, Tolerance, and Inhibition," *Journal of Epidemiol Community Health* 58 (2004).

Hutchinson, L., "Istanbul Convention Saves Lives: Zero-tolerance Treaty Turns 10," https://www.theparliamentmagazine.eu/news/article/istanbulconventionsaveslives-zerotolerance-treaty-turns-10, accessed January 11, 2022.

Ignjatović, T., *Violence against Women in Intimate Partnership Relations: Model of Coordinated Community Response* (Belgrade 2011).

Kelly, L., "Sexual Violence—Understanding the Experience of Trauma" (2009), www.womenngo.org.rs, accessed November 5, 2021.

Jones, J. S., Alexander, C., Wynn, B. N., Rossman, L., and Dunnuck, C., "Why Women Don't Report Sexual Assault to the Police: The Influence of Psychosocial Variables and Traumatic Injury," *The Journal of Emergency Medicine* 36, no. 4 (2009), https://pubmed.ncbi.nlm.nih.gov/18462905/, accessed January 11, 2022.

Litke, R., "Violence & Power," *International Social Science Journal 132 (1992).*

OSCE, "Welfare and Safety of Women" (2019) https://www.osce.org/files/f/documents/7/5/419756_1.pdf, accessed January 11, 2022.

Sally, K., "Thinking About Gender and Judging," *International Journal of the Legal Profession* 15, no. 1–2 (2008).

Zeljko, N., *Policija u zajednici* (2nd ed, University of Criminal Investigation and Police Studies 2019).

Legislation and other Resources

Amnesty International, "Right to be Free from Rape—Overview of Legislation and State of Play in Europe and International Human Rights Standards" (EUR 01/9452/20189, November 24, 2018), https://www.amnesty.org/en/latest/news/2019/03/an-expert-view-why-most-european-countries-still-need-to-change-their-rape-laws/, accessed December 25, 2021.

Council of Europe, CoE, Second General Report on GREVIO'S Activities covering period from June 2019 to December 2020, CoE, April 2021, 64–65, 2021, www.coe.int/en/web/istanbul-convention, accessed May 24, 2021.

Council of Europe, The Mid-term Horizontal Review of GREVIO of all 17 baseline evaluation reports, Secretariat of the monitoring mechanism of the Council of Europe Convention on Preventing and Combating Violence against Women and Domestic Violence Council of Europe, May 10, 2021, www.coe.int/en/web/istanbul-convention, accessed May 20, 2021.

Council of Europe Treaty Series—No. 210, "Explanatory report to the Council of Europe Convention on preventing and combating violence against women and domestic violence" (2011) 39, https://rm.coe.int/16800d383a, accessed January 11, 2022.

Council of Europe Treaty Series—No. 210, "Council of Europe Convention on Preventing and Combating Violence against Women and Domestic Violence" (2011) 12, https://rm.coe.int/168008482e, accessed January 11, 2022.

Council of Europe, Declaration of the Committee of the Parties to the Council of Europe Convention on Preventing and Combating Violence against Women and Domestic Violence (Istanbul Convention) on the 10th anniversary of the opening for signature of the Istanbul Convention, May 6, 2021, www.coe.int/en/web/istanbul-convention, accessed May 26, 2021

Criminal Code (Official Gazette RS No 85/2005, 88/2005 – corr., 107/2005 - corr., 72/2009, 111/2009, 121/2012, 104/2013, 108/2014, 94/2016 and 35/2019).

Criminal Procedure Code (Official Gazette of RS, No 72/2011, 101/2011, 121/2012, 32/2013, 45/2013, 55/2014 and 70/17).

EU Fundamental Rights Agency (FRA), Violence against Women: An EU-wide survey, http://fra.europa.eu/sites/default/files/fra-2014-vaw-survey-main-results-apr14_en.pdf, May 22, 2021.

Family Law (Official Gazette of RS, No 18/2005, 72/2011, 6/2015).

Gender Equality Law (Official Gazette of Serbia No 52/2021 of May 2021).

GREVIO's (Baseline) Evaluation Report on legislative and other measures giving effect to the provisions of the Council of Europe Convention on Preventing and Combating Violence against Women and Domestic Violence (Istanbul Convention) – Serbia, January 22, 2020.

Law on Free legal aid (Official Gazette of RS, No 87/2018).

Law on prevention domestic violence (Official Gazette of RS, No 94/2016).

"Svaka treća žena u Srbiji žrtva je nasilja!," OzonPress (Čačak, November 25, 2020), https://www.ozonpress.net/politika/svaka-treca-zena-u-srbiji-zrtva-je-nasilja/, accessed December 10, 2021.

Case

Opuz v. Turkey, App no. 3340102 (ECtHR, June 9, 2009).

NOTES

1. "Svaka treća žena u Srbiji žrtva je nasilja!," OzonPress (Čačak, November 25, 2020), https://www.ozonpress.net/politika/svaka-treca-zena-u-srbiji-zrtva-je-nasilja/, accessed December 10, 2021.

2. https://www.who.int/health-topics/violence-against-women#tab=tab_1, accessed May 20, 2021.

3. EU Fundamental Rights Agency (FRA), Violence against Women: An EU-wide Survey, http://fra.europa.eu/sites/def ault/files/fra-2014-vaw-survey-main-results-apr14_en.pdf, accessed May 22, 2021.

4. Gordana Gasmi, Dragan Prlja, and Aleksandar Jerotić, "European Leading Legal Principles of Combating Gender-based Violence—Istanbul Convention," in Stevan Lilić (ed), *Perspectives of Implementation of European Standards in Serbian Legal System* (Law Faculty, University of Belgrade 2017), 336.

5. Enrique Gracia, "Unreported Cases of Domestic Violence against Women: Towards an Epidemiology of Social Silence, Tolerance, and Inhibition," *Journal of Epidemiol Community Health* 58 (2004): 536.

6. Ibid.

7. "The reasons for not reporting were primarily environmental factors (prior relationship with assailant) rather than internal psychological barriers (shame, anxiety, fear)." Jeffrey S Jones, Carmen Alexander, Barbara N. Wynn, Linda Rossman, and Chris Dunnuck, "Why Women Don't Report Sexual Assault to the Police: The Influence of Psychosocial Variables and Traumatic Injury," The Journal of Emergency Medicine 36, no. 4 (2009): 417, https://pubmed.ncbi.nlm.nih.gov/18462905/, accessed January 11, 2022.

8. OSCE, "Welfare and Safety of Women" (2019), https://www.osce.org/files/f/documents/7/5/419756_1.pdf, accessed January 11, 2022.

9. Robert Litke, "Violence & Power," *International Social Science Journal* 132 (1992): 173.

10. https://eige.europa.eu/gender-based-violence/what-is-gender-based-violence, accessed December 10, 2021.

11. https://www.who.int/health-topics/violence-against-women#tab=tab_1, accessed May 20, 2021.

12. Gracia (n. 5), 536.

13. https://www.dw.com/sr/nasilje-nad-%C5%BEenama-%C5%BErtve-postaju-spremnije-da-progovore/a-59929702, accessed December 11, 2021.

14. Gordana Gasmi, "Global Significance of European Standards of Women Human Rights Protection in Domain of Gender Based and Domestic Violence," *Fiat Iustitia* 1 (2019): 125.

15. Council of Europe Treaty Series—No. 210, "Explanatory Report to the Council of Europe Convention on Preventing and Combating Violence against Women and Domestic Violence" (2011) 39, https://rm.coe.int/16800d383a, accessed January 11, 2022. Sanctions ought to be: "effective, proportionate and dissuasive," Art. 45 of the Istanbul Convention, Council of Europe Treaty Series—No. 210, "Council of Europe Convention on Preventing and Combating Violence against Women and Domestic Violence" (2011) 12, https://rm.coe.int/168008482e, accessed January 11, 2022.

16. Rahime Erbaş, "Effective Criminal Investigations in Combating Domestic Violence and the ECtHR: Prima Ratio v. Ultima Ratio?," in E. Stradella (ed), *Gender Based Approaches to the Law and Juris Dictio in Europe* (Pisa University Press 2020), 225.

17. Group of experts on Action against Violence against Women and Domestic Violence (GREVIO)—monitoring expert body—GREVIO's (Baseline) Evaluation

Report on legislative and other measures giving effect to the provisions of the Council of Europe Convention on Preventing and Combating Violence against Women and Domestic Violence (Istanbul Convention)—Serbia, January 22, 2020.

18. Serbian Criminal Code (Official Gazette of Serbia No 85/2005, 88/2005—corrected, 107/2005—corrected, 72/2009, 111/2009, 121 / 2012i104 / 2013, 108/2014, 94/2016, 35/2019).

19. Britain, Belgium, Canada, Cyprus, Germany, Greece, Iceland, Ireland, and Luxembourg define rape as sex without consent, while Denmark, Finland, Spain, and Portugal have promised similar reforms.

20. The Sexual Offences Act 2003 (SOA 2003) came into force on May 1, 2004, and repealed most sections of the Sexual Offences Act 1956. It represents a large-scale revision of the law of sexual offences. The act applies to England and Wales only. Scotland is covered by the Sexual Offences (Scotland) Act 2009.

21. https://www.lawteacher.net/acts/sexual-offences-act-2003.php#_ftn16, accessed May 30, 2021.

22. Deborah Rhode, *Justice and Gender—Sex Discrimination and the Law* (Harvard University Press 1991), 239, 199.

23. Council of Europe Treaty Series—No. 210, "Explanatory Report to the Council of Europe Convention on Preventing and Combating Volence against Women and Domestic Violence" (2011), 55.

24. "Again We Are Demanding that the State of Serbia Change the Definition of the Criminal Offense of Rape," December 13, 2017, www.womenngo.org.rs, accessed November 10, 2021.

25. Gender Equality Act (Official Gazette of Serbia No 52/2021 of May 2021). It is the first code after the Istanbul Convention dealing comprehensively with gender equality.

26. Official Gazette of RS, No 94/2016. The law began implementation in mid-2017, because of the six months of transition period that enabled specialized training of judges, prosecutors, and police officers.

27. Željko Nikač, *Policija u zajednici* (2nd ed., University of Criminal Investigation and Police Studies 2019).

28. Ninth Independent Monitoring Report on implementation of the Law on Prevention of Domestic Violence in Serbia for the period January—December 2020, www.womenngo.org.rs, accessed November 10, 2021.

29. Ibid.

30. Official Gazette of RS, No. 18/2005, 72/2011, 6/2015.

31. Art. 197 of the Family Law, Official Gazette of RS, No. 18/2005, 72/2011, 6/2015.

32. National Strategy for Prevention and Suppression of Violence against Women in the Family and in Partnerships, Official Gazette of RS, no. 27/2011; General Protocol on the Conduct and Cooperation of Institutions, Bodies and Organizations in Situations of Violence against Women in the Family and in partnerships (2011); special protocols of the Ministry of Health (2010), Protocol on the conduct of police officers (2013), Protocol of Centers for Social Work (2013), Special Protocol for Justice (2014).

33. Lorna Hutchinson, "Istanbul Convention Saves Lives: Zero-tolerance Treaty Turns 10" https://www.theparliamentmagazine.eu/news/article/istanbulconvention-saveslives-zerotolerance-treaty-turns-10, accessed January 11, 2022.

34. Prof. Dr. Gordana Gasmi, the coauthor of this paper, represented Serbia at the expert level when formulating the text of the Istanbul Convention during the two-year negotiations in CAHVIO from 2009 until 2011, and in 2011 she became the Council of Europe expert in the field of human rights and gender equality. The CAHVIO Committee, formed by a decision of the Committee of Ministers of the CoE in December 2008, started its work in April 2009 on the basis of the mandate entrusted by the CoE Committee of Ministers.

35. Gasmi, Prlja, and Jerotić (n. 4), 336.

36. Gordana Gasmi, "New European Legal Standards in the Area of Women Human Rights," in Fodor, E. M., Popovici, P., Buzdugan, C. (eds), *Efficiency of Legal Norms I* (Law Faculty, Cluj—Napoca, Romania 2012), 145.

37. *Opuz v. Turkey,* App no. 33401/02 (ECtHR, June 9, 2009).

38. Erbaş (n. 16), 237.

39. Martin Banks, "EU Leaders and MEPs Condemn Turkey's Decision to Withdraw from Istanbul Convention," https://www.theparliamentmagazine.eu/news/article/eu-leaders-and-meps-condemn-turkeys-decision-to-withdraw-from-istanbul-convention, accessed December 11, 2021.

40. Council of Europe Treaty Series—No. 210, "Explanatory Report to the Council of Europe Convention on Preventing and Combating Violence against Women and Domestic Violence" (2011), 10.

41. Council of Europe Treaty Series—No. 210, "Explanatory Report to the Council of Europe Convention on Preventing and Combating Violence against Women and Domestic Violence" (2011), 33.

42. Ibid.

43. Council of Europe Treaty Series—No. 210, "Council of Europe Convention on Preventing and Combating Violence against Women and Domestic Violence" (2011), 55.

44. Ibid.

45. Ibid.

46. Quoted from: Liz Kelly, "Sexual Violence—Understanding the Experience of Trauma" (2009), www.womenngo.org.rs, accessed November 5, 2021.

47. Art. 40–Sexual harassment–"Parties shall take the necessary legislative or other measures to ensure that any form of unwanted verbal, non-verbal or physical conduct of a sexual nature with the purpose or effect of violating the dignity of a person, in particular when creating an intimidating, hostile, degrading, humiliating or offensive environment, is subject to criminal or other legal sanction." The type of conduct covered by this provision includes three main forms of behavior: verbal, nonverbal, or physical conduct of a sexual nature *unwanted* by the victim, which have the purpose or effect of violating the dignity of the victim.

48. Second General Report on GREVIO's activities, June 2019 until December 2020, 29.

49. https://rm.coe.int/cop-declaration-10th-anniversary-eng/1680a25cc0, accessed December 25, 2021.

50. Ibid.

51. GREVIO's (Baseline) Evaluation Report on legislative and other measures giving effect to the provisions of the Council of Europe Convention on Preventing and Combating Violence against Women and Domestic Violence (Istanbul Convention)—Serbia (January 22, 2020), https://rm.coe.int/grevio-report-on-serbia/16809987e3, accessed December 25, 2021.

52. Amnesty International, "Right to be Free from Rape—Overview of Legislation and State of Play in Europe and International Human Rights Standards" (EUR 01/9452/20189, November 24, 2018) https://www.amnesty.org/en/latest/news/2019/03/an-expert-view-why-most-european-countries-still-need-to-change-their-rape-laws/, accessed December 25, 2021.

53. Ibid.

54. Kenney Sally, "Thinking about Gender and Judging," *International Journal of the Legal Profession* 15, no. 1–2 (2008): 87, 88.

55. Official Gazette of RS, No. 72/2011, 101/2011, 121/2012, 32/2013, 45/2013, 55/2014 and 70/2017.

56. GREVIO's (Baseline) Evaluation Report on legislative and other measures giving effect to the provisions of the Council of Europe Convention on Preventing and Combating Violence against Women and Domestic Violence (Istanbul Convention)—Serbia, January 22, 2020, 32.

57. GREVIO's (Baseline) Evaluation Report on legislative and other measures giving effect to the provisions of the Council of Europe Convention on Preventing and Combating Violence against Women and Domestic Violence (Istanbul Convention)—Serbia, January 22, 2020, 36.

58. https://nova.rs/zena/lifestyle/definicija-silovanja-u-srbiji-je-sramotna-i-mora-da-se-menja/, accessed December 14, 2020.

59. Official Gazette of RS, No. 87/2018.

60. "The ECtHR emphasizes the particular vulnerability of the victims of domestic violence and thus urges active State involvement for their protection (Bevacqua and S. v. Bulgaria, 2008, para. 65; T. M. and C. M. v. the Republic of Moldova, 2014, para. 46). The whole course of criminal proceedings in the Opuz case highlights the degree of vulnerability of victims of domestic violence in the process." Rahime Erbaş "Effective Criminal Investigations for Women Victims of Domestic Violence: The Approach of the ECtHR," *Women's Studies International Forum* 86 (2021), www.elsevier.com/locate/wsif, accessed December 16, 2021.

61. "A prompt response in domestic violence cases implies two types of judicial action within criminal justice. One is initiating prosecution which refers to a pure criminal procedural action as it is applied to every criminal case. The prosecution is to be opened without delay in domestic violence cases. Pre-trial detention is of particular importance to protect victims from further violent behavior by the perpetrator. The other one is applying interim measures, such as restraining orders, which are also called immediate measures (*Volodina v. Russia,* App no. 2019, para. 88), to protect victim," in Erbaş (n. 59) 7.

62. Council of Europe Treaty Series—No. 210, "Explanatory report to the Council of Europe Convention on Preventing and Combating Violence against Women and Domestic Violence" (2011), 33.

63. Rhode (n. 22), 237.

64. Gasmi (n. 14), 131.

65. At the moment of writing this essay, only three countries Parties of the Convention have complied with this standard in their legislation. Council of Europe (2021), The Mid-term Horizontal Review of GREVIO of all seventeen baseline evaluation reports, Secretariat of the monitoring mechanism of the Council of Europe Convention on Preventing and Combating Violence against Women and Domestic Violence Council of Europe, May 10, 2021, www.coe.int/en/web/istanbul-convention, accessed September 10, 2021.

66. Tanja Ignjatović, *Violence against Women in Intimate Partnership Relations: Model of Coordinated Community Response* (Belgrade 2011), 231.

Chapter 7

Sexual Offenses within Close Relationships

Victims' Vulnerability and Criminal Proceedings

Lara Ferla

Sexual offenses are characterized by a relevant dark figure. This is primarily due to the distinctive features of these forms of aggression, which affect a person in his or her most intimate sphere. These crimes are often unreported to the judicial authorities, or not punished, because of different reasons, some of which are directly linked to the victims' condition. The purpose of this chapter is to help highlight the causes for which the victims' behavior may constitute an obstacle to the judicial assessment of sexual offenses. In this regard, the concept of vulnerability will have a central role, as it represents both a widespread legal category and a descriptive term of a psychophysical condition that can affect the victim of a sexual crime. This chapter will consider the Italian rules that aim to protect the victims and to encourage their cooperation in the fight against these crimes. From the Italian criminal law's point of view, many rules take into account the relationship between the victim and the offender. In this research, the focus will be on the sexual offences committed by an adult against another adult, in a context that Directive 2012/29/EU defines as "close relationship,"[1] that is, one of the most meaningful relationship to the person.

SEXUAL OFFENCES, KNOWN OFFENDERS AND DARK FIGURE OF CRIME

Statistic surveys in Italy show that sexual violence is a widespread phenomenon.[2] Furthermore, due to the public measures that have imposed a social distancing for the COVID-19 pandemic outbreak during the early months of 2020, in Italy emerged data about an increase in acts of violence within close relationships.[3] The emergency telephone number available to victims of domestic violence, which was set up by the Italian Government in 2006, has registered a significant amount of requests.[4] These data confirm those already collected, which highlighted a considerable level of physical and psychological violence in personal relationships.[5] The same data show that women are predominantly involved as the victims of sexual violence.[6]

Despite the availability of statistical data expressing requests for help against these crimes, sexual violence is still a largely hidden phenomenon. The lack of knowledge on the judicial level has its roots in the criminological background of sexual offenses, relating both to the material fact and to the relationship between the parties.

Regarding the crime itself, acts that affect a person in his or her sexual dimension show many problematic aspects. Nonconsensual acts related to the sexual sphere offend both physical and psychological integrity of the person.[7] These acts represent an intrusive conduct in an intimate aspect of life and they are able to cause feelings of shame, guilt, and humiliation as well as specific psychological consequences, such as the post-traumatic stress disorder.[8] These consequences can affect the victims in such a way as to weaken their responsiveness or the ability to make appropriate choices for the protection of their rights.[9] Furthermore, sexual offenses expose the victims to social prejudice, in particular when their behavior is specifically questioned as having a relevant impact in the crime's development. Social mechanisms, such as gender prejudice or "victim-blaming" approaches, represent negative consequences affecting people who have been victims of a crime.[10] Especially in cases where sexual abuse is perpetrated under the influence of alcoholic or toxic substances, the victim's condition is carefully considered in order to mark the boundary of the offender's responsibility. The victim's condition at the time of the crime may be considered as a kind of joint responsibility in the event, as it has emerged from some Italian court cases.[11] These prejudices cause processes of secondary victimization to the person involved: The suffering related to the harmful conduct is accompanied by the suffering caused by the social and judicial consequences of the crime.[12]

In addition to the specific condition of the victim, the relationship to the offender also contributes to extend the dark figure of sexual offences.

Criminological researches carried out in Italy since the last decade of the 1900s show that the belief that the offender of a sexual crime is usually unknown to the victim is widely refuted by the judicial statistics.[13] In a considerable percentage of cases, sex offenders are persons well known to their victims.[14] These findings are also confirmed by the latest statistics, which demonstrate a significant presence of known offenders along with unidentified ones.[15] These empirical results have influenced the criminal law scholars' approach to the issue of sexual offenses and have drawn attention to the phenomenon of the "Intimate Partner Violence," of which sexual aggression is one of the most relevant forms of expression.[16] This approach of analysis has led not only to a more in-depth criminological knowledge of the phenomenon, but also to the identification of the most appropriate legal means to combat these crimes.

THE ITALIAN LAWS AND REGULATIONS ON SEXUAL OFFENCES AND THE RELEVANCE OF CLOSE RELATIONSHIPS

The provision of measures aimed at contrasting sexual violence is conditioned by the social and cultural context that defines the background of the issue. According to the Italian Penal Code, which came into effect in 1930, there was no increase in the penalty for sexual offences committed in the context of personal relationships. In the cultural environment of the early decades of the twentieth century, it was acceptable to provide better protection for the family relationships rather than for individuals.[17] An explicit example of this cultural conception was the provision that the subsequent marriage between the offender and the victim was a cause for extinguishing the offense (*causa di estinzione del reato*).[18]

Since then, legislative reforms have taken on a different perspective. An awareness permeates modern regulations: when the perpetrator of a sexual offense is not a stranger to the victim, the criminal act deserves now a more severe punishment. Although these crimes do not have the predatory connotation of searching for unknown victims,[19] offenders have taken advantage of a situation of closeness and trust in order to achieve their sexual goals. In addition to this, there are concrete probabilities that, even after the crime, the offender will continue to be a part of the victim's life as a family member, a relative, or a partner. In such cases, sexual offense should not be regarded as an isolated act, but as part of a complex and pathological relationship, where the victim is exposed to repeated victimization.[20]

According to the Italian Penal Code, sexual offenses are not differentiated with regard to the specifically performed act. In 1996 a legislative reform was implemented[21]: the reform introduced Article 609-*bis*, regulating the crime of sexual violence. This article contains the expression "sexual act" (*atto sessuale*), for which a definition has not been provided. Based on the interpretation given in criminal judgments, this concept includes both sexual intercourses and other acts with a sexual connotation—such as kisses, touches, and other less invasive acts on the victim's body—connoted by a sexual purpose.[22] The cultural and social environment plays an important role in identifying the sexual connotation of an act. Some gestures—such as kisses—assume an offensive significance depending on different social and cultural conditions.[23] An act like a kiss may occur in different contexts, serving friendly or affective purposes, devoid of any erotic connotation. In such cases, the kiss should not be considered as a sexual act in order to establish a criminal liability. For this purpose, it is necessary to consider not only the material act but also the final objective of the conduct, that is, the satisfaction of the sexual instinct of the offender.[24]

Despite the different severity of the various sexual acts, a uniformity of the legislative definition was introduced in order to protect the victim from intrusive investigations during the criminal proceedings[25]; meanwhile, this rule also represents the enhancement of the meaning of a sexual act as a conduct involving sexual freedom as a whole.[26] The difference between severely invasive sexual acts and other acts of a sexual nature carried out without the consent of the person undergoing them may be relevant in sentencing.[27]

Sexual behaviors assume the relevance of a crime if committed without the consent of the person involved.[28] In most cases, the lack of consent is implicitly deduced from the violent behavior of the offender, who acts with physical violence or threat. In such cases, the sexual act takes on the value of a harmful conduct, since the victim is intentionally placed in a condition of inability to choose or to self-defense. Article 609-*bis* of the Italian Penal Code states that sexual violence may be committed either through "coercion"—with the use of violence, threat or abuse of authority—or through "induction" of the victim to perform sexual acts. In the latter case, the offender takes advantage of the "inferiority state," that is the psychophysical condition of vulnerability that characterizes the victim at the moment of the fact.[29]

Even in the absence of particularly violent or threatening behaviors, however, many other factors may hinder the victim's awareness of the harmful nature of the conduct. A precondition for a more effective fight against sexual offenses is the strengthening of the victims' consciousness about their freedom of self-determination in sexual behaviors. On many occasions, the offensive nature of a sexual act may be underestimated by the victim, especially if it occurs within a close relationship. In this regard, it is necessary to clarify what kind of relationship criminal law refers to, starting from a comparison between the definitions used respectively by the European and Italian legislation.

The Directive 2012/29/EU represents a fundamental point of reference in this field, as the importance of a "close relationship" has been explicitly recognized in this Convention.[30] With this choice, the European Parliament and Council have eloquently underlined the tight bond existing between the people involved: "close relationship" is an evocative expression that reflects a significant interpersonal relation. The Directive 2012/29/EU also defines the person who suffers a crime in the context of close relationships as in need of special protection.[31]

In the Italian Penal Code, the personal relationship between the subjects involved in the sexual act is referred to the family, meant in a broader sense, and to other relationships established on feelings of love and affection between the partners. The Italian legislation has taken into account situations with a defined legal status—such as marriage, same-sex unions, spouses who have obtained a separation or divorce sentence—but also the condition of *de facto* family members. It is noteworthy that Italian criminal regulations have attributed importance to unmarried partner relationships (*convivenze more uxorio*), even in the absence of legal recognition, and to affective relationships (*relazioni affettive*), even in the absence of cohabitation, in order to provide a more effective protection against sexual offenses.[32] With this choice, the Italian Penal Code expresses a particular consideration for the substantive aspects of personal relationships, regardless of the legal form that they may have assumed. In traditional families, as well as in more recent family models based on cohabitation, the affective relationship establishes a context in which people have expectations of trust and care; if this confidential bond becomes an opportunity for a person to commit a sexual aggression,[33] this conduct should be evaluated for a more severe punishment. The Italian Penal Code is oriented in this direction. Article 609-*ter* provides for an increase in the penalty in the amount of one third in the event of a personal relationship between the perpetrator and the victim at the moment of the criminal act.

However, despite the availability of legal means providing protection, the cases of sexual offenses committed in a family or affective context show evaluative profiles, conditioned by the idea that the partners involved have of their relationship. Some Italian judgments have shown the existence of a sort of misunderstanding regarding the awareness that the community may have in the sexual field. Many people, especially women, are unaware of their right to self-determination in sexual matters. Italian judgments show examples of cultural conceptions that consider women to be relegated to a subordinate position with respect to men, even in the behaviors that relate to sexual life.[34] In many criminal trials, victims' testimony showed that they did not feel they had the right to refuse sexual intercourse or violent behavior from their husband or partner. On other occasions, victims have tolerated repeated sexual assaults committed by their partners in order to preserve their marriage or the family unity and to show them obedience.[35] In some judicial cases decided by the Italian Supreme Court, difficulties have arisen for the victims to deal with the sexual violence suffered, due to the roles assumed within the family or the personal relationship. In some of these cases, Italian judges expressed strong disapproval of cultural and religious conceptions that consider relationships within the family based on rigid roles and discrimination against women.[36]

In the event that a sexual violence has been committed, the criminal responsibility of the offender must be ascertained on the basis of the Italian criminal law and the principles enshrined in the Italian Constitution. In particular, Article 2 of the Constitution affirms the principle according to which a person must be protected both as an individual and in the social group where their personality develops. Article 3 of the Constitution is also relevant, because it affirms a principle of equality between people without discrimination based, *inter alia*, on sex. Articles 29 and 31 of the Constitution also enshrine principles of equal dignity and rights between persons bound by marriage. All these provisions are inspired by the fundamental principle of respect for the individuals and their rights, even within family or personal relationships. These constitutional rules are opposed to the establishment of power relations between the individuals, to unlawful practices that violate their fundamental rights.

TIME LIMITS AND PSYCHOLOGICAL VULNERABILITY AS CHALLENGES TO THE RIGHTS OF THE VICTIM

Once a sexual crime has been committed, the cooperation of the victim is essential to the outcome of criminal proceedings.[37] The victim's vulnerability may constitute an obstacle to the procedural assessment, if the criminal complaint is not filed. With respect to this requirement, Italian law is governed by rules, which aim at the dual purpose of ensuring the protection of the victim of crime as well as the efficient functioning of the criminal justice system.[38] The criminal complaint for a sexual offense usually corresponds to a choice reserved to the victim of a crime, it is an "ex parte" charge.[39] While the ordinary deadline for filing a criminal complaint is set within three months,[40] in the case of sexual offenses the deadline is set within one year.[41] This rule is the result of a recent reform adopted in Italy, implementing the 2011 Istanbul Convention. Law No. 69 of July 19, 2019, named "Red Code" (*Codice Rosso*), has applied various amendments to the Italian Penal Code and the Italian Code of Criminal Procedure, in order to ensure a more effective protection to the victims of sexual offenses.[42] The denomination of this law has raised critical remarks amongst criminal law scholars, because of its populistic approach.[43] It was highlighted that this definition could be aimed at obtaining electoral approval, exploiting a social problem to which the community devotes much attention.[44] The name "Red Code" is evocative of a necessary reaction against an urgent problem, consisting in the spread of violent behaviors committed against women. This recent legislative action is intended to demonstrate rigor and strength against these serious crimes; at the same time, it was not explained to the community that these regulations, although well structured, cannot in themselves be a solution to overcome such a complex social problem.

Setting the deadline for the submission of a criminal complaint relating to sexual offenses within one year, the "Red Code" expresses a careful consideration to the victims' psychological condition. Professionals who offer support to victims of sexual offenses report that these victims are in a vulnerable condition in the period immediately subsequent the crime, due to the need of coping with physical and psychological suffering associated with the fact.[45] This condition of vulnerability is even more serious when the sexual offense has been perpetrated by a person to whom the victim is linked to by a personal relationship.[46] There may be difficulties in talking about the criminal act or the refusal in reporting the details of its development. In cases where sexual violence constitutes a repeated behavior, the victims may also fear that they will have to justify the reasons why abusive sexual acts have been tolerated for such a long time. The victims may also be affected by a sense of guilt and be willing to protect their partners from the negative consequences of a criminal trial.

This psychological condition is not abstractly predictable in its duration. In the meantime, the loss of time is reflected, on a procedural level, in the expiry of the deadline for filing a complaint and in the dispersion of evidence (*elementi di prova*). As a result, it can become very difficult to prove the victim's version of events in court. In extreme cases, failure by victims to report the crime within a reasonable period of time could be considered as an indication of the victim's unreliability or inconsistency of the fact.

Although the circumstances highlighted constitute potential obstacles to the criminal prosecution of sexual offenses, the Italian criminal law and regulations provide some means to overcome the victims' will and their reluctance to file a criminal complaint. Some of these tools have been introduced specifically in order to combat sexual offenses; others are the result of the joint application of different procedural rules in cases where serious crimes are committed.

Firstly, the criminal complaint for a sexual offense is irrevocable, once filed. By means of this rule, the Italian lawmaker has pursued a dual purpose:

on one hand, a form of protection of the victim against any threatening or intimidating behavior perpetrated by the offender, aimed at the withdrawal of the complaint; on the other hand, the irrevocability of the complaint satisfies an interest of the offender, who has a constitutional right to defend in court, guaranteed by the Article 24 of the Italian Constitution, and an interest in proving their innocence.

The objective of a more effective fight against sexual violence in personal relationships is also pursued through the repression of some of these crimes "ex officio." In cases where a sexual offense constitutes one of the forms of aggression perpetrated by the same offender, all the crimes committed are linked according to the rules that set up the connection of criminal offenses (*connessione di reati*). If the prosecution of those crimes is mandatory, the knowledge of the *notitia criminis* by Public Prosecutor may allow the beginning of a criminal proceedings, according to Article 609-*septies*, paragraph 4, of the Italian Penal Code.

The irrevocable character of the complaint and the replacement of the "ex parte" with the "ex officio" procedure in case of connection of criminal offenses aim at achieving a more effective and efficient fight against sexual offenses. The recent amendment of the procedural regulations provided for by the "Red Code" could represents an important tool to limit the cases unreported to the judicial authorities, due to the particular vulnerability of the victim.

THE TRIAL CONTEXT: VICTIM'S STATEMENTS AND EVIDENTIARY OUTCOMES

The victim's testimony is a fundamental source of evidence. The victim can offer a significant contribution in an effort to ascertain the validity of charges brought against the defendant. On the other hand, the moment of the testimony is also an occasion where the victim is subjected to strong psychological pressure, which derives both from the public context of the examination and from the attitude of the other parties in the trial.[47]

In order to protect victims in a vulnerable condition, as the victims of sexual offenses should be considered,[48] the Italian Code of Criminal Procedure provides for a specific measure, consisting of special evidentiary hearings (*incidente probatorio*). Through this measure, any testimonial evidence can be carried out under conditions of protection and confidentiality, avoiding public hearings.[49] The testimony procedure is governed by Article 392 of the Code of Criminal Procedure. This measure represents a first endentiary phase with respect to the ordinary hearings, where the evidence is formed through the cross-examination of the parties. Through a legislative amendment,[50] this special hearing has been extended to adults who are in a particular vulnerable condition, which could also be due to being victims of sexual offenses.

In judiciary cases of sexual offenses, the victim's testimony is subjected to careful critical scrutiny, both by the defense lawyer and by the Public Prosecutor. Inconsistencies, gaps, or other uncertainties in the victim's statements can indeed influence the outcome of the criminal proceedings, especially considering that the criminal act is often committed in the absence of witnesses and further evidence.

Since a particular evidentiary value is attributed to the victim's statements regarding sexual offenses,[51] these statements must be subjected to a double critical scrutiny, relating to the victim's "subjective credibility" and the "objective reliability" of their content.[52] It is precisely in the context of this evidentiary evaluation that difficulties arise in the protection of the person who has suffered a crime against freedom or sexual integrity. Article 194 of the Code of Criminal Procedure provides, in this regard, that the witness must testify on the "fact" consisting in the subject of the trial. Intimate questions should be avoided in criminal proceedings,[53] as well as moral judgments about the victim's life conduct. However, in this context, personal questions are often asked in order to investigate the victim's personality, sexual attitude and lifestyle.

The assessment of the victim's subjective reliability must be accompanied by an assessment of the objective credibility of his or her claims. A comparison of the victim's statements with all other available evidence, such as biological evidence, medical reports, criminal police reports and statements from potential witnesses, is required.[54] With respect to the evidence available, it is noteworthy that the evidentiary standards have been adapted by criminal Court to the specificities of sexual offenses. Indeed, in the criminal judgments passed down in this field, it can be observed that criteria have been established in an effort to assess the victims' claims, which take into account the need for their protection. In this regard, the Italian Supreme Court has repeatedly highlighted that the proof of a sexual violence can be deduced from the victim's statements: the nature of the crime and the difficulty in finding external evidence could represent a risk as it would not offer the person an adequate protection within criminal proceedings.

VICTIMS OF SEXUAL OFFENSES RECANTING THEIR STATEMENTS

The victim's behavior within the trial can greatly influence its course or outcome even when previous charges are withdrawn. Italian judgments show that, on many occasions, victims of a sexual crime committed by a known person have subsequently changed their reconstruction of the fact.[55] Through this behavior victims attempt to minimize the gravity of the prior statements and to make less burdensome the defendant's position in the trial.[56]

The Italian laws and regulations provide for special rules regarding the witness statements. Thanks to the understanding that the emotional and psychological condition of the victim is difficult, when it comes to stating facts that can have negative consequences for a known person, it has been suggested the introduction of a regulatory framework that allows the person to avoid testifying in the trial. The psychological conflict suffered by victims, in fact, could lead them to make false statements. The Article 199 of the Code of Criminal Procedure in particular provides for a limitation to this possibility, which concerns cases where the person is a victim of the crime: in such circumstances, the person is required to testify during the trial, having made allegations that led to a criminal proceedings against a person.[57]

Considering the judicial cases related to sexual offense between persons linked by an affective relationship, it can be observed that, on many occasions, the victim has indeed recanted prior statements.[58] This happened because the victims believe that they have the possibility to report a crime and to "withdraw" the previous formal complaint, based on a different personal assessment of the seriousness of the offender's conduct.[59] In Italian criminal justice system, however, the criminal complaint of a victim of a sexual violence cannot be revoked, as it is expressly defined by the law as "irrevocable."[60]

The assessment of the case can only be carried out by the criminal judge. Especially on the field of sexual offenses, it is necessary to verify whether the victims have suffered intimidation or threats, which have conditioned their attitude. In many cases, however, even without direct intimidations, the victims themselves decide to recant their statements, once they face with the legal and the material consequences of the complaint, such as the fear of retaliation, the lack of economic resources, the difficulties in providing for the family without any help,[61] the need to explain to other family members the reasons for the removal of the parent or relative from the house.[62] These difficulties increase when sexual offenses involve people in condition of social and emotional isolation, who may encounter greater obstacles in managing family life without their partner.

From a procedural point of view, however, the recantation of the prior statements should be considered as a part of a larger evidentiary context, in which such conduct must be evaluated. The basic assumption is that the statements that the person made in the immediacy of the fact or at the time of filing the criminal complaint seem to have some security and reliability, insofar as they constitute a direct consequence of the crime and express the actual psychological condition of the victim. The criminal judge, however, has the task of carrying out a careful assessment of the reliability of the person who made those statements and of the truthful content of the same. In some judgments, indeed, it was argued that the unreliable or mendacious recantation "appears, as such, a further element of confirmation of the original accusation" against the defendant.[63]

With their false or unreliable statements, victims may intentionally seek to cause the dispersion of important evidence in support of the charges against the defendant. The withdrawal of the previous allegations made under these conditions or the non-cooperative attitude of the victim in the trial should be considered as indicators of a specific vulnerable condition. With regard to these victims, the necessary measures should be taken in order to provide specialist psychological and economic assistance.[64]

AN INTEGRATED APPROACH TO SEXUAL VIOLENCE WITHIN CLOSE RELATIONSHIPS

Scientific researches show that the sexual component of the crime is accompanied—and perhaps even overtaken—by reasons that are not strictly related to the sexual sphere itself but rather expressive of a power relationship.[65] Whether it is an occasional criminal act or a repeated approach, sexual violence has motivations which relate to how the person is valued and considered.[66]

Like other crimes affecting the rights of the person, it should be noted that criminal law can merely offer a delayed sanctioning response, after the crime has produced its irreversible effects.[67] Through this criminal act, the most intimate and private sphere of the victim is affected and the application of a penalty against the aggressor cannot alleviate the victim's suffering. In some judgments, this aspect is clearly highlighted by the judges, who have stated the need of psychotherapeutic support for the injured person, ordering the offender to pay for these costs by way of compensation for damage.[68]

The psychological and power-related components inherent to violent sexual conduct require not only to be sanctioned with a punishment but also to be understood in their dynamics. This implies the need for a renewed study and for a treatment approach to the perpetrators of violent sexual behaviors. In Italy, criminal law and psychology scholars are carrying out specific studies on this issue. They pointed out that drastic solutions to offenders such as those provoked by anger or impulse reactions—*throw away the key?*[69]—do not lead to useful results. The prospects of imprisonment and serious criminal penalties, in fact, are not in themselves appropriate responses to the complexity of the issue.[70] These researches show that it is necessary to investigate the offender's cultural background and look for clues and signs in order to understand the offensive nature of the act and to overcome the mechanisms that led to its implementation.[71] Considering that the penalty does not protect potential crime victims but only punishes individual offenders, criminal law scholars highlight the importance of sharing the content of the criminal law on a cultural level.[72]

In this regard, in Italy there are important signs of preventive action against the phenomenon of sexual violence in close relationships.

Italy has introduced administrative measures that can be readily applied to persons who have been engaged in violent behavior in the family or in personal relationships. These measures are based on the assumption that sexual violence is often preceded by "warning signs," consisting of progressively violent and aggressive behaviors, even without sexual connotation. The administrative warning (*ammonimento*) by the *Questore*, as a public safety authority, is giving encouraging results in this regard.[73] This peculiar administrative measure was expressively addressed to subjects responsible of stalking, in 2009, and of domestic violence, in 2013.[74] At the request of the victim, the *Questore* may summon the person suspected of such conduct and order that they cease it immediately. The administrative measure issued by the *Questore* can have important preventive and dissuasive effects. A summons from a public official, who has an institutional public safety role, may actually prompt the offenders to change their behavior.

The significance of this administrative measure, however, is not limited to a deterrent function. In fact, the *Questore*'s involvement is also relevant because of the link that this public official can establish with the judicial authorities in charge of investigating stalking and domestic violence crimes. If, in the exercise of his duties, the *Questore* is informed of an event in which violent or threatening behavior has been committed against a person, he can lodge a complaint with the judicial authority for any crime that can be prosecuted "ex officio." Through the intervention of this authority, which is not part of the judiciary, early actions can be taken against aggressive and violent behavior before it becomes more serious. Therefore, regardless of whether an aggressive behavior may be classified as a criminal act, the most important result that can be achieved is a timely awareness of situations that may escalate and become serious violations of a person's rights.

CONCLUDING REMARKS

The analysis carried out in this chapter sought to highlight the main obstacles that the victims of sexual offenses encounter in the path towards its punishment. Among them, many are closely linked to the condition of vulnerability in which the victims are found as a result of those crimes, especially on a psychological level. From the moment of the very first description of the fact to its final assessment, material circumstances and procedural conditions occur; they can delay or obstruct its actual punishment and they also contribute in creating the discrepancy, that is the lack of correspondence between the number of offenses actually committed, those reported, and those effectively punished.

The dispersion of a relevant amount of sexual violence cases, which can be observed in other legal systems as well,[75] also depends on the behavior of the victim within the criminal proceedings. The Italian criminal law and regulations show that these obstacles were foreseen, as it can be deduced from the provision, in the Penal Code, of legal means inspired by the aim of providing the victims of sexual offenses with a longer time in order to choose the behavior that could be more consistent along with their safeguard and protection. At the same time, the Code of Criminal Procedure provides for tools aimed at a timely collection of evidence.

The contribution of the "Red Code" in this field aims at strengthening a link between the victim, the criminal police and the Public Prosecutor. In addition to the provision of a longer deadline for the victim when submitting the criminal complaint, shorter deadlines have been set for the judicial authorities when scheduling the criminal proceedings.[76] The charge of *notitia criminis*, the collection of evidence and its acknowledgement on unrepeatable procedural documents are key points in a more efficient approach to sexual offenses. The most promising aspect of these recent regulations is the mandatory information that must be given to the victims about the possibility of an immediate contact with anti-violence centers, where they can receive professional assistance, especially from the psychological and legal point of view.[77] In this respect, strengthening the rights of the victim have a positive impact on individuals and on the community too, thanks to an increased level of trust in criminal justice system.[78] However, many critical points are still open in the network of the law enforcement tools.

The full protection of those victims could only be guaranteed by an action of contrast that addressed the causes of those forms of violence against persons linked to the aggressor by a personal and/or familiar meaningful relationship. Integrated action toward this phenomenon should not only be based on the condition of specific vulnerability of the victims, but also on the need to explicitly face the offender, his attitude and his pattern of behavior in the sexual field.

Actions meant for fighting these crimes must be characterized by the provision of opportunities for psychological support and must encourage a reflection on the harmful value of these behaviors. The planning of intervention in relation to these crimes should surely be characterized by a more focused approach on preventive actions, in order to ensure the deterrence that should trigger fear about severe criminal penalties; but, most of all, it should focus on sharing the fundamental values that the criminal law intends to protect. As the Istanbul Convention officially stated, there is a need for a widespread social awareness that the sexual violence issue deserves an action on cultural orientation, aimed at promoting the enhancement of the individuals and their rights, even in the most significant relationships.

REFERENCES

Literature

Aliquò, G., *La violenza domestica. L'ammonimento del Questore* (Pacini Giuridica, 2020).

Amalfitano, C., "La vittima vulnerabile nel diritto internazionale e dell'Unione europea," *Rivista italiana di medicina legale* 2 (2018).

Bandini, T., "Vittimologia," *Enciclopedia del diritto* (1993), 1008.

Bargis, M., and Belluta, H. (eds.), *Vittime di reato e sistema penale* (Giappichelli 2017).

Bartoli, R., "La famiglia nel diritto penale: evoluzione sociale, riforme legislative, costituzionalismo," in Fidelbo, G. (eds.), *Diritto penale della famiglia* (Giappichelli 2021).

Bennice, J. A., et al., "The Relative Effects of Intimate Partner Physical and Sexual Violence on Post-Traumatic Stress Disorder Symptomatology," *Violence and Victims* 1 (2003).

Bertolino, M., "La violenza di genere e su minori tra vittimologia e vittimismo: notazioni brevi," *Rivista italiana di diritto e procedura penale* 1 (2021).

———. Libertà sessuale e tutela penale (Giuffré 1992).

Bonini, V., "The Istanbul Convention's value and its implementation in Italy," in Bonini, V., and Erbaş, R. (eds.), *The 10th anniversary of the Istanbul Convention* (Pisa University Press 2021).

Canzio, G., "La tutela della vittima vulnerabile nel sistema delle garanzie processuali: le misure cautelari e la testimonianza 'vulnerabile,'" *Diritto penale e processo* 8 (2018).

Coker, A. L., et al., "Physical and Mental Health Effects of Intimate Partner Violence for Men and Women," *American Journal of Preventive Medicine* 4 (2002).

Cornacchia, L., "Vittime e giustizia criminale," *Rivista italiana di diritto e procedura penale* 4 (2013).

Curtois, C. A., ""Complex Trauma, Complex Reactions: Assessment and Treatment," *Psychotherapy: Theory, Research, Practice, Training* 4 (2004).

de Maglie, C., *I reati culturalmente motivati. Ideologie e modelli penali* (ETS 2010).

Erbaş, R., "Evidentiary Challenges to an Effective Criminal Investigation for Domestic Violence: An Introduction," in Bonini, V., and Erbaş, R. (eds.), *The 10th Anniversary of the Istanbul Convention* (Pisa University Press 2021), 101.

Felson, R. B., "Is Violence against Women about Women or about Violence?," *Contexts* 5 (2006).

Fiandaca, G., "La rilevanza penale del 'bacio' tra anatomia e cultura," *Foro italiano* (1998).

Fiandaca, G., and Musco, E., *Diritto penale. Parte speciale* Vol II.1 (Zanichelli 2020).

Fletcher G. P., *With Justice For Some. The Rights of Victims in Criminal Trials* (Mazo Publishers 2020).

Forti, G., *L'immane concretezza. Metamorfosi del crimine e controllo penale* (Raffaello Cortina Editore 2000).

Gino, S., et al., "Dall'*intimate partner violence* al femminicidio," *Rassegna italiana di criminologia* 2 (2019).

Giulini, P., and Xella, C. M. (eds.), "*Buttare la chiave? La sfida del trattamento per gli autori di reati sessuali*"" (Raffaello Cortina 2011).

Giunta, F., *Interessi privati e deflazione penale nell'uso della querela* (Giuffré 1993).

Giussy, B., et al., "Aspetti clinici nella prevenzione della violenza sulle donne: deontologia ed etica delle professioni sanitarie," in Calloni M (ed.), *Il ruolo dell'università nella lotta contro la violenza di genere* (Pearson 2020).

Hessick, C. B., "Violence Between Lovers, Strangers, and Friends," *Washington University Law Review* 85 (2007).

Jung, S., et al., "A Comparative Profile of Intimate Partner Sexual Violence," *Journal of Sexual Aggression* 1 (2021).

Mantovani, F., *Diritto penale. Parte speciale. I. Delitti contro la persona* (Cedam 2019).

Marandola, A., and Pavich, G., *Codice rosso l. n. 69/2019* (Giuffrè Francis Lefebvre 2019).

Mazza, O., "Misure di protezione della vittima fonte di prova," *Giurisprudenza italiana* (2012).

Moretti, B., *La violenza sessuale tra conoscenti. Analisi giuridica e criminologica di un fenomeno poco indagato* (Giuffré 2005).

Morillo, F. F., and Todino, I. B., "The Victims' Rights Directive: Origins and expectations," in Bargis M and Belluta H (eds.) *Vittime di reato e sistema penale. La ricerca di nuovi equilibri* (Giappichelli 2017).

Nussbaum, M. C., *Citadels of Pride. Sexual Assault, Accountability, and Reconciliation* (WW Norton & Company 2021).

Parlato, L., "Domestic violence in light of the Istanbul Convention: some procedural issue," in Bonini, V., and Erbaş, R. (eds.), *The 10th anniversary of the Istanbul Convention* (Pisa University Press 2021).

Petrini, D., "Il trattamento del delinquente sessuale, tra esigenze securitarie e controllo della recidiva," *Rivista italiana di medicina legale* 4 (2013).

Presutti, A., "Le audizioni protette," in Bargis, M., and Belluta, H. (eds), *Vittime di reato e sistema penale* (Giappichelli 2017).

Quattrocolo, S., "Vittima e processo penale: commistione di ruoli e di funzioni," *Rivista italiana di medicina legale* 2 (2018).

Rìos Vega, L. E., Ruggiu, I., and Spigno, I. (eds.), *Justice and Culture. Theory and Practice Concerning the Use of Culture in Courtrooms* (Editoriale Scientifica 2020).

Romano, M., "Legislazione penale e consenso sociale," *Jus* (1985).

Ruggiu, I., *Culture and the Judiciary. The Anthropologist Judge* (Routledge 2019).

Stella, F., *La giustizia e le ingiustizie* (Il Mulino 2006).

Taverriti, S. B., "La tutela della vittima tra procedibilità a querela e procedibilità d'ufficio," in Bargis, M., and Belluta, H. (eds.), *Vittime di reato e sistema penale* (Giappichelli 2017).

Taylor, S. C., and Gassner, L., "Stemming the Flow: Challenges for Policing Adult Sexual Assault with Regard to Attrition Rates and Under-reporting of Sexual Offences," *Police Practice and Research* 3 (2010).

Triggiani, N., "L'ultimo tassello del percorso legislativo di contrasto alla violenza domestica e di genere: la legge 'Codice Rosso,' tra effettive innovazioni e novità solo apparenti," *Processo penale e giustizia* 2 (2020).

Vitarelli, T., "Violenza contro le donne e bulimia repressiva," *Diritto penale contemporaneo—Rivista trimestrale* 3 (2020).

Woods, L., and Porter, L., "Examining the Relationship Between Sexual Offenders and Their Victims: Interpersonal Differences between Stranger and Non-stranger Sexual Offences," *Journal of Sexual Aggression* 1 (2008).

Zara, G., *Il diniego nei sex offender. Dalla valutazione al trattamento* (Raffaello Cortina 2018).

——, "La psicologia della 'vittima ideale' e della 'vittima reale.' Essere vittime e diventare vittime di reato," *Rivista italiana di medicina legale* 2 (2018).

Cases:

Corte di cassazione, judgment of January 25, 2007, no. 1841
Corte di cassazione, judgment of September 28, 2011, no. 42393
Corte di cassazione, judgment of March 23, 2013, no. 14085
Corte di cassazione, judgment of March 18, 2016, no. 11591
Corte di cassazione, judgment of March 23, 2016, no. 31340
Corte di cassazione, judgment of May 10, 2017, no. 33049
Corte di cassazione, judgment of May 20, 2017, no. 45947
Corte di cassazione, judgment of July 11, 2018, no. 43565
Corte di cassazione, judgment of October 16, 2018, no. 6355
Corte di cassazione, judgment of July 10, 2020, no. 27590
Corte di cassazione, judgment of September 8, 2020, no. 28838
Corte di cassazione, judgment of December 4, 2020, no. 3250
Corte di cassazione, judgment of December 11, 2020, no. 5623
Corte di cassazione, judgment of December 17, 2020, no. 7136
Corte di cassazione, judgment of February 10, 2021, no. 21047
Corte di cassazione, judgment of February 18, 2021, no. 24124
Corte di cassazione, judgment of March 24, 2021, no. 12158
Corte di cassazione, judgment of April 30, 2021, no. 19314

Corte di cassazione, judgment of May 28, 2021, no. 34390
Corte di cassazione, judgment of September 22, 2021, no. 37460
Corte di appello di Firenze, judgment of March 4, 2015, no. 858
Tribunale di Milano, judgment of December 16, 2009, no. 15359
J. L v. Italy, App no 5671/16 (ECHR, August 27, 2021)

NOTES

1. See paragraph 18 of the Directive 2012/29/EU: "Where violence is committed in a close relationship, it is committed by a person who is a current or former spouse, or partner or other family member of the victim, whether or not the offender shares or has shared the same household with the victim."

2. See ISTAT (*Istituto Nazionale di Statistica*), https://www.istat.it/it/violenza-sulle-donne/il-fenomeno/violenza-dentro-e-fuori-la-famiglia/numero-delle-vittime-e-forme-di-violenza, accessed December 5, 2021. In the context of a statistical survey on violent crimes, significant data emerged on the perpetrators of sexual offences. Out of a total of 4,923 male offenders reported to the police in 2019, 259 of them are under the age of seventeen. The largest number of reports over the same period concerned male offenders aged between thirty-five and forty-four (1,162 reports). During the same period, a total of ninety-nine women were reported for sexual offenses.

3. Italy was one of the first and most affected countries by the COVID-19 pandemic outbreak during the early months of 2020. ISTAT conducted a population survey on the effects of the pandemic on family life and personal relationships. Although more than nine out of ten people had the opportunity to spend this phase in a positive family context, a part of the interviewees (9.1 percent) were "relegated to a context aggravated by isolation and the impossibility to compensate with social interaction." Under these conditions, many forms of physical and psychological violence against women have occurred. See ISTAT, *Annual Report 2020—The state of the Nation,* https://www.istat.it/en/archivio/24710, accessed December 5, 2021.

4. According to a report published in June 2021, during the year 2020, phone calls for help requests increased by 79.5 percent, compared to 2019. In 47.9 percent of cases, these are reports from women who have suffered forms of physical violence. The violence reported to the emergency telephone number was mainly committed by the partner (57.1 percent in 2020) or ex-partner (15.3 percent in 2020). See https://www.istat.it/it/archivio/258897, accessed June 24, 2021.

5. See the report "Violence against women" by ISTAT, https://www.istat.it/it/archivio/169135, accessed September 23, 2021.

6. On the basis of statistical data, updated to 2019, there is a significant difference in relation to the gender of the victims of sexual crimes who reported the crime to the police. Out of a total of 4,427 reports for sexual offences, 4,016 complainants are female and 411 are male. See "Alleged offenders and victims of crimes reported by the police to the judicial authorities" http://dati.istat.it/Index.aspx?QueryId=25128&lang=en, accessed December 5, 2021.

7. See Giovanni Fiandaca and Enzo Musco, *Diritto penale. Parte speciale* (Zanichelli 2020), 307.

8. See Jennifer A. Bennice et al., "The Relative Effects of Intimate Partner Physical and Sexual Violence on Post-Traumatic Stress Disorder Symptomatology," *Violence and Victims* 1 (2003): 87, 91; Christine A. Courtois, "Complex Trauma, Complex Reactions: Assessment and Treatment," *Psychotherapy: Theory, Research, Practice, Training* 4 (2004): 412, 414.

9. See Georgia Zara, "La psicologia della 'vittima ideale' e della 'vittima reale.' Essere vittime e diventare vittime di reato," *Rivista italiana di medicina legale* 2 (2018): 615, 630.

10. See Gabrio Forti, *L'immane concretezza* (Raffaello Cortina 2000), 261; George P. Fletcher, *With Justice for Some* (Mazo Publishers 2020), 84.

11. In some judicial cases, attention has been focused on the rash conduct of the victim, who had placed herself in a vulnerable condition for taking alcoholic substances: see *Corte di appello di Firenze*, judgment of 4 March 2015, no. 858. About this case, see also *J. L v. Italy*, App no. 5671/16 (ECHR, 27 May 2021). See also *Corte di cassazione*, judgment of July 11, 2018, no. 43565.

12. See Tullio Bandini, "Vittimologia," *Enciclopedia del diritto* (1993), 1008, 1011.

13. See Barbara Moretti, *La violenza sessuale tra conoscenti. Analisi giuridica e criminologica di un fenomeno poco indagato* (Giuffré 2005), 62.

14. See Laura Woods and Louise Porter, "Examining the relationship between sexual offenders and their victims: Interpersonal differences between stranger and non-stranger sexual offences," *Journal of Sexual Aggression* 1 (2008): 61, 69. See also Carissa Byrne Hessick, "Violence Between Lovers, Strangers, and Friends," *Washington University Law Review* 2 (2007): 343, 385.

15. See ISTAT, *Delitti, imputati e vittime di reati. La criminalità in Italia attraverso una lettura integrata delle fonti sulla giustizia* (ISTAT 2020), 58.

16. See Sarah Gino and others, "Dall'*intimate partner violence* al femminicidio," *Rassegna italiana di criminologia* 2 (2019): 131, 132.

17. See Roberto Bartoli, "La famiglia nel diritto penale: evoluzione sociale, riforme legislative, costituzionalismo," in Giorgio Fidelbo (ed.), *Diritto penale della famiglia* (Giappichelli 2021), 3.

18. See Article 544 of the Penal Code, according to its version of 1930. This rule was repealed by the Law no. 442 of August 5, 1981.

19. See Gino and others (n 16), 144. See also Sandy Jung and others, "A Comparative Profile of Intimate Partner Sexual Violence," *Journal of Sexual Aggression* 1 (2021): 95, 103.

20. See Marta Bertolino, "La violenza di genere e su minori tra vittimologia e vittimismo: notazioni brevi," *Rivista italiana di diritto e procedura penale* 1 (2021): 65, 78.

21. See Law no. 66 of February 15, 1996, concerning norms against sexual violence.

22. See *Corte di cassazione*, judgment of September 22, 2021, no. 37460.

23. See Giovanni Fiandaca, "La rilevanza penale del 'bacio' tra anatomia e cultura," *Foro italiano* (1998): 505, 507.

24. See Ferrando Mantovani, *Diritto penale. Delitti contro la persona* (Cedam 2019), 429.

25. See Marco Venturoli, *La vittima nel sistema penale. Dall'oblio al protagonismo?* (Jovene 2015), 144.

26. See *Corte di cassazione*, judgment of March 23, 2013, no. 14085.

27. According to Article 133 of the Italian Penal Code, the judicial discretion in determining the penalty to be imposed on the offender must be exercised on the basis of some parameters: among them, the seriousness of the offence and the damage caused to the victim. A mitigating circumstance is provided for by Article 609-*bis*, paragraph 3, which establishes that "In case of minor gravity, the penalty is reduced to an extent not exceeding two-thirds."

28. See Marta Bertolino, *Libertà sessuale e tutela penale* (Giuffrè 1992), 27.

29. See *Corte di cassazione*, judgment of May 20, 2017, no. 45947, about a sexual violence committed toward a person with a mental illness.

30. See n.1.

31. See n.1.

32. See Article 609-*ter*, no. 5-*quater*, of the Italian Penal Code. One of the aggravating circumstances provided for this rule states that the penalty referred to in Article 609-*bis* shall be increased by one third if the fact is committed "against a person for whom the offender is the spouse, separated or divorced, or that it is or has been linked to the same person by an affective relationship, even without cohabitation."

33. See Fletcher (n. 10) 11, who notes that "For many women, the home is more dangerous than walking the street at midnight."

34. For a comprehensive analysis of the relevance of cultural differences within Italian judgments, see Ilenia Ruggiu, *Culture and the Judiciary. The anthropologist judge* (Routledge 2019); Louis Efrén Rìos Vega, Ilenia Ruggiu and Irene Spigno (eds.), *Justice and Culture. Theory and practice concerning the use of culture in courtrooms* (Editoriale Scientifica 2020); Cristina de Maglie, *I reati culturalmente motivati. Ideologie e modelli penali* (ETS 2010).

35. See, among others, *Corte di cassazione*, judgment of December 11, 2020, no. 5623. In the context of that criminal proceedings, it emerged that the victim did not refuse sexual intercourses with her husband "although they were preceded by physical aggressions and moral humiliations, justifying, *a posteriori*, her failure with the argument of a sort of voluntary surrender to psychological pressure and resignation to marital duties."

36. See *Corte di cassazione*, judgment of September 8, 2020, no. 28838. See also *Corte di cassazione*, judgment of March 18, 2016, no. 11591; *Corte di cassazione*, judgment of January 25, 2007, no. 1841.

37. See Rahime Erbaş, "Evidentiary challenge to an effective criminal investigation for domestic violence: an introduction," in Valentina Bonini and Rahime Erbaş (eds.), *The 10th anniversary of the Istanbul Convention* (Pisa University Press 2021), 110; Serena Quattrocolo, "Vittima e processo penale: commistione di ruoli e di funzioni," *Rivista italiana di medicina legale* 2 (2018): 577, 587.

38. See Fausto Giunta, *Interessi privati e deflazione penale nell'uso della querela* (Giuffrè 1993), 25.

39. See Article 609-*septies* of the Italian Penal Code.

40. See Article 124 of the Italian Penal Code. On this topic, see Sara Bianca Taverriti, "La tutela della vittima tra procedibilità a querela e procedibilità d'ufficio," in Marta Bargis and Hervé Belluta (eds.), *Vittime di reato e sistema penale* (Giappichelli 2017), 503.

41. See Article 609-*septies* of the Italian Penal Code.

42. See Nicola Triggiani, "L'ultimo tassello del percorso legislativo di contrasto alla violenza domestica e di genere: la legge 'Codice Rosso,' tra effettive innovazioni e novità solo apparenti," *Processo penale e giustizia* 2 (2020): 451, 456. See also Antonella Marandola and Giuseppe Pavich, *Codice rosso l. n. 69/2019* (Giuffrè Francis Lefebvre 2019), 1, 28.

43. Tiziana Vitarelli, "Violenza contro le donne e bulimia repressiva," *Diritto penale contemporaneo—Rivista trimestrale* 3 (2020): 461, 463.

44. See Alessandro De Santis, "Codice Rosso. Le modifiche al codice penale," *Studium iuris* 1 (2020): 1, 9.

45. On this topic, see Woods and Porter (n. 14), 71. See also n.18.

46. Ann L. Coker et al., "Physical and Mental Health Effects of Intimate Partner Violence for Men and Women," *American Journal of Preventive Medicine* 4 (2020): 260, 266; Ann Coker and others, "Physical Health Consequences of Physical and Psychological Intimate Partner Violence," *Archives of Family Medicine* 9 (2000): 451, 456.

47. See *Corte di cassazione*, judgment of February 18, 2021, no. 24124.

48. See Luigi Cornacchia, "Vittime e giustizia criminale," *Rivista italiana di diritto e procedura penale* 4 (2013): 1760, 1778.

49. See the Article 392 of the Italian Code of Criminal Procedure. On the topic of testimony, see Giovanni Canzio, "La tutela della vittima vulnerabile nel sistema delle garanzie processuali: le misure cautelari e la testimonianza 'vulnerabile,'" *Diritto penale e processo* 8 (2010): 985, 989; Oliviero Mazza, "Misure di protezione della vittima fonte di prova," *Giurisprudenza italiana* (2012): 478, 479; Antonella Presutti, "Le audizioni protette," in Marta Bargis and Hervé Belluta (eds), *Vittime di reato e sistema penale* (Giappichelli 2017), 375.

50. See Law no. 212 of December 15, 2015.

51. See *Corte di cassazione*, judgment of February 18, 2021, no. 24124; *Corte di cassazione* judgment of July 10, 2020, no. 27590.

52. This principle has been repeatedly affirmed in the criminal judgment about sexual violence. See, among others, *Corte di cassazione*, judgment of September 8, 2020, no. 28838. In this judgment, Italian Court of Cassation stated that "the statements of the victim can legitimately be placed as a basis for the criminal responsibility of the accused, after verification, accompanied by suitable reasons, of the subjective credibility of the declarant and the intrinsic reliability of the story." See also *Corte di cassazione*, judgment of December 17, 2020, no. 7136; *Corte di cassazione*, judgment of December 4, 2020, no. 3250.

53. See Article 472, paragraph 3-*bis*, of the Code of Criminal Procedure.

54. See, among others, *Corte di cassazione*, judgment of October 16, 2018, no. 6355. In this case, Italian Court of Cassation came to the conclusion of the "full

reliability" of the victim's statements after a comparison with the results of the medical report, which had ascertained the presence of injuries resulting from a physical aggression. From a medical point of view, however, it has been shown that sexual violence could leave no signs on the victim's body, "because the victim is often immobilized for fear of lethal consequences," see Barbara Giussy et al., "Aspetti clinici nella prevenzione della violenza sulle donne: deontologia ed etica delle professioni sanitarie," in Marina Calloni (eds.), *Il ruolo dell'università nella lotta contro la violenza di genere* (Pearson 2020), 93.

55. See, among others, *Corte di cassazione*, judgment of December 17, 2020, no. 7136; *Corte di cassazione*, judgment of 10 May 2017, no. 33049; *Corte di cassazione*, judgment of March 23, 2016, no. 31340; *Corte di cassazione*, judgment of September 28, 2011, no. 42393.

56. See Lucia Parlato, "Domestic Violence in Light of the Istanbul Convention: Some Procedural Issue," in Valentina Bonini and Rahime Erbaş (eds.), *The 10th anniversary of the Istanbul Convention* (Pisa University Press 2021), 135.

57. See the Article 199 of the Code of Criminal Procedure.

58. See, among others, *Corte di cassazione*, judgment of April 30, 2021, no. 19314; *Corte di cassazione*, judgment of 24 March 2021, no. 12158; *Corte di cassazione*, judgment of December 17, 2020, no. 7136; *Corte di cassazione*, judgment of December 11, 2020, no. 5623; *Corte di cassazione*, judgment of February 10, 2021, no. 21047.

59. *Corte di cassazione*, judgment of February 18, 2021, no. 24124.

60. See the Article 609-*septies*, paragraph 3, of the Italian Penal Code.

61. See *Corte di cassazione*, judgment of February 10, 2021, no. 21047.

62. See *Corte di cassazione*, judgment of May 10, 2017, no. 33049.

63. See *Corte di cassazione*, judgment of December 17, 2020, no. 7136. In this judgment, the court has reiterated the need for criminal judges to verify the "motivation" for which the victim's statements made at the preliminary phase of the trial were withdrawn at the time of testimony. See also *Corte di cassazione*, judgment of February 10, 2021, no. 21047; *Corte di cassazione*, judgment of May 28, 2021, no. 34390.

64. See Chiara Amalfitano, "La vittima vulnerabile nel diritto internazionale e dell'Unione europea," *Rivista italiana di medicina legale* 2 (2018): 523, 545.

65. See Richard B. Felson, "Is Violence against Women about Women or about Violence?," *Contexts* 5 (2006): 21, 25.

66. See Martha Nussbaum,"Citadels of Pride. Sexual Assault, Accountability, and Reconciliation" (WW Norton & Company 2021), 3, who notes that "Sexual violence is not just a problem of isolated 'sick' individuals" and it is, rather, an issue of "background culture," which "denies women key features of full and equal humanity."

67. See Federico Stella, *La giustizia e le ingiustizie* (Il Mulino 2006), who points out that the application of the penalty to the offender cannot remedy the injustice inherent in the crime committed.

68. See, among others, Tribunale di Milano judgment of December 16, 2009, no. 15359.

69. "Throw away the key" is the provocative title of a volume that collects the results of a long activity of psychological support and treatment carried out with some of the sex offenders detained in prison in Italy following a final sentence, see Paolo Giulini and Carla Maria Xella (eds), *Buttare la chiave? La sfida del trattamento per gli autori di reati sessuali* (Raffaello Cortina 2011).

70. Davide Petrini, "Il trattamento del delinquente sessuale, tra esigenze securitarie e controllo della recidiva," *Rivista italiana di medicina legale* 4 (2013): 1823, 1833.

71. See Georgia Zara, *Il diniego nei sex offender. Dalla valutazione al trattamento* (Raffaello Cortina 2018), 69.

72. Mario Romano, "Legislazione penale e consenso sociale," *Jus* (1985): 412, 413.

73. See Giovanni Aliquò, *La violenza domestica. L'ammonimento del Questore* (Pacini Giuridica), 2020.

74. The warning from the public safety authority (*ammonimento del Questore*) can be issued in cases of domestic violence, stalking and cyberbullying. See Law no. 38 of April 23, 2009 (in case of stalking); Law no. 119 of October 15, 2013 (in case of domestic violence); Law no. 71 of May 29, 2017 (in case of cyberbullying).

75. See S. Caroline Taylor and Leigh Gassner, "Stemming the flow: challenges for policing adult sexual assault with regard to attrition rates and under-reporting of sexual offences," *Police Practice and Research* 3 (2010): 240, 241.

76. See, in this regard, Article 362 of the Code of Criminal Procedure, which states that the Public Prosecutor must take information from the victim within three days of *notitiae criminis*.

77. See Valentina Bonini, "The Istanbul Convention's values and its implementation in Italy," in Valentina Bonini and Rahime Erbaş (eds.), *The 10th Anniversary of the Istanbul Convention* (Pisa University Press 2021), 80.

78. See Francisco Fonseca Morillo and Ingrid Bellander Todino, "The Victims' Rights Directive: Origins and expectations," in Marta Bargis and Hervé Belluta (eds.) *Vittime di reato e sistema penale* (Giappichelli 2017), 13.

Chapter 8

Female Genital Mutilation as a Gender-Based Violence

Francesco Angelone and Angela Caruso

There is nothing sacred about the violation of intimacy.[1]

There is really nothing "culturally oriented" and, therefore, legitimate in the decapitation of sexuality.

There is really nothing in the wounds caused by the FGM which deserves to be balanced with the *sacred* values[2]—the affirmation—of life, freedom, and nondiscrimination, enshrined in the Constitution of individual States, as well as by the charter that is dedicated to the protection of human rights.

This is the meaning of our European *idem sentīre*;[3] this is the reason why *Schiller and Beethoven* composed the *Hymn*—thus said—*to joy*.

Just as the moment in which a woman chooses—she must be able to choose—to join physically with the one she has chosen as an extension of herself and this must be a moment of joy. And of pleasure. Not of unspeakable pain. Simply breathing in the pure air of equality—uncontaminated by the degenerate and degenerating myth of an imposed false purity—we can understand, study, and solve the atavistic problem of the FGM.

The international community, which only woke up in the middle of the last century,[4] has finally taken note of these practices which originate—unquestionably—from the primitive will of the male gender to oppress the female gender.

The vexations that are imposed on girls and women, condemned by the ethnic groups they belong to—and which too often operate silently—toward a future of atrocious, permanent physical and psychological suffering sometimes even lead to death.[5] Thus, this chapter aims to reflect on the necessity to analyze the sociological, philosophical, normative and jurisprudential evolution of the phenomenon in all regions of the world. In this regard, the

Italian reality deserves particular attention. The examination of the regulatory frameworks and their application by the judicial authorities will enable the reader to figure out whether FGM is properly punished in the world and whether the victims receive fair compensation or not.

ANTHROPOLOGY, RELIGION AND PHILOSOPHY

The Woman as a Scapegoat: A Victim Who Becomes Sacred?

The issue of female genital modifications, better identified as "female genital mutation,"[6] represents a complex issue, as it describes the use of various traditional rituals within a cultural, religious and anthropological matrix.

Due to the interdisciplinary nature of the subject, several studies, although well-informed, have shown limits relating to a specialist or hyper-specialistic approach. One of the reasons for confusion is mostly related to effort of scholars wanting to contextualize historically the birth of genital mutilation's practice, regardless of its sacral meaning and the negative impact on the inviolable human rights. In fact, according to a study conducted by the Italian Association of Women for Development Onlus,[7] mutilated women do not undergo this practice sic et simpliciter to obtain some advantage, but because these practices constitute the cornerstone of complex [social] structures, of relationships of power that organize the world's perception of those who practice them and who at different levels are involved in these rites.[8]

The justifications underlying the use of this practice—for us "barbaric"—can be traced back to four main explanations[9]: those of a sociocultural nature, aesthetic and hygienic reasons, spiritual and religious beliefs and finally, psychological and sexual reasons. For our purposes, it is useful to take into consideration the most relevant reasons before us, both from an absolute point of view and for our concern; that is, those of a sociocultural and spiritual-religious character.[10]

In relation to sociocultural motivations; it should be assumed that in some communities there is the belief that only through the removal of the clitoris a woman can reach maturity and thus become a full member of society. This practice, therefore, is considered a form of female "purification"[11] which, by depriving the woman of her external genital organs, would remove any hypothesis of infidelity, as well as the onset of psychiatric diseases (at the beginning of the last century, female hysteria[12] was linked to problems relating to the sphere of sexual pleasure). Furthermore, given that mutilation deprives the woman of pleasure, genital mutilation would be considered a guarantee of virginity.

It is easy to understand how this approach has acquired extreme importance, so much so that an entire structure of economic and social rules revolves around a system that recognizes the legitimacy of such a practice, with its binding force rooted in customary institutions such as so-called "bride price"[13] and forced marriage.

On the spiritual front, for a long time the belief that this imperative was dictated by religious requirements prevailed.[14] Indeed, these are the beliefs that have developed to justify a pre-existing practice. The spread of these practices[15] is linked to a criterion of geographical and ethnic distribution, not having a religious matrix. So much so that the phenomenon is present both among the Coptic Christian population and among the Falasha, Ethiopians women of Jewish religion; on the contrary, it is not present in all the territories considered to be the cradle of Islam, among Jewish women in other parts of the world or among other Christian denominations. However, the religion within which these practices are most widespread is Islam,[16] I would dare to say corrupt, so much so that, although the origins of the practice of genital mutilation is probably not Islamic,[17] it is precisely in the Muslim traditions that it is significantly rooted, despite its absence in the Koran.[18]

This last statement requires a certain reflection when examining the hadiths; the accounts of what Muhammad said and did. In this regard, it should be noted that some hadiths include questionable and even contradictory statements, such that their authentication and interpretation has become the object of study within Islam.[19]

One of the criticisms is aimed precisely at this authentication process. Suffice to say, according to the scholar Coulson, this activity "was limited to a careful examination of the chain of transmitters that narrated the account and did not [examine the authenticity] of the account itself."[20] It is useful, in order to show how some hadiths present interpretational difficulties and have a certain inconsistency.[21]

In the collection of Muhammad ibn Ismāʿīl al-Bukhārī, the seventh volume of book 72, hadith n. 779, reads: "I have heard the prophet say: "Five practices are characteristic of fitra: circumcision, shaving pubic hair, shortening the moustache, cutting the nails and shaving the hair of the armpits."[22]

Again, in the Al-Tirmidhi collection, in the first volume of book I, in hadith n. 108 we read: "When the circumcised meets the circumcised, then Ghusl is required. Allah's messenger and I had done it [the sexual act], so we practiced Ghusl."[23]

Finally, it is interesting, despite remaining questionable in its authenticity, hadith 5251, collected by Sunan Abi Dawud, which established that Muhammad himself allowed genital mutilation. Specifically, when addressing a woman who performed genital mutilation in Medina, he said: "Do not cut in an extreme way, because it's better for the woman and her husband likes her more."[24]

Therefore, in the light of what has been said, it is clear that it is possible to make mistakes when one wishes to include this practice exclusively to purely religious convictions or with patriarchal societies.[25] In any case, it is easy to understand how, regardless of the reasons underlying the practice in question, physical and moral damage is suffered by the woman, as if she were a sacrificial victim.

The Theory of Sacrifice as A Possible Justification?

In fact, it is precisely to the detriment of women that the drama of a rituality with an apparent purifying character is manifested; thus, under the banner of an alleged sacredness, the "rite" of infibulation masks real violence, forcing the victim, in our opinion, to assume the role of mere scapegoat. The French anthropologist René Girard (1923–2015) reflected precisely on this last point, elaborating the so-called Theory of Sacrifice.[26]

As for most scholars of the sciences of religion, as also for Girard, "a religious fact must be considered the basis of every human creation and, despite its various manifestations, it is always that which determines or influences human action."[27] The arguments, both in the work The Violence and the Sacred and in On Things Hidden Since the Foundation of the World, often take on dark colors and there is no lack of criticism, but they cover quite severe judgments.

His analyses of the phenomenon of sacrifice, which is ever present in all religions and is found in every culture, show parallels between Proust and Dostoevsky, between Freud and Sophocles.[28] Girard aims to provide new interpretations in his research into sacrifice carried out by anthropologists, ethnologists, and psychologists. In the work *La Violenza e il Sacro (Violence and the Sacred)*, for example, the author attempts to establish the relationship between innate violence in man and the sacred, arguing that it is an identity and at its most extreme point: sacrifice.

In light of his study into various primitive cultures,[29] Girard's belief is validated; that ritual sacrifice constitutes precisely the sublimation of violent intentions. In other words, it is all about beating an innocent victim (scapegoat) in place of the guilty person, in order to avoid generating a chain of endless rivalry and revenge among the same members of a community.

According to Girard, it all began with a primordial episode of violence and, subsequently, the repetition of the sacrificial rituals would have constituted a guarantee for the birth of a certain society and for the maintenance of order within it. Such sacrificial rituals would have the ultimate effect of making the victim sacred; this, it first assumes the guise of a scapegoat, transforming itself through sacrifice from a maleficent to a beneficial entity.[30] The very fact that Girard studies the sacrificial rites of the various religions and finds sacrifice in myths, as well as in all cultural forms, drew criticism from those scholars who had turned their commitment to sacrifice by focusing exclusively on its rituality.[31]

In relation to the scapegoat mechanism applicable to all cultural forms, one might think of the similarity to some medical treatments such as, for example, immunization and vaccination that aim to defeat the disease using the same "weakened" disease. To support the hypothesis of the mechanism[32] of the expiatory victim, Girard also affirms that all the great human, religious and profane institutions,[33] that is, political power, judicial power, the art of healing, philosophy, anthropology, are presented in rituality and this, as we have seen, envisages an expiatory victim.

This, in the case of our discussion, is the woman who becomes the educator par excellence of humanity. In fact, by this rite, man comes into contact with the sacred; it is through the rite that he escapes his own violence, distances himself from it, assuming, thanks to the female sacrifice, the best human countenance of himself, humanity.

What About *Homo Necans*?

Of considerable importance is the work by Burkert in October 1980 preface to the Italian edition of Homo necans, where a similarity with the thought of René Girard emerges. In fact, Burkert, starting from the analysis of Greek rites, demonstrates how such practices occupy a leading position in the organization of the social life of communities: there is, indeed, no stage in individual life or the development of economic or social activity that in ancient times was not celebrated with a ritual.[34]

In particular, Burkert starts from the consideration according to which "all orders and forms of power of human society are based on institutionalized violence."[35] This is also true for religion in which bloody violence predominates. In fact, the act of devotion essentially consists in shedding blood.[36]

The fundamental experience of the "sacred" is identifiable in the killing of victims, for which the homo religious act becomes aware of itself as homo necans. For Burkert, real sacred "action" represented by the act of killing and sacrifice is undoubtedly the most ancient form of religious act.[37] At the origin of civilization there has been an essential action: killing to eat; for which man is homo necans. However, this act by the hunter is immediately accompanied by a sense of guilt; in this way, the sacred value of the act of killing[38] becomes a ritual and thus takes the form of a sacrifice with the task of reparation.

Some fundamental acts such as hunting, killing, and eating combine to form, in their various concretizations, sacrifice,[39] which is seen by Burkert as the religious act par excellence. Yet, for Burkert, religion, preserving its aspect over the millennia, seems an extraordinary factor of social consolidation in historical reality. In this relationship with society, however, religion does not only perform the simple function of reflecting mirror: it appears much more related to deeper layers of human coexistence and its psychic presuppositions.

A certain similarity between Burkert's theses and those of Girard appears, although it is necessary to highlight an imposing difference, which for the French scholar lies in the consideration according to which religiously managing violence[40] serves to regenerate religion and the sacred, and not to legitimize what is negative in the profane world.[41] At least two useful considerations, we believe, can be reached starting from the theories of Burkert and Girard: understanding how, if one wanted to contextualize the practice of female genital mutilation in the broader framework of sacrifice, it would still be defined as a violent practice. And yet, despite it being considered a religious/purifying practice, today seen as a practice of cultural value,[42] it is still part of society.[43]

THE INTERNATIONAL SCENARIO

The Awakening of Society

FGM is mainly practiced in about thirty countries[44] across Africa[45] and the Middle East, but also in some countries of Asia and Latin America and among communities from these regions.[46]

Considering the widespread practice of FGM, with the resolution relating to FGM on September 20, 2001, the Parliament of the European Union asked the same EU and other Member States to collaborate in the harmonization of existing legislation and, where not adequate, in the creation of specific legislation to protect the rights[47] of the person, their integrity, freedom of conscience, and the right to health.

To date, various Western countries have passed punitive FGM laws: Sweden with a law of July 10, 1982; the United Kingdom with the *Prohibition of Female Circumcision Act* of July 16, 1985; the United States with the *Federal Prohibition of Female Genital Mutilation Act* of July 10, 1995; and Norway with a law on December 15, 1995. Canada followed with an amendment on April 25, 1997, to the criminal code; New Zealand, with art. 204 A of the Crimes Act, 1999 version; and Belgium, with a law dated November 28, 2000, thanks to which art. 409 Criminal code was introduced.

The French Republic has not introduced a specific legislation but boasts substantial jurisprudence in relation to cases of female circumcision. They are framed in Art. 222–9 which punishes violence that involves permanent mutilation or infirmity.[48]

Some countries like Turkey, we do not have a separate crime of FGM. But we consider it within crime of Injury's aggravating form, causing loss of human organs through injury. There is a critique by GREVIO report of the Istanbul convention to introduce a specific crime by stating that they are aware that FGM is foreign concept in Turkey, but Turkey receives many immigrants and refugees from other countries especially from middle east.

Here it should be noted that if we do not have a crime type called FGM, there will be no legal loophole. It will be punished within the other classic crimes. However, there is an importance to introduce a specific crime type to achieve the deterrence effect of Criminal codes.

The Istanbul Convention

The Council of Europe Convention on preventing and combating violence against women and domestic violence,[49] briefly known as the Istanbul Convention, which was opened for signature in Istanbul on May 11, 2011, intervened in order to increasingly implement protection against gender-based violence.[50] With specific reference to FGM, Art. 38 of the Convention reads as below:

Parties shall take the necessary legislative or other measures to prosecute the following intentional acts:

a. Excision, infibulation or any other mutilation of all or part of the labia majora, labia minora or removal of the clitoris;
b. To force a woman to undergo any act indicated in point a, or to provide her with the means to do so;
c. Induce, coerce or provide a girl with the means to undergo any of the acts set out in point a.[51]

Unfortunately, in many countries, FGM is not yet provided for and punished by the respective Criminal codes, paradoxically this includes Turkey.[52] Turkey subsequently, on March 20, 2021, withdrew from the Convention it had first ratified. If this withdrawal was enormously disappointing, what instead aroused pleasant surprise was the historic announcement of the Prosecutor of Somalia: in the month of July 2018, he decided for the first time to address in a courtroom the issue of FGM and to ask for the condemnation of those who practice them.

And in fact, on July 14, 2018, Deeqa Dahir Nuur—a ten-year-old girl—was forced to undergo the surgery of FGM, a result of which she bled to death a few days later.[53]

This is the first step and, therefore, a possible epochal turning point for Somalia: the nation with the highest incidence rate. Meanwhile, a huge step forward has been made in Sudan whose government—in April 2020—finally banned FGM with a ban included in an amendment to the Criminal code. The new law—which became enforceable on July 10, 2020—provides for a three-year prison sentence for those who practice genital mutilation, as well as a fine.[54]

THE ITALIAN PANORAMA

Art. 583-*bis* of the Criminal Code: Women not Objects.

In Italy, Art. 583-*bis* of the Criminal Code (henceforth: c.p.) was inserted by Art. 6, law on January 9, 2006, n. 7, ensuring clear prevention to practices that violate the fundamental rights to the integrity of the person and to the health of women and girls.

The subjective component of the crime is represented by generic willful misconduct in the first paragraph, understood as conscience and will of action, and by specific willful misconduct in the second paragraph, since in addition to the typical fact—lesions to the female genital organs—there is the further purpose of procuring profit for oneself or others. However, it is a free-form crime, for which liability for omission can also be configured—pursuant to Art. 40, c. 2, c.p.—against the person subject to the corresponding guarantee obligation.

Consider, for example, of the mother of a little girl who remained inactive to her husband's initiative to subject her daughter to mutilation: there will be the typical hypothesis of the culpable participation—on the part of the mother—in the willful crime perpetrated by the father.[55]

In both the first and second paragraphs, the practices in question are punished if implemented *in the absence of therapeutic needs*. In the first paragraph, mutilation practices are *typified* and are as follows: clitoridectomy, excision, and infibulation, in any other practice that causes effects of the same type.

This rule would not be worthy of full agreement if the one contained in the first paragraph was excluded, and this for a very simple reason: in this case, willful misconduct is specific, so if by hypothesis and in this case, the subject against whom the criminal actions exercised proves not to have been motivated by the further aim—represented, in fact, by the desire to impair sexual functions—the accusation risks collapse with consequent acquittal of the accused.

This provision follows that referred to in the first paragraph—which deals with the sanctioning of practices, in turn, aimed at punishing those who harm the genital organs assigned to female pleasure—which, therefore, is complete.

A real compression of the freedom of self-determination,[56] the external control over the development of sexuality,[57] that appears—and is—impassive to be excused or condemned for example 'by virtue' of the exercise of the right of religious freedom or a right arising from a custom, pursuant to Art. 51 c.p. There are those in Italy who have splendidly defined the causes for the exclusion of guilt in this way: "valves that allow a system of rules to breathe in human terms."[58] Well, those who undergo these practices see the breath of their own existence restricted: biological and feminine, in all the splendid and multiple facets that this last meaning entails.

CULTURAL DEFENSES VS. HUMAN RIGHTS?

No (pseudo) cultural tradition, let alone religion, can justify or excuse such a crime. In this regard, with a sentence in 2002, the Manchester Crown Court did not recognize the exemption of the provocation (*plea of provocation*) in favor of a Muslim of Pakistani origin, who immigrated to England in 1965, who had killed his twenty-four-year-old daughter after finding her (non-Muslim) boyfriend in her bedroom.[59]

This ruling is an example of jurisprudence that has intervened with regard to so-called "culturally oriented" crimes, the result of an awareness of the diversity of thought of a people, of the respect it imposes. Anyway, the protection of inviolable rights prevails upon the outcome maintaining relative balance, whatever the basic model from which the study of the single case derives: the French assimilationist one (where integration is the result of a one-way path), or the typically British multiculturalist one (where integration is the result of a one-way process) bidirectional between minority and majority).

Returning to Art. 583-*bis* c.p., it should be noted that, in the third paragraph, the penalty is increased by a third if the practices referred to in the two previous paragraphs where this crime *is committed to the detriment of a minor or if the offence is committed for profit.* The fourth paragraph establishes that the sentence or the application of the penalty at the request of the parties pursuant to Art. 444 of the Code of Criminal Procedure (henceforth: c.p.p.)—so-called "Plea bargaining"—when fact is committed by the parent or guardian involved, respectively.[60] According to this rule, further consequences are the following: the forfeiture of the exercise of parental responsibility and the permanent ban from any office relating to the guardianship and support administration.[61]

The fifth and last paragraph establish that the provisions of the aforementioned Article *also apply when the offence is committed abroad by an Italian citizen or a foreigner residing in Italy, or to the detriment of an Italian citizen or a foreigner residing in Italy*. The *leitmotif* is, therefore, that the crime is committed abroad. *In this case*, Article 583-*bis* c.p. thus concludes, *the guilty party is punished at the request of the Minister of Justice*. It would have been more appropriate—from a topographical point of view and not only, as will be seen in the following paragraph—to insert art. 583-*bis* directly within Art. 7 c.p. entitled *Crimes committed abroad.*

The Cases of Milan

In Italy, the Art. 583-*bis* has existed since 2006—as mentioned—but there have been very few practical cases.[62] The first ended with a conviction issued by the Court of Milan on November 25, 1999, for serious personal injury, pursuant to Art. 583, c. 1, no. 2, c.p.:[63] it was obviously a fact that occurred before March 9, 2006.

This conviction concerned an Egyptian immigrant, denounced by his Italian wife, who had his ten-year-old daughter's clitoris amputated during a vacation in Egypt. More precisely, the judge ruled in the following terms:

> Legally classified as serious voluntary injuries pursuant to art. 582, 583 and 585, c.p., in relation to art. 577, nos. 1 and 3, in art. 61, n. 5, c.p., the fact of a man whose daughter underwent circumcision surgery, consisting of the removal of the clitoris and the proximal upper 3rd of the labia minora, as well as in the saturation of the upper 3rd of the vulva with reduction of the vulvar intake, resulting in illness lasting 10 days and the permanent weakening of the genital system. [64]

There is another case that occurred in Turin, "defined" by the archiving decree "*due to the lack of conditions to exercise criminal proceedings*."[65] One wonders whether the non licet procedure derives precisely from the lack of a request by the Minister of Justice in the case of a crime already committed abroad. Here, then, is that the insertion of Art. 583-*bis* c.p. within Art. 7 c.p., which is not only appropriate but necessary in order to allow the 'machinery of justice' to move towards the person, the acquired elements against which are suitable to support the accusation in court.

This is the exact antithesis of Art. 125 of the implementing provisions, c.p.p., which governs the request for archiving. Article 7 c.p., in fact, begins as follows: *According to Italian law, a citizen or foreigner who commits any of the following crimes in a foreign territory (. . .)*, including—after the listing of some types of crimes in numbers 1–4—*any other crime for which special provisions of law or international conventions establish the applicability of the Italian criminal law* (see no. 5). This is a provision that allows the Prosecutor's Office to prosecute, therefore, without the constraint—sometimes really hostile to a truly just and proper Justice—of a condition of admissibility.

The Verona Case

Finally, with the sentence of April 14, 2010,[66] there is the first sentence of conviction for the newly minted crime. The enthusiasm generated by such a stance of "living law," the result—in turn—of the denunciation of what usually happens, but remains submerged, is chilling for the reason that will be explained shortly.

Meanwhile, it should be noted that the arrest in question was technically perfect in the first part and technically/socially almost flawless in the second part:

> It integrates the crime referred to in the 2nd paragraph of Art. 583-bis c.p. the incision of the anterior superior surface of the clitoris, which has not determined a permanent weakening of the clitoral sensitivity, it being sufficient that the agent has, with conscience and will, caused lesions to the female genital organs with the intention of impairing the sexual functions of the offended party (. . .). The specific intent of the crime is not excluded by the fact that in the perpetrators' communities of origin the incision of the female genitals primarily takes on the value of initiation and recognizes the identity of the subject in the group, since it cannot in any case disregard this practice, if only with regards to girls, and is also a function of controlling their sexuality.[67]

Indeed, the reservation is based on the following—and just mentioned above—incidental reason: "*if only with regards to girls*." There are those who argue, in this regard, the discriminating relevance of the consent of the person entitled pursuant to Art. 50 c.p.: physical integrity and psycho-sexual health are relatively available rights, so that the freedom of self-determination of women would not be violated if the practice was carried out with her consent. No such thought is shared in the light of Art. 5 of the Civil Code which states: "Acts of disposition of one's own body are prohibited when they cause a permanent loss of physical integrity, or when they are otherwise contrary to the law, public order or morality."

Not only that. It is no coincidence that Art. 583-*bis*, c. 3, c.p., refers to practices carried out to the detriment of minors in terms of aggravating circumstances: whatever the age group, therefore, such practices deserve to be punished, precisely because they involve the permanent elimination of genital tissue and, consequently, a permanent decrease in physical integrity in the light of the aforementioned Art. 5.

That was the story in fact: in April 2006, the then-fledgling anti-infibulation law was applied for the first time: a Nigerian woman, G. O., was arrested on her way to Caldiero to apply genital mutilation to a three-month-old girl. The parents of the same little girl were, therefore, tried and convicted in the first degree. However, once the second level of judgment was reached, the two defendants were acquitted "because the fact does not constitute a crime," a formula that in the Italian criminal trial system is used to acquit the merits of a defendant who acted in the absence of guilt.

The practical reason is here explained and embodied, for the reservation advanced at the beginning on the structural conformation of art. 583-*bis* c.p. The "small incision" has reversed the hypothesis provided for by the second paragraph, id est: injuries to the female genital organs other than those referred to in the first paragraph, practiced in order to impair sexual functions. This is precisely the prediction of the subjective element in terms of specific intent—in the concrete case of the child born in Verona—that the injury, even if practiced to the female genital organs, moreover of a newborn and at the behest of the parents, remained unpunished. Thus, the nefarious concept of woman echoes, from birth to maturity, as a mere womb to be fecundated. Where it has remained suitable for reproduction, it does not know "other" offenses: socially and legally punishable.

SOME REFLECTIONS

As already noted, Paragraph 4 of the same Art. 583-*bis* c.p. provides for the forfeiture of the exercise of parental responsibility only when the offence was committed by the father or mother. If one parent remains inactive "in front of" the execution of the practice carried out by will, psychological or material, the other parent will respond as stated for nonfulfillment of duty as guarantor in willful crime. In fact, the aforementioned Art. 40, § 2, c.p.: *not preventing an event, where there is a legal obligation to prevent, is equivalent to causing it*.

Conversely, if the other parent has accepted the implementation of the practice also in terms of possible misconduct, he/she will be able to respond by way of willful participation, except for the hypothesis referred to in Art. 583-*bis*, c. 2, c.p. In fact, any willful misconduct[68] is incompatible with the criminal offenses characterized by specific willful misconduct.

Finally, whoever acts as a principal or as an accomplice, at least with direct intent, responds as a "simple" competitor in the same crime. The term "simple" is explained immediately in the light of the wording of Art. 110 c.p., entitled penalty for those who participate in the crime.[69]

This is the result of the Italian legal tradition, which does not provide forms of differentiated liability. On the other hand, such a statement enters into an open and irreversible collision course with the principle (of) *best interests of the child*, enshrined in art. 3, paragraph 1, of the Convention on the Rights of the Child, signed in New York on November 20, 1989.

Art. 25-quater.1 of Legislative Decree n. 231/2001: The Administrative Liability of Entities

The legislative decree June 8, 2001, no. 231, regulates the administrative liability of legal persons, companies and associations, even without legal personality, pursuant to Article 11 of the Law of September 29, 2000, n. 300.[70] The main problem arises from its hybrid nature: administrative, for supporters of the formalistic thesis—given the wording used by the legislator and the impossibility of attaching to a legal person the cardinal principle of personality of criminal responsibility, as per art. 27, c. 1, Constitutional—criminal, for supporters of the substantive thesis, expecting the identity of the judicial body and the nature of the discipline invoked and applied in the courtroom.

It is believed that it is nature—real and finally revealed—that must prevail, thus leaning towards the substantive thesis and, therefore, for the criminal value of the liability of the Entity.

First of all, Art. 1 reads as follows: *This legislative decree regulates the liability of entities for administrative offences resulting from a crime*. Therefore, between the offence attributable to the entity (of an administrative nature, because the sanction does not affect the freedom of those who are obviously not physical persons) and the offense perpetrated by the individual physical person, there is the same relationship that binds—the branch of administrative law—the "presupposed act" to the "presupposing act," such that the existence of the second is strictly bound to the existence of the first.

However, it is not always the case; which will be one of the first signs of openness to admissibility of the constitution of a civil party directly toward the entity: *person offended by the crime including the practice of mutilation of female genital organs.*

Can the person injured by female genital mutilation become a civil party directly against the entity?

In Italy, the problem of the personal nature of criminal liability[71] is overcome through the concept of "organizational fault": in essence, the entity is responsible for having determined or, in any case, facilitated the commission of the crime by individual categories of physical persons and under the conditions set out in Articles 6—in which case it concerns the subjects in the top position—and 7—in which case it concerns, instead, the subjects subject to other directions—of the decree in question.

Looking overseas, we are reminded that in the United States the prevailing orientation of the Federal Courts is to extend the notion of *agent* as much as possible: The legal person must be held criminally responsible for the acts committed by any employee, even of the lowest degree, while the status, duties or sector of the agent are irrelevant. The essential thing is that they act within the scope of their duties (*scope of employment*) and in the interest of the legal person (*intent to benefit the corporation*). Minority is instead the restrictive solution followed by the *Model Criminal Code*, which holds the legal person responsible only for violations committed by a person who performs management functions (*high managerial agent*).[72]

Returning to Italy and, in detail, how and when the responsibility of the entity actually exists, first of all, is clarified thus by Art. 5 of the same legislative decree no. 231.

It goes without saying that, in the case referred to in paragraph 2, the aforementioned relationship—presupposed act/presupposing act—is dissolved, the administrative offence of the entity does not exist even if the offence was committed by the individual physical person: if the latter acted exclusively in self-interest or in the interest of others, what is legally relevant by itself cannot be reduced to the charge of the institution. Add, then, Art. 8:

1. *The entity's liability also exists when:*
   a. *the perpetrator of the crime has not been identified or is not attributable;*
   b. *the offence is extinguished for a reason other than amnesty.*

   (. . .).[73]

In those cases, referred to in letters (a) and (b), therefore, the criminal machinery against the single person stops but the proceedings against the entity continue.

Proceedings that take place before a criminal judge, applying—as provided for by art. 34 and—*insofar as they are compatible, the provisions of the code of criminal procedure and of the legislative decree of 28 July 1989, n. 271* (the latter represent the implementing rules, c.p.p.).

The Italian "Swing of Pendulum"

On the specific question of the admissibility of a civil action directly against the entity, the first relevant arrest was that signed by the Coroner's Section of the Court of Milan which, by order of March 9, 2004,[74] gave a negative answer, concluding that it was inadmissible.

There were two reasons: (1) the "administrative" label chosen by the legislator to qualify the responsibility of the entity; (2) the prohibition of analogy in *malam partem*.

It would be waived if the scope of Art. 185 c.p.—this provision is substantive, not procedural—where art. 35 of Legislative Decree no. 231/2001 (the civil party poses, in fact, as the defendant's counterpart) allows the entity to apply the procedural provisions relating to the accused, insofar as they are compatible. Compatibility in that, for the Court of Milan, the reference is not limited to the provisions which guarantee the defendant, therefore denied by basing the principle called *ubi voluit dixit, ubi noluit tacuit*, a Latin expression for *when the Legislator wanted he said, when he did not want he did not say*. This injured party may sue the entity not directly but only as civilly liable—for a fait accompli by the accused, according to the canons of art. 2049 of the Italian Civil Code—pursuant to Art. 83 c.p.p.

The citated Art. 83 and "*integral provisions*" of Legislative decree n. 231/2001 which were the subject of question of constitutional legitimacy, precisely in so far as they do not provide for such direct power vis-à-vis the entity; a question that, however, was incorrectly posed, since the referring judge had not identified the specific provision of the decree which, in connection with that of Art. 83 c.p.p., would have determined the violation of the principle of equality. For this reason, the Constitutional Court, with sentence no. 218, filed on July 18, 2014, declared the matter inadmissible.

On January 24, 2008, however, there was the first sign of an opening by the "same" Coroner's Section of the Court of Milan which—re melius perpensa—recovered the concept of compensation as an alternative to the criminal penalty, to be understood as included in the provision of Art. 185 c.p.; the latter, thanks to an extensive and "*evolutionary*" interpretation, not already analogous, includes within its scope a new source of damage worthy of direct compensation from the entity. All this is justified "*in the absence of specific contrary provisions contained in the same decree and of incompatibility profiles with the discipline contained in the code of criminal procedure*."[75]

Hour (H)after[76] hour, those who care for and give birth cannot and must not enjoy, but suffer.

Borrowing the famous expression that, in Alessandro Manzoni's I *Promessi Sposi,* the "Bravi" uttered toward the fearful Don Abbondio, FGM on the other hand, has nothing to do with it. Conversely, if it is still practiced, it should be denounced, persecuted, and punished.

The "Maurizio Giovanardi and Others" Ruling

On the other hand, Directive 2012/29/ EU defines "*restorative justice*"—in Art. 2, let. d)—*any procedure that allows the victim and the perpetrator of the crime to actively participate, if they agree freely, in the resolution of the issues resulting from the crime with the help of an impartial third party.*[77] However, the Giovanardi ruling, issued by the Court of Justice of the European Union, Section Two, on July 12, 2012, concluded negatively.

Here, in fact, we read in §49:

> it is necessary to answer the question posed by declaring that Article 9, paragraph 1, of the Framework Decision must be interpreted in the sense that it does not prevent, in the context of a regime of liability of legal persons such as the one at issue in the main proceedings, the victim of a crime cannot claim compensation for damages directly caused by that crime, in the context of the criminal trial, from the legal person responsible for an administrative offence from a crime.[78]

An Opening Signal from the South of Italy

Finally and, on the contrary, the recent sentence issued on January 29, 2021, by the Court of Lecce, Second Criminal Section,[79] concluded that the constitution of a civil party was admissible, taking into account that:

> when the legislator wished to depart from the provisions of the code of rite, he expressly stated it (. . .), the explanatory report of Legislative Decree no. 231 of 2001 does not contain any indication relating to the inadmissibility of a civil action, there is no obstacle to this extensive interpretation in the specific rules on the assessment of ascertaining the administrative offence [80]

Ultimately, "*no provision of the decree expressly prohibits the establishment of a civil action against the entity*,"[81] within which "*there are, moreover, a series of provisions*," such as Articles 12 and 17, "*which makes it possible to frame the system of liability entities in the sense of recognizing a sanctioning model compatible with the recognition of damage deriving from the offence*."[82]

CONCLUDING REMARKS

The reason we investigated FGM was born from the observation—once again the Preamble of the Istanbul Convention as quoted—*that women and girls are often exposed to serious forms of violence, including (. . .) female genital mutilation (. . .)*.[83]

However, if at the regulatory level the *gap* has been finally (albeit belatedly) remedied in many countries, the cases offered (because they emerged) from reality and, therefore, brought to the attention of the Judicial Authorities are still (except for France) few, especially in Italy.

It is the "proof" that in our Peninsula FGM still remains hidden, because it is tolerated and not reported. Except in extreme hypotheses: those, that is, in which it is death that "speaks." What causes greater horror is that they are almost always carried out within the home and with the mother's approval. That is; those who, despite having given life, allow—because they do not prevent—that their offspring, "guilty" of being born female, see their lives *fade*.

The number of cases in which the Prosecutor's Office managed to prosecute—before and after the introduction of Art. 583-*bis* c.p.—is inversely proportional to the gravity of the crime. The sentences of conviction are not enough. The problem of the admissibility of the constitution of a civil party directly against the Entity is still not definitively resolved; the turmoil of jurisprudential merit and legitimacy, on this point, is undeniable. And there is no doubt that the issue also concerns the victims of FGM, where such practices are carried out within an Authority.

The hope, therefore, is that by talking—and writing—ever more about these practices, silence will be "broken" and women will once again take possession of themselves, of all their rights and freedoms.

Including sexuality. Why not?!

Mysterium tremendum fascinans et augustum.[84]

REFERENCES

Literature

Abu-Sahlieh, S. A. A., "Islamic Law and the Issue of Male and Female Circumcision," *Third World Legal Studies* 13, no. 4 (1995), https://scholar.valpo.edu/cgi/viewcontent.cgi?article=1036&context=twls, accessed March 19, 2021.

Al-Suhrawardy, A. Al-M., *Maometto. Le parole del Profeta* (Newton & Compton Editori 1997).

Althaus, F. A., "Female Circumcision: Rite of Passage or Violation of Rights?," *Guttmacher Institute* 23, no. 3 (1997), https://www.guttmacher.org/sites/default/files/pdfs/pubs/journals/2313097.pdf, accessed April 6, 2021.

Amoretti, B. S, *Tolleranza e guerra santa nell'Islam* (Sansoni 1974).

Babès, L., *L'altro Islam. Un'indagine sui giovani musulmani e la religione* (Edizioni Lavoro 2000).

Barbieri, M. S., "Considerazioni sul sacro e sul santo. Per un confronto tra Burkert e Girard," *Heliopolis* 15, no. 1 (2017).

Basile, F., "Il reato di 'pratiche di mutilazione degli organi genitali femminili' alla prova della giurisprudenza: un commento alla prima (e finora unica) applicazione giurisprudenziale dell'art. 583 bis c.p.," *Stato, Chiese e pluralismo confessionale*

24 (2013), https://www.statoechiese.it/images/uploads/articoli_pdf/basile_il_reato.pdf?pdf=il-reato-di-pratiche-di-mutilazione-degli-organi-genitali-femminili-alla-pr, n. 24/2013, accessed April 30, 2021.

Benhabib, S., *The Claim of Cultural Identity* (il Mulino 2005).

Bettiol, G., *Diritto penale, Parte generale* (Cedam 1986).

Bouchard, M., "Dalla famiglia tradizionale a quella multietnica e multiculturale: maltrattamenti ed infanzia abusata in 'dimensione domestica,'" *Diritto Immigrazione Cittadinanza* 1 (2000).

Bonini, V., "The Istanbul Convention's Values and Its Implementation in Italy," in Bonini V and Erbaş R (eds.), *The 10th anniversary of the Istanbul Convention* (Pisa University Press 2021).

Broch-Due, V., Rudie, I., and Bleie, T., *Gendered Symbols and Social Practices* (Carved flesh/cast selves 1993).

Burkert, W., *Homo necans: The Anthropology of Ancient Greek Sacrificial Ritual and Myth* (University of California Press 1983).

———, *Anthropologie des religiösen Opfers. Die Sakralisierung der Gewalt* (Carl Friedrich von Siemens Stiftung 1987).

———, *Glaube und Verhalten: Zeichengehalt und Wirkungsmacht von Opfer-ritualen* (Fondation Hardt 1981).

———, *Homo Necans: Interpretationen altgriechischer Opferriten und Mythen* (Walter de Gruyter, Berlino, New York, 1972) trad. it. *Homo necans, Antropologia del sacrificio cruento nella Grecia antica* (Boringhieri 1981).

———, "The Problem of Ritual Killing," in Robert G. Hamerton-Kelly (ed), *Violent Origins: Walter Burkert, René Girard, Jonathan Z. Smith on Ritual killing and cultural formation* (Stanford University Press 1987).

Canestrari, S., Ferrando, G., Mazzoni, C., Rodotà, S., and Zatti, P., "Il governo del corpo," in S. Rodotà and P. Zatti (eds.), *Trattato di biodiritto* (Giuffrè 2011).

Carrillo, D., and Pasini, N., *Migrazioni Generi Famiglie. Pratiche di escissione e dinamiche di cambiamento in alcuni contesti regionali* (FrancoAngeli 2009).

Casanova, J., *Oltre la secolarizzazione* (il Mulino 2000).

Ciminelli, M. L., "The Cultural Reason for F.G.M: Critical Note of Definition of F.G.M. from Oms/Who," *La Ricerca Folklorica* 46 (2002).

Coccia, B., *L'Europa contemporanea tra la perdita delle radici e la paura del futuro* (Apes 2007).

Consorti, P., "The Meaning of 'Religion' in Multicultural Societies Law," *Stato, Chiese e pluralismo confessionale* 39 (2017), https://www.statoechiese.it/images/uploads/articoli_pdf/AA.VV.M4_The_Meaning.pdf?pdf=the-meaning-of-religion-in-multicultural-societies-law, accessed April 22, 2021.

Coulson, N. J., "European Criticism of Hadith Literature," in A. Beeston, T. Johnstone, R. Serjeant and G. Smith (eds.), *Arabic Literature to the End of the Umayyad Period* (Cambridge 1983).

Erbaş, R, "Evidentiary Challenge to an Effective Criminal Investigation for Domestic Violence: An Introduction," in Valentina Bonini and Rahime Erbaş (eds.), *The 10th Anniversary of the Istanbul Convention* (Pisa University Press 2021).

Favali, L., *Fra legge e modelli ancestrali: prime osservazioni sulle mutilazioni genitali in Eritrea* (Giappichelli 2002).
Foucault, M., *The History of Sexuality, Volume I: An Introduction* (Robert Hurley tr, Pantheon Books 1978).
Gaskell, I., and Carter, S. A., *The Oxford Handbook of History and Material Culture* (Oxford University Press 2020).
Gastaldo, M. C., "Processo penale e accertamento della responsabilità amministrativa degli enti: una innaturale ibridazione," *Cassazione penale* 5 (2009).
Garofoli, R., *Tracce penale con giurisprudenza, Parte generale* (Nel Diritto 2010)
———, *Manuale di diritto penale, Parte generale* (Giuffrè 2008).
Germanò, R., *The Theory of Sacrifice according to René Girard* (Pontificia Università Lateranense 1989).
Girard, R., *I See Satan Fall Like Lightning* (Gracewing Publishing 2001).
———, "Interview: René Girard," *Diacritics* 8 (1978).
———, *Des Choses cachées depuis la fondation du monde* (Grasset, Paris, 1978), trad. it. *Delle cose nascoste sin dalla fondazione del mondo* (Adelphi 1983).
———, *La violence et la sacré* (Grasset, Paris, 1972), trad. it. *La Violenza e il Sacro* (Edizioni Adelphi 1980).
———, "Generative Scapegoating," in Robert G. Hamerton-Kelly (ed), *Violent Origins: Walter Burkert, René Girard, Jonathan Z. Smith on Ritual killing and cultural formation* (Stanford University Press 1987).
Izzo, A., *Storia del pensiero sociologico* (il Mulino 2000).
Kitts, M., "Sacrifical Violence in the Iliad," *Journal of Ritual Studies* 16, no. 1 (2002).
Mancini, S., "The Power of Symbols and Symbols as Power: Secularism and Religion as Guarantors of Cultural Convergence," *Cardozo Law Review* 30, no. 6 (2009).
Mitchum, P. D., "Slapping the Hand of Cultural Relativism: Female Genital Mutilation, Male Dominance, and Health as a Human Rights Framework," *William & Mary Journal of Women and the Law* 19, no. 3 (2019), https://scholarship.law.wm.edu/cgi/viewcontent.cgi?article=1363&context=wmjowl, accessed March 4, 2021.
Mongillo, V., *La responsabilità penale tra individuo ed ente collettivo* (Giappichelli 2018).
North, R., *Violence and the Bible: the Girard Connection* (The Catholic Biblical Quarterly 1985).
Pace, E., *Sociologia dell'Islam* (Carocci 1999).
Paloutzian, R. F., and Park, C. L., *Handbook of the Psychology of Religion and Spirituality* (The Guilford Press 2005).
Pasquinelli, C., *Antropologia delle mutilazioni genitali femminili. Una ricerca in Italia* (Aidos 2000), https://aidos.it/wp-content/uploads/2009/01/Ricerca-pasquinelli-completa.pdf, accessed March 25, 2021.
Pasquinelli, C., *Infibulazione, Il corpo violato* (Meltemi Editore 2007).
Ruggeri, A., *Scritti in onore di Gaetano Silvestri* (Giappichelli 2016).
Sembè, Ne O., *Moolaadé. La forza delle donne* (Feltrinelli 2006).

Scuri E, "Somalia, per la prima volta si terrà un processo contro le mutilazioni genitali femminili" (July 26, 2018), https://www.lifegate.it/somalia-primo-processo-mutilazioni-genitali-femminili, accessed April 23, 2021.
Smith, B. G., *The Oxford Encyclopedia of Women in World History*, vol. 4 (1st edn, Oxford University Press 2008).
Smith, B. K., and Doniger W., "Sacrifice and Substitution: Ritual Mystification and Mythical Demystification," *Numen* 36, no. 2 (1989).
Tarditi, C., *René Girard, Interprete del Novecento, Dialoghi a distanza con dieci rappresentanti della cultura europea contemporanea* (Editrice Uni Service 2009).
Tugnoli, C., *La Magnifica ossessione. Il mito della Vittima tra letteratura e vangeli* (Bruno Mondadori 2005).
Vercellin, G., *Istituzioni del mondo musulmano* (Einauidi 1996).

Legislation

Council of Europe Convention on preventing and combating violence against women and domestic violence [2011], https://rm.coe.int/168046031c, accessed June 18, 2021.
Declaration on the Elimination of Violence against Women, proclaimed by General Assembly resolution 48/104 of December 20, 1993, https://www.ohchr.org/en/professionalinterest/pages/violenceagainstwomen.aspx, accessed July 17, 2021.
Directive 2012/29/ EU, of October 25, 2012, establishing minimum standards on the rights, support and protection of victims of crime, also in consideration of former FD 2001/220/JHA on the standing of victims in criminal proceedings.
European Parliament Resolution, 2001/2035, Female genital mutilation [2001], https://op.europa.eu/en/publication-detail/-/publication/5dd0b2f0-1a46-421c-8fc8-4c2e5040beb2/language-en, accessed May 25, 2021.
Law 1 October 2012, n. 172: ratification and execution of the Convention of the Council of Europe for the protection of minors against sexual exploitation and abuse, signed in Lanzarote on October 25, 2007.
Legislative decree June 8, 2001, n. 231: "The administrative liability of legal persons, companies and associations, even without legal personality," pursuant to Article 11 of the Law of September 29, 2000, no. 300.

Cases

Case C-79/11, *Criminal proceedings against Maurizio Giovanardi and others* [2012], ECR, ECLI:EU:C:2012:448.
Cass. civ. (2), January 21, 2020, K. S., https://sentenze.laleggepertutti.it/sentenza/cassazione-civile-n-17954-del-27-08-2020, accessed June 8, 2021.
Tribunale di Milano, November 25, 1999, El Namr [2000] 2, Diritto Immigrazione Cittadinanza, 148.
Tribunale di Milano, March 9, 2004 [2004] 2, Foro italiano, c. 435.
Tribunale di Milano, January 24, 2008, B S.p.A., https://www.aodv231.it/images/pdf/trib%20Milano%2024-01-08.pdf, accessed September 7, 2021.

Tribunale di Verona, April 14, 2010, Obaseki Gertrude, Omoruyi Ogowen, Ekogiawe John Osagie, n. 979 [2011], 2, Rivista italiana di diritto e procedura penale, 838.
Tribunale di Lecce (2), January, 29 2021 (February 15, 2021), https://www.giurisprudenzapenale.com/wp-content/uploads/2021/02/trib-lecce-231-ordinanza.pdf, accessed April 20, 2021.

NOTES

1. Although the present work is the result of ideas and thoughts shared (Introduction and Concluding Remarks), the authorship of Chapter "Anthropology, Religion and Philosophy" is by Francesco Angelone, the motherhood of Chapters "The International Scenario" and "The Italian Panorama" is by Angela Caruso.

2. Antonio Ruggeri, *Scritti in onore di Gaetano Silvestri* (Giappichelli 2016), 873.

3. Benedetto Coccia, *L'Europa contemporanea tra la perdita delle radici e la paura del futuro* (Apes 2007), 260.

4. The international agencies orbiting within the United Nations Organization began to take an interest in female sexual mutilation in 1958, but only in 1977 did the World Health Organization approve the creation of a working group for this phenomenon. However, it was in 1995 that the Fourth Women's Conference in Beijing condemned such practices by equating them with acts of sexual violence. Sami A. Aldeeb Abu-Sahlieh, "Islamic Law and the Issue of Male and Female Circumcision," *Third World Legal Studies* 13, no. 4 (1995): 73, 95–96, https://scholar.valpo.edu/cgi/viewcontent.cgi?article=1036&context=twls, accessed March 19, 2021.

5. Ousmane Sembè Ne, *Moolaadé. La forza delle donne* (Feltrinelli 2006), 11.

6. Preston D. Mitchum, "Slapping the hand of cultural relativism: Female genital mutilation, male dominance, and health as a human rights framework," *William & Mary Journal of Women and the Law* 19, no. 3 (2019): 585, https://scholarship.law.wm.edu/cgi/viewcontent.cgi?article=1363&context=wmjowl, accessed March 4, 2021.

7. Carla Pasquinelli, *Antropologia delle mutilazioni genitali femminili. Una ricerca in Italia* (Aidos 2000), https://aidos.it/wp-content/uploads/2009/01/Ricerca-pasquinelli-completa.pdf, accessed March 25, 2021.

8. Frances A. Althaus, "Female Circumcision: rite of passage or violation of rights?," *Guttmacher Institute* 23, no. 3 (1997): 130, https://www.guttmacher.org/sites/default/files/pdfs/pubs/journals/2313097.pdf, accessed April 6, 2021.

9. Maria Luisa Ciminelli, "The Cultural Eeason for F.G.M: Critical Note of Definition of F.G.M from Oms/Who," *La Ricerca Folklorica* 46 (2002): 39.

10. Raymond F. Paloutzian and Crystal L. Park, *Handbook of the Psychology of Religion and Spirituality* (The Guilford Press 2005), 3–18.

11. Vigdis Broch-Due, Ingrid Rudie and Tone Bleie, *Gendered Symbols and Social Practices* (Carved flesh/cast selves 1993), 83–106.

12. Bonnie G. Smith, *The Oxford Encyclopedia of Women in World History*, vol. 4 (1st edn, Oxford University Press 2008), 521.

13. Carla Pasquinelli, *Infibulazione, Il corpo violato* (Meltemi Editore 2007), 94.

14. Pierluigi Consorti, "The Meaning of 'Religion' in Multicultural Societies Law," *Stato, Chiese e pluralism confessionale* 39 (2017): 1, https://www.statoechiese.it/images/uploads/articoli_pdf/AA.VV.M4_The_Meaning.pdf?pdf=the-meaning-of-religion-in-multicultural-societies-law, accessed April 22, 2021.

15. Seyla Benhabib, *The Claim of Cultural Identity* (I Mulino 2005), 149; Susanna Mancini, "The Power of Symbols and Symbols as Power: Secularism and Religion as Guarantors of Cultural Convergence," *Cardozo Law Review* 30, no. 6 (2009): 2, 629.

16. Giorgio Vercellin, *Istituzioni del mondo musulmano* (Einauidi 1996), 27.

17. Biancamaria Scarcia Amoretti, *Tolleranza e guerra santa nell'Islam* (Sansoni 1974), 30.

18. Therefore, it is a foreign concept in some other Muslim dominated countries such as Turkey or Bosnia Herzogovina or Kosovo.

19. Enzo Pace, *Sociologia dell'Islam* (Carocci 1999), 32.

20. Noel J. Coulson, "European criticism of Hadith literature," in A. Beeston, T. Johnstone, R. Serjeant, and G. Smith (eds.), *Arabic Literature to the End of the Umayyad Period* (Cambridge 1983), 317.

21. Abdullah al-Mamun Al-Suhrawardy, *Maometto. Le parole del Profeta* (Newton & Compton Editori 1997), 21–22.

22. Sahih al-Bukhari, 7, *Book 72*, Hadith, 779.

23. Jami` at-Tirmidhi, *Book of Purification*, I, Hadith, 108.

24. Sunan Abi Dawud, *Book 42*, Hadith, 5,251.

25. Leila Babès, *L'altro Islam. Un'indagine sui giovani musulmani e la religione* (Edizioni Lavoro 2000), 168–176.

26. Remigia Germanò, *The Theory of Sacrifice according to René Girard* (Pontificia Università Lateranense 1989), 92.

27. René Girard, "Interview: René Girard," *Diacritics* 8 (1978): 31.

28. Robert North, *Violence and the Bible: The Girard Connection* (The Catholic Biblical Quarterly 1985), 47 [1].

29. René Girard, *Des Choses cachées depuis la fondation du monde* (Grasset 1978), trad. it. *Delle cose nascoste sin dalla fondazione del mondo* (Adelphi 1983), 313.

30. René Girard, *I See Satan Fall Like Lightning* (Gracewing Publishing 2001).

31.Brian K. Smith and Wendy Doniger, "Sacrifice and Substitution: Ritual Mystification and Mythical Demystification," *Numen* 36, no. 2 (1989): 189.

32. René Girard, *La violence et la sacré* (Grasset, Paris,1972), trad. it. *La Violenza e il Sacro* (Edizioni Adelphi 1980), 390.

33. Claudio Tarditi, *René Girard, Interprete del Novecento, Dialoghi a distanza con dieci rappresentanti della cultura europea contemporanea* (Editrice Uni Service 2009), 24.

34. Walter Burkert, *Homo Necans: The Anthropology of Ancient Greek Sacrificial Ritual and Myth* (University of California Press 1983), 384.

35. Walter Burkert, *Glaube und Verhalten: Zeichengehalt und Wirkungsmacht von Opfer-ritualen* (Fondation Hardt 1981), 110; Walter Burkert, *Anthropologie des religiösen Opfers. Die Sakralisierung der Gewalt* (Carl Friedrich von Siemens Stiftung, 1987), 34; Walter Burkert, "The Problem of Ritual Killing," in Robert G. Hamerton-Kelly (ed), *Violent Origins: Walter Burkert, René Girard, Jonathan*

Z. Smith on Ritual killing and cultural formation (Stanford University Press 1987), 178–179.

36. Walter Burkert, *Homo Necans: Interpretationen altgriechischer Opferriten und Mythen* (Walter de Gruyter, Berlino, New York, 1972) trad. it. *Homo necans, Antropologia del sacrificio cruento nella Grecia antica* (Boringhieri, Torino, 1981), 22–23.

37. Margo Kitts, "Sacrifical Violence in the Iliad," *Journal of Ritual Studies* 16, no. 1 (2002): 19.

38. Maria Stella Barbieri, "Considerazioni sul sacro e sul santo. Per un confronto tra Burkert e Girard," Heliopolis 15, no. 1 (2017): 7.

39. Claudio Tugnoli, *La Magnifica ossessione. Il mito della Vittima tra letteratura e vangeli* (Bruno Mondadori 2005), 115.

40. René Girard, "Generative Scapegoating," in Robert G. Hamerton-Kelly (ed), *Violent Origins: Walter Burkert, René Girard, Jonathan Z. Smith on Ritual Killing and Cultural Formation* (Stanford University Press 1987), 79.

41. *Ibid.,* 108.

42. Jose Casanova, *Oltre la secolarizzazione* (il Mulino 2000), 21–76.

43. Alberto Izzo, *Storia del pensiero sociologico* (il Mulino 2000), 283.

44. Daniela Carrillo and Nicola Pasini, *Migrazioni Generi Famiglie. Pratiche di escissione e dinamiche di cambiamento in alcuni contesti regionali* (FrancoAngeli 2009).

45. Lyda Favali, *Fra legge e modelli ancestrali: prime osservazioni sulle mutilazioni genitali in Eritrea* (Giappichelli 2002).

46. European Parliament News, "Female Genital Mutilation: In which Countries Is It Practiced? Why? What Are the Consequences?" (February 11, 2020, Updated February 13, 2020), https://www.europarl.europa.eu/news/en/headlines/society/20200206STO72031/female-genital-mutilation-where-why-and-consequences, accessed May 24, 2021.

47. European Parliament Resolution, 2001/2035, "Female Genital Mutilation" (2001), https://op.europa.eu/en/publication-detail/-/publication/5dd0b2f0-1a46-421c-8fc8-4c2e5040beb2/language-en, accessed May 25, 2021.

48. Sami A. Aldeeb Abu-Sahlieh (n. 3), 99.

49. The Council of Europe Convention on preventing and combating violence against women and domestic violence (2011) 1, https://rm.coe.int/168046031c, accessed June 28, 2021.

50. Rahime Erbaş, "Evidentiary Challenge to an Effective Criminal Investigation for Domestic Violence: An Introduction," in Valentina Bonini and Rahime Erbaş (eds.), *The 10th anniversary of the Istanbul Convention* (Pisa University Press 2021) 101, 111, 113, analyzed "the case of Durmaz v. Turkey (2015) from the European Court of Human Rights (. . .) ." About that affair, very similar to Talpis v. Italy, 2017, "The Court held that there has been a violation of art. 2 of the Convention due to the national authorities' failure to carry out an effective investigation into the death of the applicant's daughter."

51. Article 38 of the Istanbul Convention. See n. 48.

52. Valentina Bonini, "The Istanbul Convention's values and its implementation in Italy," in Valentina Bonini and Rahime Erbaş (eds.), *The 10th anniversary of the*

Istanbul Convention (Pisa University Press 2021) 69, 75, wrote: "the experiences of Turkey and Italy, despite their differences, make it clear that the path to overcome inequalities between women and men is a long, challenging road, which requires a joint effort by all stakeholders."

53. Elisabetta Scuri, "Somalia, per la prima volta si terrà un processo contro le mutilazioni genitali femminili" (July 26, 2018), https://www.lifegate.it/somalia-primo-processo-mutilazioni-genitali-femminili, accessed April 23, 2021.

54. *Il Sudan ha vietato le mutilazioni genitali femminili* (Milano, May 1, 2020), https://www.ilpost.it/2020/05/01/sudan-vietate-mutilazioni-genitali-femminili/, accessed April 23, 2021.

55. Marco Bouchard, "'Dalla famiglia tradizionale a quella multietnica e multiculturale: maltrattamenti ed infanzia abusata in 'dimensione domestica,'" *Diritto Immigrazione Cittadinanza* 1 (2000): 19.

56. Stefano Canestrari, Gilda Ferrando, Cosimo Mazzoni, Stefano Rodotà, and Paolo Zatti, "Il governo del corpo," in S. Rodotà and P. Zatti (eds.), *Trattato di biodiritto* (Giuffrè 2011).

57. Michel Foucault, *The History of Sexuality, Volume I: An introduction* (Robert Hurley tr, Pantheon Books 1978) 38–39, reported that in the eighteenth and nineteenth centuries "(. . .) what came under scrutiny was the sexuality of children, mad men and women, and criminals; the sensuality of those who did not like the opposite sex; reveries, obsessions, petty manias, or great transports of rage."

58. Giuseppe Bettiol, *Diritto penale*, *Parte generale* (Cedam 1986), 493.

59. Roberto Garofoli, *Tracce penale con giurisprudenza*, *Parte generale* (Nel Diritto 2010), 673.

60. See Article 583-*bis*, §4, c.p. This paragraph was inserted into law October 1, 2012, n. 172: ratification and execution of the *Convention of the Council of Europe for the protection of minors against sexual exploitation and abuse*, signed in Lanzarote on October 25, 2007.

61. Article 583-*bis*, §4, no. 1–2.

62. An applause goes to the civil justice sector which included the M.G.F. among the cases eligible for the recognition of international protection. See Cass. civ. (2), January 21, 2020, K.S., https://sentenze.laleggepertutti.it/sentenza/cassazione-civile-n-17954-del-27-08-2020, accessed June 8, 2021.

63. Tribunale di Milano, 25 November 1999, El Namr [2000] 2, Diritto Immigrazione Cittadinanza, 148.

64. See the full text on http://feir.cois.it/database/regioni/lombardia/Libert%C3%A0%20religiosa/Sentenza%2026%2011%201999%20Tribunale%20Milano%20Libert%C3%A0%20religiosa.html accessed June 20, 2021.

65. Fabio Basile, "Il reato di 'pratiche di mutilazione degli organi genitali femminili' alla prova della giurisprudenza: un commento alla prima (e finora unica) applicazione giurisprudenziale dell'art. 583 bis c.p.," *Stato, Chiese e pluralismo confessionale* 24 (2013): 1, https://www.statoechiese.it/images/uploads/articoli_pdf/basile_il_reato.pdf?pdf=il-reato-di-pratiche-di-mutilazione-degli-organi-genitali-femminili-alla-pr, n. 24/2013, accessed April 30, 2021.

66. Tribunale di Verona, April 14, 2010, Obaseki Gertrude, Omoruyi Ogowen, Ekogiawe John Osagie, n. 979 [2011] 2, Rivista italiana di diritto e procedura penale, 838.

67. See the full text on http://www.adir.unifi.it/rivista/2012/ghizzi/cap2.htm accessed March 5, 2021.

68. Magnificently so in the c.d. "second formula of Frank": "it can be so or otherwise, happen so or otherwise, in any case I act."

69. Article 110 c.p.

70. Vincenzo Mongillo, *La responsabilità penale tra individuo ed ente collettivo* (Giappichelli 2018), 106.

71. Massimo Ceresa Gastaldo, "Processo penale e accertamento della responsabilità amministrativa degli enti: una innaturale ibridazione," *Cassazione penale* 5 (2009): 2, 232.

72. Roberto Garofoli, *Manuale di diritto penale, Parte generale* (Giuffrè 2008), 253.

73. Article 8 of d.lgs. of June 8, 2001, no. 231.

74. Tribunale di Milano, March 9, 2004 [2004] 2, Foro italiano, c. 435.

75. Tribunale di Milano, January 24, 2008, B S.p.A., https://www.aodv231.it/images/pdf/trib%20Milano%2024-01-08.pdf, accessed September 7, 2021.

76. Vincenzo Mongillo, *La responsabilità penale tra individuo ed ente collettivo* (Giappichelli 2018), 113–115.

77. Directive 2012/29/ EU, of October 25, 2012, establishing minimum standards on the rights, support and protection of victims of crime, also in consideration of former FD 2001/220/JHA on the standing of victims in criminal proceedings, Art. 2, d).

78. Case C-79/11, *Criminal Proceedings against Maurizio Giovanardi and Others* [2012], § 49, ECR, ECLI:EU:C:2012:448.

79. Tribunale di Lecce (2), January 29, 2021 (February 15, 2021), https://www.giurisprudenzapenale.com/wp-content/uploads/2021/02/trib-lecce-231-ordinanza.pdf, accessed April 20, 2021.

80. Ibid., para. 2, (a), (b), (c).

81. Ibid., para. 2, in the central part of (a), 2.

82. Ibid., para. 2, in the last part of (c), 3.

83. The Council of Europe Convention, Preamble, 2 (above, n. 48).

84. Ivan Gaskell and Sarah Anne Carter, *The Oxford Handbook of History and Material Culture* (Oxford University Press 2020), 297.

Index

About the Editor and Contributors

Rahime Erbaş is currently an assistant professor in criminal law at Istanbul University. She studied law at Selçuk University, pursued a master's in public law on the topic "The Mandatory Reporting Duty of Healthcare Providers from a Comparative Law Perspective" at Istanbul University and at Justus Liebig Universität Gießen in Germany (Erasmus Exchange) in 2012. In 2019, she completed her PhD with the title "Legal Duty to Act in Crimes of the Omission (delicta commissionis per omissionem) in the Turkish Penal Code" at Istanbul University. Dr. Erbaş carried out a doctoral research at the Osnabrück Universität in Germany between 2016 and 2017 and has been a visiting scholar at the Max Planck Institut in Freiburg and Zürich Universität. She has two edited books published: E. Johnston, R. Erbaş, and D. Jasinski, *A Comparative Analysis of Pre-Trial Procedure in Europe: The Search for an Ideal Model* (2020) and V. Bonini and R. Erbaş, *The 10th Anniversary of the Istanbul Convention* (2022). Her research interests focus on the substantive part of criminal law, organized crime, medical criminal law, sexual crimes, and violence against women. She speaks Turkish (mother tongue), English, German, and Italian. Rahime lives in İstanbul, and is very passionate about travelling.

***

Francesco Angelone is qualified as a lawyer. He is a philosophy's scholar of history and religions, with particular attention to the thought of Hegel, Kant, and the history of the foundations of German philosophy. His research interests also revolve around the historical, religious, philosophical and legal origins of organized crime in southern Italy. In this perspective, his research focuses on the *Theory of Sacrifice* according to René Girard. He is responsible for the website, dirittocanonico.com, which became revised in 2017 with ISSN 2532–1633. He is the author of numerous publications in international and national journals and he has also participated in numerous conferences at universities and research institutions.

Angela Caruso is a lawyer and lecturer in criminal procedural law at the DiGiES of Reggio Calabria. She is a member of the local branch of CAMMINO and a fellow of MacroCrimes. She has published numerous manuscripts and has participated in three collective works titled *Legislazione antimafia e sistema del doppio binario—Analisi della normativa penale, processuale e penitenziaria* (2009), *Il trasferimento fraudolento di valori* (2018) and *La via referendaria al fine-vita. Ammissibilità e normativa di risulta del quesito sull'art. 579 c.p. Atti del Seminario, Ferrara, 26 novembre 2021* (Forum di Quaderni Costituzionali-Rassegna, 1, 2022). She writes for the magazine *Il Penalista* and has moderated/lectured at several conferences, including one with the participation of Dr. Antonio Balsamo, law; Abdelaziz Essid; and Şerife Ceren Uysal, at which she discussed the right to time.

Chara Chioni-Chotouman has studied law at the National and Kapodistian University of Athens. She completed her LLM in criminal law and criminal procedure and acquired her PhD titled "Victims' Rights in Criminal Proceedings—The Impact of European Law in Greek Criminal Trial" (published monograph) for which she received a full merit-based scholarship from the State Scholarships Foundation (I.K.Y). She also conducted research at Humboldt University on sexual offenses. She is working as a lawyer at the NGO "Diotima" providing legal advice and representation to victims of gender-based violence and conducting trainings on the issue. She has published several articles in English and Greek and delivered speeches both in Greece and abroad.

Aleksandra Deanoska Trendafilova is a professor in criminal law at the Iustinianus Primus Faculty of Law in Skopje, Republic of N. Macedonia. She studied law at the Ss. Cyril and Methodius University, where she also defended her master thesis with the topic "Illegal Transplantation and Trafficking in Human Organs and Tissues" and her PhD dissertation titled "Criminal Law Aspects of Genetic Manipulations." She has been member of the working groups on drafting the Criminal Code, Law on Classified Information, and so on. Deanoska-Trendafilova is also a lecturer at the Academy for Judges and Public Prosecutors. She has published many scientific papers, monographs, university textbooks, and books of commentaries in the area of criminal law and justice system, medical law, bioethics, private security, classified information, and so on. She is a coordinator at the National Convention on the EU in Macedonia, member of the Council of the International Association of Youth and Family Judges and Magistrates and member of editorial boards of several scientific journals.

Carmen Adriana Domocoş studied law at University of Oradea, finishing her degree with the maximum score, then pursued a master's degree in European law. She studied criminology in her postgraduate studies and has a PhD in criminal law from the University of Timişoara with her thesis on "The Crimes of Omission in Romanian Criminal Law." She is currently an associate professor at her alma mater, teaching criminology and criminal law, and having published four books alongside many articles in the field. She has practiced law since her graduation as a lawyer, then served as a prosecutor and is currently a judge; she has served for two terms as president of the Regional Second Instance Court. She is also a member of the Romanian Association of Criminal Sciences and Board Member of the Romanian Criminal Law Review. Her research interests include the evolution of the regulation of omission in criminal law, the current state of contemporary research on criminology and the legislation regarding the enforcement of criminal sentences.

Lara Ferla is lecturer of "Normativa a tutela della persona" at the Catholic University of the Sacred Heart in Milan, Italy, since 2018. She studied at the faculty of law and pursued a law degree in criminal law. In 2010, she completed her PhD in criminal law and criminology with a doctoral thesis titled "I percorsi delle cultural defenses tra garanzie di legalità e richieste di riconoscimento delle identità culturali." Dr. Ferla has been a research fellow in criminal law. She has been a visiting scholar at the Max-Planck-Institut für Ausländisches und Internationales Strafrecht in Freiburg im Breisgau (Germany) in 2013. She is a member of the editorial board of the journal *Rivista italiana di medicina legale e del diritto in campo sanitario* (*Italian Review of Legal Medicine and Law in Healthcare Area*). She is author of various publications about criminal law, in the fields of multiculturalism, mental illness, criminal responsibility, and labor criminal law.

Gordana Gasmi is full professor and a research fellow in the Institute of Comparative Law Belgrade, has published numerous books, scientific essays, and expert papers in the field of the theory of law, European law, and policies and international law in Serbian and English. She is dealing as well with gender equality research and academic writing on international standards of combating violence against women and domestic violence. In her capacity of the Council of Europe and the UNDP expert, she held numerous high-level seminars on women human rights and gender equality issues in more than ten countries of Europe and Asia for the judiciary, parliament members, and police.

Aleksandra Gruevska Drakulevski is a professor of criminology, penology, and criminal Law at the Ss. Cyril and Methodius University, Iustinianus Primus Law Faculty in Skopje, Republic of North Macedonia. She studied law at the Ss. Cyril and Methodius University. She holds a MPhil degree in criminology from the University of Cambridge, Faculty of Law, Institute of Criminology, UK. She completed her postgraduate studies in 2004, and the topic of her thesis was "Recidivism: Etiology, Prediction, Prevention and Reduction." She has a PhD in criminal law from the Ss. Cyril and Methodius University, Iustinianus Primus Law Faculty in Skopje, Republic of North Macedonia. She completed her PhD on the topic "The Effects of Imprisonment on Recidivism" in 2010. Her research interests include criminology, penology, victimology, criminal law, juvenile justice. She is an author of textbooks, manuals, and more than fifty original scientific articles and review articles, policy papers, and other publications published in journals in the country and abroad. Also, she is involved in many research projects nationally and internationally.

Barbara Herceg Pakšić is associate professor of criminal law at Josip Juraj Strossmayer University in Osijek, Croatia. She obtained her PhD by defending doctoral dissertation "Grounds of Excuse in Criminal Law" in 2014 at Faculty of Law, University of Zagreb, and received a *summa cum laude* diploma. In 2012, she completed pedagogical-psychological and didactic-methodological training at the Faculty of Teacher Education in Osijek. In 2013, she completed professional training for lawyer linguists at the Faculty of Law in Osijek (English, German, and French). She teaches at law study, professional administrative study, and social work at Faculty of Law in Osijek. In 2019, Dr. Herceg Pakšić was the recipient of a research fellowship at the Europa Institute, Saarbrücken, Germany. Study visits include Max Planck Institut in Freiburg im Br.; Institut für Recht-und Kriminalsoziologie, Vienna; University of Mannheim; Hochschule für öffentliche Verwaltung Kehl; Rechtswissenschaftlichen Fakultät Albert-Ludwigs-Universität Freiburg im Br.; Faculté de Droit de Sciences Politiques et de Gestion, Université de Strasbourg, France; University Niccolo Cusano in Rome. Her latest publications include anarticle titled "Holding All the Aces? Hate Speech: Features and Suppression in Croatia" in *Balkan Yearbook of European and International Law* (2021) and a book *Isprika u kaznenom pravu—Prekoračenje granica nužne obrane i krajnja nužda*/ (*Excuse in Criminal Law—Exceeding the Limits of Self-Defence and State of Necessity*) (2021).

Gordana Lazhetikj is a full-time professor of criminal procedural law at "Iustinianus Primus" Faculty of Law in Skopje since 2012. She served as vice dean of finance and vice dean of science from 2008 to 2014, and was a member of the University Senate from 2016 to 2020. She was a member of working groups for amending criminal legislation, witness protection, execution of sanction, juvenile justice, and victim compensation, as well as working groups for drafting strategies for criminal law, judiciary, execution of sanctions, and financial investigation. Prof. Lazetic is a member of the Governmental Council for judiciary reform, State Council for Prevention of Child Delinquency and National Council for higher education and scientific research. She was the manager of the South East European Law School Network (SEELS) and editor-in-chief of the SEE Law Journal from 2017 to 2021. As a previous visiting scholar of the Max Planck Institute for Foreign and International Criminal Law in Freiburg, she become a member of the Balkan Criminology Network, which is a part of the Max Planck Partner Group for Balkan Criminology in Freiburg, Germany. She is author/coauthor of chapters in books published by the Forum Verlag Godesberg, Duncker & Humblot and Routledge, Taylor & Francis Group, and has contributed to over one hundred conferences, scientific and research projects, and has published over forty monographs, university textbooks, and brochures. She has also published over one hundred articles in domestic and international journals.

Cristian Dumitru Miheș is associate professor at Faculty of Law–University of Oradea, Romania; presently dean of the faculty. His teaching subjects are criminal and forensic sciences, criminal law (BA Level); the influence of new technologies on administration of justice (BA Level), business criminal law, and European criminal law (LLM level). His publications and research areas include criminal justice, European law, cybercrime, corporate crime, the influence of AI on law. He is founder and editor in chief of *The Journal of the Faculty of Law Oradea*. Dr. Miheș attended specialization courses on topics of international and European criminal law organized by The International Institute of Higher Studies in Criminal Science (ISISC) & University of Palermo–Faculty of Law—Siracusa, Italy (2005–2007), and, respectively on topics of "The Life Cycle of E-evidence: Handling E-evidence in Child Sex Abuse Material" (2018), *Artificial Intelligence and Criminal Justice* (2019), and "Computer Forensics in Legal Proceedings" (2020) organized by The Academy of European Law, Trier, Germany. Also, he is attorney at law since 2007.

Željko Nikač is a full-time professor at the Police Academy Belgrade worked in the Ministry of Internal Affairs of Serbia as a criminal inspector, then Deputy and Head of the Department for Control of Legality in the Work of the Belgrade Police and Assistant Chief of the Police Directorate of the MOI RS in the rank of colonel and the chief police adviser. He participated in several international and internal projects and is now a researcher on projects of the RS Ministry of Science. He is the author of a number of scientific texts, books, and monographs in the field of Community Policing, International Police Cooperation and Human Security, as well as a participant at numerous international scientific conferences.

Nikola Tupancheski is a professor in criminal law at the Iustinianus Primus Faculty of Law in Skopje, Republic of N. Macedonia. He studied law at the Ss. Cyril and Methodius University, where he also defended his master thesis. He completed his PhD at the Lomonosov State University in Moscow, Russian Federation. Tupanceski has been the Head of the Delegation representing Republic of Macedonia in GRECO and member of the Ministry of Justice working groups on Criminal Code and Law on Pardon. In the past years, he was head of the Criminal Law Department, Head of the Master Degree Studies in Criminal Law and Vice Dean at the Iustinianus Primus Faculty of Law. He is author/coauthor of many scientific papers, articles, monographs, and university textbooks. Since January 16, 2022, he is a minister of justice in the Government of Republic of North Macedonia.

www.ingramcontent.com/pod-product-compliance
Ingram Content Group UK Ltd.
Pitfield, Milton Keynes, MK11 3LW, UK
UKHW020841290926
15470UKWH00004B/1471

9 781793 652034